Sell Yourself First

Sell Yourself First

*The Most Critical Element
in Every Sales Effort*

Thomas A. Freese

PORTFOLIO / PENGUIN

PORTFOLIO / PENGUIN
Published by the Penguin Group
Penguin Group (USA) Inc., 375 Hudson Street, New York, New York 10014, U.S.A. • Penguin Group (Canada), 90 Eglinton Avenue East, Suite 700, Toronto, Ontario, Canada M4P 2Y3 (a division of Pearson Penguin Canada Inc.) • Penguin Books Ltd, 80 Strand, London WC2R 0RL, England • Penguin Ireland, 25 St. Stephen's Green, Dublin 2, Ireland (a division of Penguin Books Ltd) • Penguin Group Australia Ltd, 250 Camberwell Road, Camberwell, Victoria 3124, Australia (a division of Pearson Australia Group Pty Ltd) • Penguin Books India Pvt Ltd, 11 Community Centre, Panchsheel Park, New Delhi—110 017, India • Penguin Group (NZ), 67 Apollo Drive, Rosedale, North Shore 0632, New Zealand (a division of Pearson New Zealand Ltd) • Penguin Books (South Africa) (Pty) Ltd, 24 Sturdee Avenue, Rosebank, Johannesburg 2196, South Africa

Penguin Books Ltd, Registered Offices: 80 Strand, London WC2R 0RL, England

This edition published in 2010 by Portfolio / Penguin, a member of Penguin Group (USA) Inc.

10 9 8 7 6 5 4 3 2 1

Copyright © QBS Research, Inc., 2009, 2010
All rights reserved

Originally published as *The Complete Guide to Selling Yourself* by QBS Publishing, Inc.

Library of Congress Cataloging-in-Publication Data
Freese, Thomas A.
    Sell yourself first : the most critical element in every sales effort / Thomas A. Freese.
        p.   cm.
    Includes index.
    ISBN 978-1-59184-365-8
    1. Selling.   2. Customer relations.   3. Relationship marketing.   I. Title.
    HF5438.25.F74   2010
    658.85—dc22
                    2010032986

Printed in the United States of America
Designed by Carla Bolte

This book is dedicated to altering the customer's perception of the true sales professional, a change which is long overdue.

PREFACE

When I first sat down to write this book, the world economy was headed into one of the worst recessions since the Great Depression. Now, everything seems eerily different as we realize that the field on which we work and play has changed dramatically. Even those of us who were minding our own business when the downturn began breathed a collective gasp when the thirty-year era of unabated growth and prosperity seemed to collapse overnight.

It's easy to sell when business conditions are consistently favorable. And for the better part of two generations, businesses, individuals, and investors alike have all enjoyed an unprecedented run of good times. As a result, the economy boomed with unrestrained exuberance, rampant overspending became an accepted part of our culture, and ravenous growth distorted the corporate mindset to the point where just a few years ago, companies couldn't hire new employees fast enough. More was definitely better. Then, reality set in and the bubble burst.

Who would have thought that our financial system would require a trillion-dollar bailout, or that large Wall Street brokerage houses could literally go out of business over a weekend? These factors have all come together at the same time to create a perfect storm of economic conditions that sent our previous capitalistic mentality into a veritable tailspin.

More than at any other time since the industrial revolution, companies in all industries are now aggressively looking for ways to retain customers, boost top-line revenue, and maintain reasonable profit margins. To survive and, ultimately, flourish in this new economy, decision makers at all levels within the company must reexamine the way they deal with suppliers and customers; and frankly, some of the adjustments that need to be made are long overdue. Surely I'm not the only one who thinks there have been a few times in recent history where we could have used a good kick in the pants?

> **Now more than ever, companies are looking for ways to retain customers, boost top-line revenue, and maintain reasonable profit margins.**

People are naturally concerned about what the future holds. Some of them should be. I can see it in the eyes of audience participants during some of the recent QBS training programs I've recently delivered. I'm not trying to be insensitive, just realistic. Economic times have changed, and I suspect that this genie isn't going back in the bottle anytime soon.

That said, I am not one of those doomsdayers who run around predicting economic Armageddon, nor do I believe we are headed for another Great Depression. We will survive the current challenges, as well as the many humps and bumps that will likely occur on the road to economic recovery. I do believe, however, that we have entered a historic period of adjustment, where a Darwinian-style recalibration is now under way, where those companies and individuals who are the most able to adapt to a changing marketplace will have a definite advantage. Thus, how we choose to conduct ourselves in the coming months and years will likely determine where we end up when the dust settles and the current turbulence subsides.

The Appetite for Change Has Never Been Greater

When there is plenty of business for everyone in the marketplace, company meetings tend to morph into celebratory events where sales teams congratulate themselves for a job well done. When the size of the market shrinks unexpectedly and suddenly there's no longer enough business to go around, the overall mood at these meetings abruptly shifts from congratulatory and self-indulgent to serious and grim, overtaken by a sense of urgency to identify ways to adjust to rapidly changing market conditions.

In a real-life game of musical chairs, it has become clear that not everyone will get a seat when the music stops. And even those who are able to survive the tumultuous nature of today's competitive marketplace will undoubtedly notice that the opportunities coming their way have appreciably decreased in number, size, and scope.

Guess what happens when salespeople and companies begin to transact smaller pieces of business, or in some cases are no longer getting enough opportunities to justify their existence? That's right, they tend to become perceptibly hungrier and more aggressive. Basically, a competitive businessperson's survival instincts kick in, and struggling sellers who are not able to differentiate themselves or their products will inevitably resort to significantly discounting their prices, thus eroding profit margins across the industry. Sound familiar?

This increased pressure in the marketplace comes with an ironic upside, however, and one that has sparked a renewed sense of desire within companies, and, I daresay, throughout the entire sales profession. It turns out that the same people who are hungry for business are also eager for a new perspective and creative ideas about what they can do differently to give themselves a competitive advantage. Never before have individual salespeople been so willing to put their egos aside and adjust their approach to make themselves invaluable to their company and customers. Frankly, most salespeople are smart enough to realize that some adjustments are necessary with regard to how we approach and deal with clients, as it now appears that our best opportunity to get out of the current predicament is going to be to somehow sell our way out.

Companies have experienced a bit of a comeuppance as well, where much of the typical squabbling and internal politics that have traditionally plagued organizations has been replaced by an "all hands on deck" mentality. Essentially, the same perfect storm that recently stirred up so much dust in the marketplace has also fostered a perfect opportunity to recalibrate the traditional selling mindset.

Updating the effectiveness of your existing sales force doesn't have to be as daunting as it sounds, however. It is true that some corporate training departments will need to shift their traditional focus away from continually redefining the sales process or just offering a slew of refresher courses that teach old-school content. Teaching salespeople to sound the same as your closest competitors is an exercise in futility, and anything that merits the title of a "refresher" course is more likely to send people backward in their thinking rather than forward.

Does anyone else think it's strange that the effectiveness of the sales organization drives the success of every company, yet the skills required to be successful in a sales role continue to be the least taught professional discipline in the world? Most companies rely on individual salespeople to figure it out for themselves. While some of the more experienced sellers on your team have likely attended a bunch of sales seminars over the years, teaching people how to sell in a tough economic climate is very different from what most sellers have encountered from their in previous sales training experiences.

Emphasis on Sales Effectiveness

Who should be held responsible for the recent softness in sales volume? Unfortunately, finger pointing to assign blame has become a veritable pastime in some companies and industries. However, in sales, after you get done blaming the economy, corporate marketing, the competition, and sometimes even the customer, if you look around any sales organization, you will notice that some salespeople are significantly more effective than others, even though they are selling the same basic products and services to the same types of customers.

What is it that makes a top performing salesperson more effective than one of their struggling counterparts? What is it (exactly) that they are doing to separate themselves from the competition, in a way that overcomes the adversities and grievances many other salespeople see as obstacles? It's a fair question, but very few people have the answer.

I wrote this book with the intentional and unmistakable mission to increase the sales effectiveness of the person staring back at you when you look in the mirror. It is possible that the techniques and strategies outlined in this book can also help your colleagues, business partners, and maybe even your management team. Let's consider that a bonus if it happens. But the truth of the matter is, if you aspire to become a more effective salesperson, the time has come for you to take matters into your own hands. The customer's impression of you will enable or compromise the entire business relationship.

Unfortunately, this topic of individual effectiveness has been pushed to the back burner for too long, and in the process, lots of good people have been caught off guard, and in some cases, are unprepared for how best to respond given the rapidly changing business environment.

If it is indeed true that some salespeople in your industry are more effective than others, then I encourage you to bring your own personal selling effectiveness back to the forefront, in order to give yourself the strongest possible opportunity to be perceived as a valuable resource by your company, your colleagues, and your customers. While it's true that you still have to position your company and products in their best light, to be effective in today's economic climate, you must learn how to *sell yourself first*.

CONTENTS

Sell Yourself First

Introduction

The Game Has Changed

Do you realize that in the state of Georgia, where I live, you have to have a license to catch a fish or own a dog, but you can refer to yourself as a sales professional without any credentials whatsoever? It's true. Even though the sales industry will probably never be tightly regulated, customers have become very adept at spotting the differences between a salesperson who can provide a truly valuable product or service from those who are mostly focused on getting their next commission check.

One of the biggest differentiators in sales is actually quite simple. Those salespeople who understand that it is important to *sell yourself first* will have an unfair advantage over their competition moving forward. In every competitive industry, and probably for the rest of your sales career, the person representing a product or service is likely to have a greater influence on the customer's perception of value than the product itself.

For previous generations, the act of selling was often seen as the "art" of persuasion. In that vein, convincing potential buyers to purchase your products and services was a necessary evil, where a talented salesperson was someone who not only possessed the gift of gab, but had an uncanny knack for getting into the customer's pocket before he or she realized they were being "sold" on something.

Over time, many of the older-school sales tricks and manipulative marketing gimmicks have now run their course, as most customers are quick to recognize the difference between someone who is truly trying to help them and someone who just wants to make a quick buck. Think about it. If someone tells you that you sound like a used-car salesman, that's usually not a compliment.

When I think about the concept of being professional, my mind suddenly shifts to the other end of the spectrum, far away from the traditional used-car dealership. I think of the business practices of professional people like architects, attorneys, doctors, accountants, or engineers; basically people who are bonafide experts and who provide advice within their particular field of expertise. A professional could also be the gifted athlete who with enough hard work and a commitment to excellence is able to transform some physical skill into a marketable enterprise. Either way, being seen as a true professional is not only a casual compliment; it changes the way people perceive and interact with you.

The designation of someone as a "sales professional" could seem like the ultimate oxymoron in some people's minds, yet there is a vast difference between a salesperson who is a bona fide expert offering valuable solutions and the wheeler-dealer mentality that is often associated with more traditional selling methods.

> **The person representing a product or service is likely to have a greater influence on the customer's perception of value than the product itself.**

Today, I can assure you that the sales function is no longer a necessary evil. Rather, the ability to have success in selling goods and services is the lifeblood of every successful business venture. Simply put, if you cannot sell it with some degree of consistency, then it doesn't matter how good your product or service actually is. That said, the business of selling can no longer be seen as an act of persuasion. Customers don't want to be "persuaded" to buy something they don't want or need, especially by a salesperson they don't yet know or trust. Thus, we very quickly come to a crossroads in terms of how we (as salespeople) want to be perceived by prospects, customers, colleagues, and even our employer. Do you want to be seen as someone who is customer-focused, with valuable expertise, high integrity, and a commitment to excellence, or as just another self-serving vendor trying to get into the customer's pocket? The difference in perception usually comes down to how effective you are at positioning yourself.

Boiled down to simplest terms, a sales professional is someone who is able to do two things consistently—help people and communicate effectively.

It makes perfect sense that a doctor is essentially in the business of helping people. Lawyers, consultants, architects, engineers, and accountants too have all obtained enough expertise in their respective professions to make a healthy livelihood out of helping people, although they may not all communicate with the same effectiveness.

Having spent the bulk of my career in the trenches of sales and sales management, and then publishing this, my fifth book on professional selling, I have had the opportunity to work with many top salespeople at some of the most successful companies in the world. In doing so, I have noticed a few common characteristics among excellent salespeople that may surprise you, starting with the fact that top performers are often *not* the most outgoing or gregarious people in the company. In fact, it's not unusual to find that the very best salespersons in a company or within an entire industry are often highly introspective, somewhat reserved, and in some cases, even slightly introverted. There goes the theory that the gift of gab is actually a gift.

With this in mind, when you make an appointment to see a professional, a doctor of your choosing for example, you basically want two things from them. You want them to take the time to understand your situation, in order to then give you valuable advice or a viable solution. Your goals would be the same if you met with an accountant—you would want them to understand your situation so that, based on their experience and expertise, they can help you in some valuable way.

Today, it's no different in sales. The only reason a customer would want to meet with a sales professional is for that person (presumably you) to invest the time to understand their situation so that you could then help them in some way—either by providing valuable advice or viable solutions. Hence, the concept of being a sales professional is actually quite simple.

The challenge is, you are not the only one in the marketplace who is trying to "help" these customers. If you sell in a highly competitive business environment, which I assume most people do, then you're not the only vendor calling these customers on a regular basis and trying to get a foot in the door. In fact, you're probably not the only salesperson who has called in the last twenty minutes. Especially on the heels of an economic downturn that some people have labeled "The Great Recession," sellers who are under pressure to produce more revenue are not only making more calls, they are also being more aggressive with potential buyers. This creates somewhat of a vicious cycle, where customers who don't want to be hounded by salespeople are intentionally distancing themselves from vendor solicitations. Of course, as it becomes more difficult to get the attention of key decision makers, sellers are becoming even more aggressive, which causes customers to be even more standoffish.

Maybe you are not being overly aggressive, or inappropriate in any way. Like your prospects, I don't know you personally. But, I can assure you that your target audience of potential customers has their defense mechanisms on full alert, having been jaded from the dozens of sellers who came before you, many of whom treat the sales function as simply a means of creating revenue, as opposed to actually helping the customer solve a problem.

Still, some salespeople are significantly more effective than others, in every industry. That realization raises a very simple question. What is it that separates top performing salespeople from their struggling counterparts? The answer comes down to two simple words—customer perception.

I wish I had a nickel for every time I've seen a geographical territory get reassigned to a different salesperson, and suddenly, for some strange reason, a sales territory that was once considered an absolute wasteland turns into a virtual gold mine. Meanwhile, could it be sheer coincidence that all of the opportunities in last year's gold mine of a territory suddenly dry up when someone else with lesser skill or experience takes over? Of course, there is often some amount of luck involved when it comes to being in the right place at the right time. But in sales, you can't attribute consistent performance and maximizing one's own effectiveness to pure chance. These situations happen far too often to be brushed aside as statistical anomalies.

Neither can you blame good genes, a pleasant personality, or someone's genetic makeup for having an innate knack for success, or lack thereof. I have literally met a set of twins, presumably with the same DNA, where one could sell ice cubes in the Arctic, while the other couldn't give away an air conditioner on the equator. Likewise, I know some very pleasant people who are struggling mightily, now that the economy has tightened and selling has become much more than a personality contest. In the end, I would argue that DNA isn't the issue at all, as I have seen countless salespeople enhance their performance and results by simply adjusting their approach, without having to alter their personality or change their genetic makeup.

Some people even fault customers for their own lack of success. I can certainly empathize with the idea that blaming external factors can make you feel better in the short term, but attributing your deficiencies to external factors doesn't do anything to improve your chances of making the next sale.

Given the current business climate, sellers can no longer count on their products alone to be the differentiator. The more likely scenario is that you will be one of several competitors offering viable solutions, which customers may even perceive as comparable. For example, what's the difference really between Allstate insurance, State Farm, and Nationwide? In terms of selecting an insurance company, I suppose it comes down to whether you want to be "in good hands," have "a good neighbor," or you like the idea of having "Nationwide on your side." From a pure product perspective, however, there are more similarities than differences between these comparable options. You might even say they're function-ally equivalent. A discerning customer could easily conclude the same about the financial services industry, where you can purchase the same one hundred shares of General Electric or Coca-Cola stock from any number of brokerage houses, often located within blocks of each other. Realtors within the same metro area face a similar challenge, where they are all essentially competing to sell the same inventory of homes at the same listed prices. Even the drug companies face stiffer competition as a continuous stream of new medicines and formulary alternatives con-tinue to come on the market.

When rival companies engage in a battle of buzzwords to try and out-describe each other, comparable solutions tend to get commoditized and often end up sounding very similar to target customers. Whenever this happens, which occurs more often than not in competitive markets, the salesperson can no longer count on the product itself for differentiation. Unless you are truly the only provider that offers a unique product or service, your competitors all claim to offer the best solutions, too.

Don't get me wrong: the value of your company and the quality of the products you sell are still important. But in most industries, the person representing the product or service will have a greater influence on the customer's perception than the product itself.

> **When rival companies engage in a battle of buzzwords to try and out-describe each other, comparable solutions tend to get commoditized and end up sounding very similar to target customers.**

For too long, companies have been content to arm their sales teams with some basic product training before sending them out into their respective territories to talk about features and benefits. But, if you went down to the local branch office and opened a brokerage account with a financial firm like Morgan Stanley, I bet you would never meet Mr. Morgan or Mr. Stanley. Instead, your faith in the company and confidence in the products being offered would almost exclusively be the result of the impression you form as a result of your dealings with one of their sixteen thousand financial advisers. To a customer, the financial adviser at Morgan Stanley *is* the company.

This same phenomenon applies in most businesses, whether you sell technology, real estate, manufactured goods, pharmaceuticals, consulting services, or you are a home builder, engineer, financial planner, or franchisee. In the foreseeable future, the effectiveness of the individual salesperson will have a greater impact on customer perception than the products and services being offered or the company he or she represents.

The challenge for the salesperson who is getting ready to call on new customers is, how will the next prospective customer you call on now you're smart? How will they know that you are trustworthy, competent, knowledgeable, and experienced? Will they simply assume that you have great ideas and are a thought leader in your respective industry? How will they come to the point of understanding that you have solutions that could help them greatly? As salespeople, should we just tell them? Should we call potential buyers and say, "Hi, Mr. Customer, this is Joe Smith with XYZ Company, and I am the smartest and most credible salesperson you will ever meet. I also represent the finest company in the industry and we have better solutions than anyone else. In fact, you're lucky you picked up the telephone because you're really going to enjoy talking with me."

Really? Is that how we're supposed to do it, by trying to claim our own credibility? I hope for your sake that this is not reflective of your current approach to calling customers, because claims of credibility in today's selling environment tend to fall on deaf ears. Put yourself on the receiving end of that call for a moment, and I bet you would either laugh, sigh, or simply hang up in disgust.

Would you agree that building credibility with potential buyers is an important step toward being successful in sales? Conveying competence, relevance, innovation, stability, quality, and value, more so than your competition, is critically important as well. While a salesperson can brag about their company and products, most of us know from personal experience that one of the quickest ways for a salesperson (or any professional) to turn customers off is to start bragging about themselves.

Your success in business and in life will ultimately hinge on the impressions other people form about you. If you sell for a living, then you are keenly aware that customers are always forming impressions of a sales caller, and the perceptions they form throughout the sales process will likely determine whether or not they choose to purchase your products and services. Thus, closely contested sales opportunities usually come down to a host of intangibles, which include a variety of attributes such as the salesperson's character, professionalism, credibility, expertise, knowledge, vision, helpfulness, honesty, mutual respect, customer focus, and consistency when following through on verbal commitments. Oddly enough, the extent to which you actually possess these character traits is *not* the issue. The primary challenge sellers now face is figuring out how to convey these important yet highly intangible qualities, in order to differentiate yourself and enhance the value you bring to customers, partners, colleagues, and your management chain.

It has long been the case that people tend to buy from people they like. The thing that has changed is *why* customers may or may not like you. If a salesperson is friendly and personable, that's definitely a plus. But in today's selling environment, the salesperson who gives customers the best advice is usually the one who wins the sale. Another way to characterize this is to say that people tend to do business with whomever makes them feel most comfortable with the solution. If you indeed represent the finest company in your industry, and you are truly offering the best solutions for the customer, you still have to be perceived as relevant, purposeful, credible, and valuable in order to earn their trust, Basically, you have to *sell yourself first* in order to be successful.

How exactly are you supposed to sell yourself in an increasingly competitive business climate? That is what this entire book is about. As an extension of the Question Based Selling (QBS) methodology, which I have now been teaching for the past thirteen years to salespeople and companies around the globe, this book was written as a direct commentary for how salespeople in today's selling environment can leverage superior technique and strategy to stand out, build more value, and essentially, gain an unfair advantage over the competition—just by making a few adjustments to how they choose to position themselves.

My goal for this book was to create a repeatable formula for selling yourself, which extends far beyond the notion that readers will simply take away a few pearls of wisdom from the text. To become a consistent top performer, you ultimately need a repeatable system that focuses on the implementation of what I call the softer sales skills—like piquing the customer's interest, establishing your own credibility, forging and leveraging relationships, differentiating your solutions, justifying the cost, and of course, securing commitments throughout the sales cycle.

I would argue that skills development has become the new field on which the game of selling is now being played. At the end of the day, customers are going to turn to someone for advice, and it's reasonable to assume it's either going to be you or one of your competitors. Hence, there is some responsibility on your part to decide how you want to be perceived, and then to be proactive enough to implement a strategy that will enable you to achieve the desired result.

Does this sound too good to be true? Well, let me ask you this question. How hard do you want selling to be? If you notice, every time a sales conversation goes well, at the end of the call, the customer always thanks the salesperson for calling, coming to see them, or helping them solve a problem. We, too, can and should be respectful and appreciate the customer's time and participation. But every time a sales conversation goes well, what the customer is really verbalizing is their appreciation for your capacity to help them in some meaningful way and your ability to communicate effectively in the process. Contrary to many of the sales gimmicks and process models that have come in and out of vogue over the last twenty years, you don't communicate effectively by making the sales process more difficult or convoluted. You increase your effectiveness by understanding the cautious nature the typical prospect has toward vendors, where old school sales approaches are causing prospects to become even more skeptical, and then replacing that entire paradigm of trickery with a set of proven techniques and strategies that will produce the desired improvement in results.

Skills development has become the new field on which the game of selling is now being played.

Keep in mind that your doctor went to school and studied for ten or more years before you were willing to take his or her advice. Likewise, it takes five to eight years of formal education to become an architect, an accountant, an engineer, or an attorney. With that in mind, perhaps it's reasonable to expect that it should take a little effort and commitment on your part to learn how to cause potential buyers to trust you with their time, money, problems, issues, goals, needs, and concerns.

The sales profession is one of the most exciting and rewarding occupations in the world. Whenever a sale goes well, the customer gets the benefit of valuable solutions, the salesperson gets paid handsomely for making the sale and producing revenue for his or her company, and the customer thanks the salesperson for helping them. But for salespeople, justifying your value to customers and to your company is not going to be as easy as before.

The fact that you are reading this book tells me you are committed to excellence. I must assume, however, that some of your toughest competitors are similarly devoted to their own success. Thus, even if you are indeed a capable individual, it's unlikely that you are the only talented person in your industry. Companies offering similar solutions will be competing against you harder than ever to gain the customers' trust and ultimately earn their business. Eventually, someone is going to win these battles, and, as you might expect with any competitive situation, your ability to prevail has a lot to do with *you*.

In today's competitive landscape, your long-term career aspirations, along with your day-to-day livelihood, depend on your own personal effectiveness, now more than ever. And how you approach the profession of selling will ultimately determine whether you will be seen by customers as a sales professional, or just another hungry vendor who's trying to make a buck. Even if you are not a career salesperson, whether you manage a small business, support the organization in a customer service role, or are an executive in a Fortune 500 company, you will definitely be selling yourself every day.

On a personal note, I am grateful to have had the opportunity to share my ideas on selling with so many salespeople, managers, executives, and nonsalespeople. I am also humbled by the eagerness people have shown over the years to implement Question Based Selling and to refer the QBS methodology and our training programs to others. Thank you for placing such confidence in me. To that end, my mantra for this book is relatively simple. When selling yourself, you must remain true to yourself by doing things in the way that makes the most logical sense in today's business climate. With all due respect to other authors and selling systems, it no longer matters what may have worked twenty years ago. In that vein, make it your goal to be perceived as competent and purposeful when talking with customers, and keep it simple and current by allowing reasonability and relevance to be your guide.

Now, grab your favorite highlighter and prepare for an odyssey that will change the way you deal with customers over the rest of your career. With absolute confidence I can tell you that learning to sell yourself first will also change the way customers perceive and deal with you.

1

The Elephant in the Room

Starting with an "elevator pitch" to convey value is officially dead as a viable differentiation strategy. After a salesperson finishes spewing all the wonderful benefits of his or her product offering, the customer's two biggest issues have not been addressed. What decision makers really want to know is "who" to trust, and "how" to make a good decision.

Even if you have a great story to tell about your products and services, customers are skeptical of sales pitches, now more than ever. Thus, for the sake of maximizing your credibility and differentiating your company's value, you must be willing to give customers what they really want—the rest of the story. Customer skepticism is the "elephant in the room," and you will help yourself by dealing with it up front.

Let me guess—your company is the "leading provider of quality widgets in your respective industry, as evidenced by an impressive track record of success and unmatched innovation, with a commitment to quality and excellence that is second to none." Am I close?

Join the club. Have you been to your competitor's Web site lately? I bet they lay claim to many of the exact same bullet points you claim as exclusive benefits. Even if their marketing strategy was blatantly plagiarized from your company's efforts, you should not be surprised if the messages being conveyed by competing vendors sound very similar to yours, especially if you are the industry leader. Especially in these economic times, your rivals are going to do whatever they can to suggest that their offerings are indeed more robust and valuable than yours.

How do most customers perceive or interpret these self-serving claims of superiority? Well, you can easily judge for yourself just by observing a few of the many infomercials on television. On any Saturday morning, for example, with the exception of the cartoon channels and ESPN, you can flip around the dial and find wall-to-wall infomercials, featuring an assortment of enthusiastic pitchmen selling everything from kitchen knives to juicers, slicers, exercise equipment, weight-loss programs, and get rich quick real estate schemes.

When the host of the infomercial looks directly into the camera and confidently says, "You, too, can lose up to forty pounds in a single week, without any exercise and without changing your diet," I bet your natural skepticism doesn't allow you to buy into such claims that are obviously overstated. Seriously, I wonder how many people really lose forty pounds in a single week.

In fact, today's consumer has become so jaded that product claims from any enthusiastic salesperson are likely to fall on deaf ears. Some of this natural skepticism can be attributed to recent changes in our perspective as a society. For example, let me ask you this question. Over the past few months, or even the last several years, would you say that consumers in general have become more open and receptive to salespeople they don't yet know and trust, or more cautious and reserved? As an example, when you are on the receiving end of a cold call from a salesperson, what's the very first thought that pops into your head? Do you think to yourself, "Oh boy, this is great! A salesperson is calling. Now I get to talk with some stranger and learn about something I don't already know." I bet you don't. If you are like most people, you probably think, "Arrrgh, not another sales caller!"

No matter how seedy the reputation some sellers have earned over time, it's important to note that most customers don't despise salespeople. In fact, the opposite is true. Most customers actually depend on salespeople—for ideas, information, a vision into the future, and for solutions. They just don't depend on every vendor who happens to come calling, and they are reticent to take advice from someone they don't yet know or trust. As a result, good salespeople representing viable companies with legitimate products are being consistently fended off by gatekeepers and by decision makers themselves. Sellers are therefore finding it increasingly difficult to get appointments with key people in target accounts. It has also become more difficult to differentiate your value proposition from the last dozen vendors who called and sounded strikingly similar, and then to secure a commitment to move forward, either by scheduling the next step in the decision process or moving ahead with a favorable purchase decision.

> **Sellers are finding it more difficult to get appointments, not to mention differentiating a value proposition that sounds strikingly similar to the last dozen vendors who called.**

Even though customers have become increasingly standoffish, it's still true that whenever a sales call goes really well—I mean when the conversation goes exactly as planned, and a perfect match exists between your solution and the customer's needs—the customer always thanks the salesperson for calling. It's uncanny but true. Customers will spend all kinds of time with someone they perceive to be a valuable resource, and they are much less open to spending time with random cold callers. Not surprisingly, there is a huge difference between engaging a customer in an in-depth conversation about how your solutions will address their needs and being instantly dismissed by a reluctant gatekeeper.

Sales tricks, marketing gimmicks, and anything else that might sound manipulative to customers is likely to be fended off also, as most decision makers have become pretty adept at discarding vendors who seem purposeless or lack credibility. That said, let's not be surprised when the traditional elevator pitch or taking an infomercial sounding approach to positioning the value of your product or service offering doesn't garner a receptive audience when you reach out to prospective customers.

The next logical question that salespeople and managers tend to ask is, "Well, given the customer's natural skepticism toward vendors, how can sellers put themselves in a stronger position to be viewed as a valuable resource and not just another cold caller?"

If we're honest about it, most customers will only choose to engage some fraction of the salespeople who come calling on a daily basis. Again, they don't despise salespeople. Key decision makers just aren't going to entertain the idea of changing vendors, products, or platforms every week, and they don't want to be hounded incessantly in the meantime. But even when a real-live need is brewing, or where a specific project or initiative has been identified, not every salesperson is going to get a seat at the table to present their wares. Not surprisingly, most customers want to narrow the field of possible vendors down to a manageable number of viable alternatives, so they can then choose from the top two or three contenders. The real question therefore is, how often are you being selected as the person the customer wants to rely on for advice, ideas, a vision of the future, and ultimately for a valuable solution?

You Are More Important than Your Product or Company

If you sell in a competitive marketplace, which most people do, with the exception of where your corporate headquarters is located and how much revenue your company produced last year, there's nothing you can say at the buzzword level to a customer in the first two or three minutes of a sales conversation that is significantly different from what your competitors will probably say about their product or service. Thus, opening with a standard "elevator pitch" about your offerings is the quickest way to commoditize your value proposition, which is exactly the opposite result from what most sellers are attempting to achieve.

Customers have heard most of the buzzwords already, and they're not likely to be impressed just because you happen to have a pleasant personality. Given that the customer's comfort level surrounding you, your company, and your solution alternatives is critically important, perhaps we should ask a simple question: What exactly can we do to make potential buyers more interested and comfortable?

It's easy to talk about how great one's company and products are, but it's a little less obvious how to earn credibility with new prospects without running the risk of sounding pretentious or arrogant. It's also a bit tricky to demonstrate important personal qualities such as honesty and integrity, or being prepared, helpful, responsive, understanding, creative, and demonstrating mutual respect. If you could combine the true value of your offerings with other intangibles, like somehow conveying that you are indeed knowledgeable, experienced, capable, competent, and reliable, then you would have a pretty strong value proposition.

In a best-case scenario, you would absolutely want customers to associate you with desirable character traits like perceiving you as someone who is customer-focused, empathetic, passionate, hardworking, and sensitive to the customer's specific needs, right? Add a small dose of humility together with honorable intentions and you are either a vendor whose solution offerings are worthy of further exploration, or you are a perfect candidate for one of my daughters to marry.

Most customers who make purchase decisions are simply looking for the best value. But let's not confuse being valuable with being the cheapest option or least expensive. Customers usually aren't looking for the least expensive alternative, which is good because the cheapest option is rarely the most cost effective. Have you ever won a deal when your proposal was more expensive than other options being considered? Like any other successful salesperson, I have closed many deals over the years where my proposal was not the cheapest option. On the flip side, have you ever lost an opportunity when your proposed solution was the least expensive? I have. Even today, I have no desire to be the absolute cheapest sales trainer, just the most valuable!

The concept of procuring solutions from the best source is a constant challenge for decision makers because "value" is a very difficult concept to quantify, especially once you realize that price is only one of many factors that affect the customer's perception of your value. Cost is always going to be an important factor, particularly these days. But if you think about it, most people don't drive the cheapest car. Most consumers don't eat the cheapest food or wear the cheapest clothes. Instead, customers today are interested in choosing whichever option provides the most value relative to their needs, which combines the perceived value of your product or service coupled with the host of intangibles that you bring to the table.

Even so, chances are good that you are not the only vendor in your industry that adds value. In these cases where equivalent products can be purchased from equally viable competitors, as in real estate sales, where the same properties can be listed or purchased from any number of licensed real estate agents for basically the same price, you will find that customers usually don't deal with just anyone. Instead, most people choose to buy from whoever seems to offer the most value, in terms of the best service and advice. This is one area of sales that has changed dramatically over the last few years. As I mentioned in the introduction, customers tend to buy from whoever they like the best. It's just that likability is no longer just a function of friendliness and sociability. Instead, customers will "like" whoever represents the greatest value, which is now a function of being perceived as credible, intelligent, capable, professional, creative, honest, prepared, customer-focused, and responsive to their needs.

> **Whether or not the customer chooses to deal with you has a lot to do with how you choose to deal with them.**

The same logic applies in virtually every competitive market, whether you sell financial services, pharmaceuticals, technology, or sales training courseware. Customers are ultimately going to partner with someone in an effort to meet their needs, and whether or not they choose to deal with you has a lot to do with how you choose to deal with them. Consequently, I can tell you that the difference between winning and losing in today's business environment usually comes down to the ongoing perceptions customers form about you.

Learning How to Win When It's Close

Can we agree that a salesperson's ability to gain credibility is a critical component of any successful sales effort? While gaining the customer's confidence early is indeed important, a salesperson's ability to earn some initial credibility in order to then get deeper, wider, and more strategic within their accounts can give an otherwise ordinary salesperson an unfair advantage.

Potential buyers aren't just looking for a sterile listing of features and benefits when talking with vendor representatives. What they really want is to gain a certain comfort level that comes from a set of intangible benefits that don't necessarily show up on the company's preprinted product brochures. That's because the brochure only tells part of the story—the shiny side, you might say. But customers know that there are pros and cons that accompany any recommended solution, so just being positive and smiley-faced is fine, but it doesn't usually satisfy the typical decision maker's need to feel "comfortable." At the end of the day, they want to have some degree of confidence that they are indeed making the right decision, which includes avoiding all the potholes and surprises that usually aren't highlighted on a company's glossy product literature or in the proposal.

Discerning customers are especially looking for creative ideas, transparency, and thought leadership, the combination of which can all roll under the heading of getting sound advice. Add to these qualities the many other intangible character traits you bring to the sale, such as knowledge, experience, integrity, vision, preparedness, and responsiveness, in addition to someone who cares more about the needs of the customer than about padding their own commission check, and we may indeed be on to something. Whether the customer verbalizes it or not, these intangible qualities tend to be extremely important, and will determine the outcome of many sales opportunities. When the time for a decision arrives, customers want to know they are dealing with someone who cares about their longer-term success, and they want to feel comfortable that you have the depth and perspective to help them make the right choice.

The challenge for sellers is that your intrinsic credibility is highly intangible. While establishing one's own credibility is an important prerequisite for being successful in any sales situation, sellers can't just open their briefcases and pull out a bunch of credibility to hand to potential customers. In fact, credibility is simply a perception that other people form about you. In that sense, it is entirely possible that a salesperson can do certain things to enhance their credibility in the eyes of prospective customers, and it's also possible for that same salesperson to do things that will erode their credibility within those same accounts, if not destroy their reputation altogether.

To me, the customer's natural skepticism is the proverbial elephant in the room. Consider the customer's perspective: When you are considering a purchase, you don't just want an enthusiastic pitch from a commission-hungry salesperson. What you really want to know are the pros and cons of the options available, how they would impact your business or personal needs, along with the associated costs.

Oddly enough, most sellers choose to just ignore the "elephant in the room," and in the face of increased customer skepticism, they continue to plow ahead with a canned product pitch full of buzzwords and accompanying glossy brochures. Do you think that ignoring the customer's issue of wanting to know the "rest of the story" does more to help a salesperson's credibility or hurt it?

If you sell in a highly competitive marketplace, it's possible that the differences between your solutions or offerings and a competitor's products are very slight, in which case, it's often difficult to win the sale just by focusing on product features and company benefits. All things equal (*ceteris paribus*), what makes you stand out from other vendors with equivalent offerings? Still, customers who make purchase decisions are going to buy from someone. Whether or not you are able to win the close ones (when there's a virtual tie between competing vendors) has more to do with the customer's perception of what you (the salesperson) brings to the table, in terms of your intelligence, capability, professionalism, creativity, honesty, preparedness, and responsiveness with regard to their needs. Once again, we're back to a list of highly intangible but very important character traits.

As with credibility, sellers can't just open their briefcases and hand the customer a bag full of intelligence. That raises a pretty important question, one that salespeople and managers ask themselves on a daily basis: What can I do to give myself an advantage, so that at the end of the day, when the customer chooses a supplier or vendor, they choose to do business with me as opposed to all the other similar-sounding alternatives?

Let's agree that it's easy to win a sale if you have a huge product advantage. For example, when someone invents a safe and affordable flying car, that product will likely sell itself. Likewise, whoever stumbles upon a cure for cancer won't need a sales organization to generate revenue from millions of eager clients. It's easy to sell a product that has no competition or is clearly different from everything else on the market. Unfortunately, that's not the reality most companies face, as sales professionals today are generally not selling exclusive products. It's more likely that you will be competing in a scenario where the customer's decision process will narrow the field of possible vendors down to a few viable alternatives, either of which could do the job. At that point, the competition between these vendor finalists has come down to a virtual tie. Without any additional differentiation from you, the customer's decision could be made by simply flipping a coin, or the customer could just toss the proposals into the air and choose whichever vendor's paperwork happens to land face up. Granted, most customers aren't going to relegate important purchases to such a random decision-making process. Nonetheless, when the purchase decision comes down to a virtual tie between multiple vendors, someone is going to win the business, and it might as well be you.

The Quickest Way to Gain Traction

The true challenge in this new economy is positioning yourself to win given that your competitors are likely to be formidable and the sale could be won or lost by very slim margins. That said, your success as a sales professional will likely be determined by the customer's perception of the intangible benefits you bring to the table. Let your competitors be the ones who commoditize their respective value propositions with a bunch of generic buzzwords.

Okay, but what happens after a sales manager gives a rousing speech encouraging reps to go out and penetrate new accounts, basically instructing them to build relationships with key people within important target accounts? The real coaching challenge arises when one of these sales reps raises their hand and asks, "How exactly are we supposed to gain an advantage within target accounts when everyone else is out there trying to build the same relationships?"

Therein lies one of the big differences between a top performing sales professional and one of their struggling counterparts—the realization that an intangible benefit cannot actually be claimed by a salesperson, it must be earned. Sure, you can tell customers how great your solutions are, but your competitors are going to make similar claims about their products and company, and potential buyers will discount most of these claims anyway, just like you do when you flip past an infomercial on TV.

In order to be in the strongest possible position to prevail in those opportunities that come down to a virtual tie, sellers need some way to convey important intangible benefits like credibility, experience, integrity, vision, creativity, responsiveness, and thought leadership. I would guess that we are all in agreement that these factors can be important tiebreakers. Even so, these highly intangible benefits are not something that a salesperson can just claim. Take humility, for example, which is a very attractive human quality. Imagine the reaction you might have if someone was to say to you, "I am the most humble person in the world!" Huh? Knowing that most buyers are natural skeptics and we sellers are ultimately going to be judged by our actions, it's safe to assume that desirable human qualities (like humility) must be demonstrated and earned (as opposed to being claimed) to register value in the eyes of prospective clients.

Once we conclude that winning or losing a closely contended sales opportunity could come down to the customer's perception of the value an individual salesperson brings to the table, we quickly come to a fork in the road where you must choose to either continue onward with the traditional mentality of persuading customers that your product's benefits are different from the competition's, or step outside the box of traditional thinking and try something else that can truly give you a significant competitive advantage.

What if You Threw Your Entire Industry Under the Bus?

Although I don't always succeed, I try to be a logical thinker. In simplest terms, I consider what might make the most sense given the situation or scenario, and then I try to execute on that. Thus, my logical thought process toward selling to skeptical customers tends to work like this: It is my belief that you won't overcome a customer's natural skepticism just by being pleasant, positive or effusive. In fact, whenever I'm the customer and a salesperson shows up who is overflowing with enthusiasm, his disposition makes him seem unrealistic, if not totally fake, mostly because people in general aren't that happy to meet me. As a result, this level of disingenuousness on the part of the salesperson causes me to be even more cautious and skeptical that their offerings can actually provide value.

Like it or not, sellers inherit all of the baggage and negative perceptions that customers have formed as a result of all the interactions they've had with other salespeople who called on them long before you showed up. The good news is, the customer's natural skepticism isn't personal. They don't even know you when you first engage. Nonetheless the customer's natural standoffishness toward salespeople is very real, and it has formed as the result of encountering a steady stream of salespeople who were more focused on delivering their sales pitch rather than conveying a perception of real value.

My perspective on dealing with customer skepticism changed within the past few months, more specifically when a commercial construction company in Atlanta hired me earlier this year to help them prepare for an upcoming industry trade show. The principal of the firm along with most of the key players had already devoured my first book, *Secrets of Question Based Selling*, but they wanted me to come in and help them customize the QBS methodology for their specific industry, presumably to get maximum value out of their upcoming investment.

"We're basically a general contractor for retail office space," Mike (the CEO) told me, "and you know how people feel about general contractors, don't you?"

"Tell me," I said.

"Tom, lots of people have been burned by general contractors over the years, either by them cutting corners on quality, deviating from the contract, overcharging for change orders, or not following through on promises made," he explained. Having been burned when we built a house in 2002, I could relate to some of the negative predispositions people might have toward general contractors. He added, "In people's minds, general contractors are down there with used car salesmen and telemarketers."

I thought to myself, if that's true, then I would want to do everything possible to not be like the last dozen or so general contractors who called or showed up presenting their ideas, only to be escorted to the nearest exit. I especially wouldn't want to sound like my closest competitors, just to have an already elongated decision process come down to a virtual tie. What I would instead want to do is to figure out a way to differentiate my products and company, and most important, I would want to differentiate myself.

Well, if we know that claims of greatness from a salesperson tend to fall on deaf ears, and we also know that you can't actually hand your credibility, expertise, or integrity to a prospective buyer, that essentially leaves us with one option: to basically tell it like it is, communicating very directly to customers about their potential concerns. In the process of differentiating yourself from whatever negative experiences or perceptions they might harbor from their dealings with others in your same business, you might as well throw the already-formed reputation of your entire industry under the proverbial bus.

The concept is simple. You essentially verbalize what the customer is already thinking, starting with their biggest concern: which is, finding someone who will truly provide the highest level of value and integrity. It works like this: Instead of randomly rattling off a litany of features and benefits to your next customer, you simply point to the "elephant" in the room by saying: "Mr. Customer, the reputation among general contractors has suffered over the years as the result of those people in the industry who were willing to cut corners without regard to quality, staying on schedule, or delivering results that were consistent with the spirit of the project. Consequently, we made a conscious decision as a company not to do business as usual, in order to distinguish ourselves from all the other general contractors who have essentially eroded the reputation of the entire industry. That said, customers like yourself are generally much more interested in addressing their needs than just hearing another sales pitch. Thus, since you are probably a very busy person, would it make sense for me to skip past the marketing hype and talk more specifically about what you would like to accomplish, and how our solutions could impact your business?"

My intent here is not to disparage other vendors by name or to bad-mouth my direct competitors. Mud-slinging is a defensive strategy that rarely works. I am, however, very interesting in connecting with the prospect by saying out loud what they're probably already thinking, in this case about the reputation of general contractors. Customers in most industries believe that salespeople are looking out for their own interests first. From their experiences in dealing with many vendors over time, they know we're paid on some kind of bonus or commission basis, and they've experienced a myriad of self-serving sales pitches long before you show up. So, what's a customer supposed to think? Upon meeting a salesperson for the first time, should he or she assume, "Wow, I bet this vendor is very different and much more effective than all the other salespeople who have darkened my door over the last several weeks"? That probably won't be the reaction, as sellers usually don't get the benefit of the doubt when dealing with skeptical prospects.

....

Most customers believe that vendors are looking out for themselves first. Thus, salespeople are presumed to be valueless until they do something to prove otherwise.

....

In the American justice system, we say that you're innocent until proven guilty. In sales, I would assert that a salesperson is valueless in the eyes of every new prospect, until you do something to prove otherwise. Hence, with the exception of other sellers who have read this book, I bet that I'm pretty much the only salesperson this week, this month, or this entire year who is willing to throw an entire industry under the bus— acknowledging to customers that there is way too much fluff and self-aggrandizement in the world of selling today. From there, it's pretty easy to suggest to them that it might be more valuable to spend less time focusing on marketing hype and instead identify more specifically what the customer is trying to accomplish, and whether or not you can provide a viable solution.

"Whew!" customers will think to themselves. "Not another commission hungry sales pitch. Hooray!"

Once a prospective buyer begins to form the impression that you might be a straight-talking down-to-earth person, it's relatively easy to facilitate a conversation about the customer's needs, and how the pros and cons of your solution alternatives compare to the other options being considered, including the possibility of delaying the decision into the future, or choosing to do nothing at all.

What do you suppose happens when one of your highly enthusiastic competitors shows up a couple hours later or the following day and he jumps right into a hype-filled sales pitch about all of his wonderful features and benefits? After a very successful in-depth conversation with you, customers will have very little patience for generic sales pitches, in which case, the decision could be close to being over. You may win, simply because you were willing to verbally acknowledge what the customer already believes to be true—that salespeople who are not purposeful and customer-focused right off the bat usually end up being self-serving wastes of time from the customer's perspective.

Don't get me wrong. I'm not the least bit ashamed to represent a viable company and its valuable product or service offerings as a salesperson. Frankly, there is no higher calling than helping customers solve important problems and getting paid handsomely in the process. I just don't want to be linked to or associate myself in any way with all the baggage and negative perceptions customers have formed toward traditional sales approaches. If you agree that customers want to be helped, as opposed to being "sold to" by a commission-hungry vendor, then you can just as easily separate yourself from the rest of the noise in the marketplace.

Finally, Something "New" in the Sales Process

There will be very few times during the course of your lifetime when an idea gets introduced that is so new and innovative that it totally changes the way people think and do business. In mathematics, for example, long division has been around the days of the abacus, and in much the same manner, the rules of proper English grammar have changed, but only slightly in the last couple hundred years.

Meanwhile, the nature of the strategic sale continues to change dramatically, and it's all happening right under our noses. After publishing multiple books on the subject, I'm not ashamed to admit that this is the very first time I have written about what I would argue is a brand new component of the sales process that needs to be inserted into your daily interactions with current and prospective customers. I now teach this concept in every QBS training course I deliver, and the feedback from this one idea has been so incredibly positive that talking about how to deal with the "elephant in the room" has become the central theme of most of my recent keynotes. Verbally acknowledging the well-known reality that most customers are skeptical toward the traditional happy-faced salesperson is a competitive tactic that can give an individual salesperson or an entire sales team significantly more traction than anything else you can do when trying to penetrate new opportunities or establish relationships with potential buyers. I realize that this is a sizable claim, but what else can you expect when an elephant is involved?

It's true that most of the clients we train have some kind of structured sales process in place already, albeit some are more formal and more deeply engrained than others. That's perfectly fine with me, because Question Based Selling doesn't compete with a client's internal sales process. We do just the opposite, in fact. A successful implementation of QBS is designed to enhance the execution of the specific steps within the client's chosen process. We do this by teaching strategies and techniques that show salespeople "how" to be more effective than their closest competitors. Think of QBS as a philosophical tool box.

Unfortunately, much of the strategic sales training and development efforts have focused on defining, reinforcing, and reiterating the steps of the sales process, where sheer process definition has dominated the thinking of sales managers for the last two decades. Certainly, formalizing your internal sales process can provide some organizational benefits, like creating a common language and/or instilling forecast consistency. But after you have invested heavily in redefining or reinforcing your internal sales process, the real problem sales managers face will soon be revealed. Just look around your current sales organization, and you will quickly notice that some salespeople are more effective than others, using the same exact sales process, to position the same products to similar types of customers. This occurs because the steps of your strategic sales process will no longer determine the effectiveness of a salesperson. Rather, it's the execution of those steps that will ultimately determine each salesperson's success.

Case in point: What's the first step in your current sales process? I bet it has something to do with "identifying potential opportunities." Seems like a logical first step, doesn't it? Absolutely, which is why it is likely to be the first step in all of your competitors' internal sales processes as well. Step number two probably has something to do with "qualifica-tion." Step three is to "uncover needs." Step four calls for you to "propose solutions." Likewise, steps five, six, and seven are strikingly similar from company to company as well.

I'm not suggesting that having a defined internal sales process isn't valuable, because it does provide a level of organizational effectiveness. It just doesn't address the main problem salespeople, managers, and sales organizations face on a daily or even hourly basis—which is how to execute more effectively than the competition.

The actual execution of each of the steps within your defined process is where most sales are won or lost. And, given that prospective custom-ers have become more cautious with their decision making and more judicious with their budgets and spending than ever before, winning on this new intangible playing field can give you a significant competitive advantage moving forward, Meanwhile, consistently coming up on the short end of the stick in your sales opportunities can drop your percent-age chance of success dramatically.

With this in mind, a new puzzle piece needs to be inserted into the traditional sales model. Adding a new component to the existing mind-set of a salesperson isn't necessarily intuitive, but as I mentioned in the previous section, is a breath of fresh air for the customer. Let's simply call this new piece in the sales model "pointing at the elephant in the room." Think of it as giving yourself an unfair advantage, particularly at the beginning of the sales conversation when you are forging new relationships. Let's examine this idea by taking a closer look at the anatomy of a typical sales conversation.

From the illustration, you can see that the beginning and ending of a sales call are pretty standard. Whether you're calling a new prospect or checking in with an existing account, every sales conversation has some kind of opening, presumably where you introduce yourself and legitimize your purpose in calling. At the end of the conversation, assuming things go well, the salesperson will close for some level of commitment by suggesting an appropriate next step in the decision process.

During the meat of the conversation, matching your company's value proposition to the customer's needs is standard fare; although many books have been written on the topics of needs development and positioning value, and these philosophies often contradict each other.

For sellers like me who yearn to have an unfair advantage in the sales process, I would encourage you to insert a new component into your strategic sales process. After your initial introductory comments, without hesitation, you verbally point to the elephant in the room as a way to differentiate yourself and convey many of those important intangible qualities that will ultimately break the tie when you come to the end of a competitive sale. This new component of pointing to the elephant in the room is designated in the illustration by the simple circular icon labeled "E/R."

As a conversational technique that fosters more productive needs development conversation, (which will ultimately give you an opportunity to position your solutions in their best light), pointing at the elephant in the room is designed to produce a neck-snap reaction from customers, where they say to themselves, "Wait a minute. This is not how most salespeople talk. He's actually saying that the traditional approach to selling sounds too, self-serving (which it does), and we would be better served by sidestepping much of the vendor-hype in order to focus on the problem at hand and the specific goals we want to accomplish. Hooray!"

Here's what pointing at the elephant in the room might sound like in a real world conversation with a customer:

Customer: Tell me about ABC Company.

Rep: I'd be happy to. How much do you know about ABC and the products we offer?

Customer: A little, but why don't you bring me up to speed.

Rep: Well, we're a Fortune 200 company and a leading provider of widgets in North America, serving a broad range of customers from single-location businesses to large multinational firms. As you may know, we have a pretty impressive track record of success over time . . . *But that's not why people do business with ABC Company!*

Frankly, Mr. Customer, there is a problem in the widget marketplace, where it has become very unclear (to customers) how to choose the best solution if your goals are to maximize the function of the product in the most cost-effective manner, over time.

It used to be customers didn't have to worry about things like product support or service, and until recently, standards or compliance were not even considered as significant issues. Thus, the difference between competing offerings was pretty straightforward. Customers either bought the solution with the cheapest price, or they bought from whomever they liked best at the time.

However, as copycats continue to spring up with fancy brochures and "me too" product messaging, without the ability to deliver the same level of service or results, it has become very difficult for customers to discern the difference between real value and what I might simply characterize as marketing smoke and mirrors.

Thus, our business model at ABC Company is very focused on working with customers not just to help them understand our range of proposal options, rather we take a proactive approach to understand the customer's specific business objectives, and then customize a solution for what has become one of the top expense items that makes you competitive (or not) in your respective markets.

Would it be valuable for me to review some of the different options that could impact your business and potentially save you money in the process?

Customer: Sure.

Notice that the salesperson in this example intentionally cuts themselves off midway into their introductory pitch to say, *"But that's not why people choose to do business with us!"* Can you imagine? From there, it's pretty easy to talk about the real challenges, starting with the fact that copycat vendors springing up all over the place have made it very difficult for customers to discern the difference between real value and marketing smoke and mirrors. I can pretty much guarantee that you will be the only salesperson who is willing to verbally acknowledge that customers should indeed be very skeptical. Basically, in the process of being forthright and realistic, you can feel free to subtly indict the traditional sales mindset where the salesperson who shows up spewing features and benefits will unknowingly shoot themselves in the foot. In the case of a virtual tie customers will choose the person who is realistic over someone who is indiscriminately super-enthusiastic.

Throwing the traditional sales establishment under the bus is a huge attention getter with potential clients, but it's important to understand why. Would you agree that psychologically speaking, most people enjoy a good belly laugh. I do, and when something happens that is really funny, you probably do as well. But have you ever thought about what makes something funny? Most people have never thought about what actually triggers the laugh. They just laugh whenever something tickles their funny bone. But guess what—you don't actually have a funny bone. The trigger that makes us laugh at something is the fact that it creates an unexpected surprise that we can relate to in some comical way.

In most sales situations, we're not trying to make the customer laugh per se, but we absolutely want to grab their attention and we absolutely want to do something that creates a subtle neck-snap experience, along with having a certain "wow" factor. Well, cutting yourself off and pointing at the elephant in the room does exactly that by creating an unexpected surprise in the minds of your customer—in a breath-of-fresh-air kind of way. Verbally acknowledging the elephant in the room gives you the opportunity to diffuse the customer's skepticism by talking very directly to them with the suggestion that we go down a different path. Perfect for the customer! It's that easy.

Think about it. What every decision maker really wants to know is: "What are my options, how would each of those affect my business or me personally, and what are the associated costs?" The key to effectively executing this strategy is therefore quite simple—instead of focusing on your solutions, you literally cut yourself off, and go right into a discussion of the problems that customers in this industry now face. Bingo!

To confirm the soundness of the underlying logic, let's ask ourselves this question: what's more important to most customers today, their problems, issues, and concerns, or a salesperson's product pitch? Moreover, do you agree that customers tend to be skeptical toward salespeople until you do something to prove you are not just another smiling face? If you are on board with this logic, then throwing the traditional salesy approach under the bus by suggesting that a conversation about the customer's specific business might be more beneficial than a generic marketing overview (thus, acknowledging the elephant in the room) becomes the fastest way for a salesperson to earn credibility with potential decision makers, and gain the traction necessary to facilitate a more in-depth conversation about their needs and your potential solutions.

Now, Let's Pull Back the Curtains

Oddly enough, one of the best examples of how to convey your intangible benefits in the most customer-focused and meaningful way can be seen in my new favorite sales movie: *The Wizard of Oz*. This movie classic has endured the test of time to become one of the most watched motion pictures in history. But do you want to know why *The Wizard of Oz* has become my new favorite sales movie?

Trust me; it hasn't always been. I used to think this film was just a story about a girl who had a bad day after being conked on the head during a storm. Just recently, however, I started to notice an interesting parallel between what happens during a typical sales conversation and the story line that gets revealed midway through the movie, in the great city of Oz.

If you remember the movie, the single most important scene occurs when Dorothy's little dog Toto pulls the curtain back and we suddenly discover that the great and powerful Wizard of Oz is just a regular guy. In an instant, the underlying plot is revealed to the characters on the screen and to the movie audience at the same time. "Pay no attention to that man behind the curtain," the deafening voice booms over the loudspeaker. Once the Great Oz is exposed for who he really is—just an old man with a microphone—the story takes an interesting twist and goes on to resolve itself shortly thereafter.

This memorable scene captures the essence of the number one concern buyers have when dealing with corporate vendors or individual salespeople. They want to work with someone who is honest and forthright, and someone who will give them the whole story as opposed to just a self-serving sales pitch.

So what does it really mean to be honest and forthright? Let me frame it with a hypothetical example. Suppose for a moment that I was in the car business, and Mr. and Mrs. Customer came down to my local used-car dealership, interested in possibly trading in their old clunker for a new SUV.

With an outstretched hand, I would introduce myself and ask, "Is there something I can help you with today?"

Like most people, they would feel a need to issue a disclaimer of some sort, probably something cautious like, "My wife and I are just in the looking stage, but we are considering the possibility of upgrading our current mini-van to a new SUV."

Given my newfound affection for *The Wizard of Oz*, it would then be easy for me to respond by saying, "I would be happy to help." But, I would quickly add value by saying something like, "If you are interested in upgrading your van to one of the newer SUVs, there are three or four things that I would absolutely encourage you to consider as you look at the different models, but there are also two or three potential 'gotchas' that I would recommend you try to avoid. Would it be valuable for me to *pull back the curtains* and give you the straight scoop on your available options?"

Predictably, Mr. and Mrs. Customer would physically react to my offer. With a heavy sigh of relief and/or some other physical gesture that suggests, "Finally, someone who actually wants to help us rather than just trying to get in our pockets," their natural defenses would instantly go down making it much easier to have an honest and forthright conversation about their specific needs in order to help them find the perfect car. Note that if a used-car salesperson can quickly and easily cause customers to go from being standoffish and reluctant to instantly wanting their help and advice, then it's likely that this same strategy of gaining instant traction with customers could be applied in your business with the same positive results.

In the financial services industry, for example, a Merrill Lynch associate could easily say to a potential customer, "Mr. Customer, the financial markets have experienced a pretty significant roller-coaster ride over the last several months, as you know. And while there are some encouraging signs on the horizon, there are a handful of short-term hurdles that have me very concerned. Would it be valuable for me to *pull back the curtains* and give you the straight scoop on the different investment options Merrill Lynch can offer and how they would impact your current portfolio?"

Once again, if you say something of this nature to a prospective customer, don't be surprised when they physically react with an audible sigh of relief, a palpable reduction in their natural resistance, and a willingness to openly share their financial objectives with a salesperson they've essentially just met.

Even if you sell swimming pool supplies, you could easily say to a customer, "Mr. Customer, there are two or three options that could work, but it might be to your benefit to take a look at some of the fine print on the product before making a decision. Would it be valuable for me to *pull back the curtains* and explain the different options and how they would affect your ongoing pool maintenance?"

It's not the actual words that make such a powerful impact on customers, it's what your words actually convey. By using a straightforward approach that is based on logic and some insight into basic human nature, you are essentially indicting the traditional sales establishment. While most sellers are content to ramble on and on about the features and benefits of their respective offerings, you, on the other hand, are offering to facilitate a candid conversation about the pros and cons of an important customer decision. This simple act of selflessness conveys the highest levels of honesty and integrity to prospective customers.

Therein lies the magic. What customers really want is the rest of the story. You might even be accused of sounding sensible and down-to-earth! This approach is an instant credibility builder for a salesperson in any industry, and it puts you in a strong position to initiate more in-depth and valuable needs development conversations, which we will talk about shortly.

Understanding what a customer wants isn't difficult once they perceive you to be a valuable resource as opposed to just another sales caller. Thus, my first priority as a salesperson is to diffuse the customer's initial skepticism using proven techniques, in order to earn the right to provide useful advice. I also want to set myself apart from the competition. The ability to do this consistently gives me and the many salespeople I have taught over the years an *unfair* advantage throughout the sales process, and it will work just as well for you.

An Added Bonus from a Competitive Point of View

How can a customer tell when a salesperson is really telling the truth? Even if you are the most polished professional in the business, customers still are natural skeptics, and it's likely that they have been burned in the past, especially if they didn't do their due diligence. Thus, those salespeople who focus most of their attention on positioning their company as the industry leader, or who rely on claims that their products are "second to none" should stop and think for a minute what the customer is likely to do next. If you spend your time talking with customers about all the wonderful options you offer, the only way for customers to verify whether what you have shared is true is to pick up the telephone and call your competitors. At that point, they will compare whatever you said with what your rivals claim about how great their products and services are.

Oops! If your sales approach causes customers to call your competitors to verify the information you share with them, I would argue that your positioning strategy may be creating more competition for you. Personally, I don't want customers to feel the need to verify my integrity by calling other vendors, which, of course, gives competitors the opportunity to show up at the last minute and say, "Me, too." I especially don't want this to happen if someone with no time or effort invested is just going to try and undercut my price in order to steal the business.

This strategy of verbally acknowledging the elephant in the room not only gives you an unfair advantage, it also allows you to plant competitive land mines that will cause your closest competitors to literally shoot themselves in the foot if the customer does happen to shop around. Essentially, you set the bar so high that your less strategic competitors simply won't be able to measure up. Here's how it works.

Just like in the sample dialogue earlier in this chapter, you can start off by characterizing your company in broad terms, letting customers know you are the "leading provider of widgets in North America, with twenty-two offices staffed with excellent advisers who are committed to helping customers customize solutions for their business . . . *But that's not why people choose to do business with us!*"

Customers will all predictably react the same way, by silently asking themselves, "Hmmm, then I wonder why it is that people *do* choose to do business with you?"

The next thing out of your mouth is a very direct dose of reality, essentially pointing at the elephant in the room. You say: "Mr. Customer, there is a problem in the world of widget manufacturing." From there, it's relatively easy to talk about the fact that are a number of copycats who claim to deliver the same level of service, which has made it very difficult for customers to know which vendor (not to mention which product option) would provide the best choice.

You alone will be the only vendor rep who literally cuts themselves off to directly and openly talk about the fact that there is confusion in the widget industry with regard to all the claims being made by various vendors. This creates tremendous credibility for you and conveys unparalleled openness which translates into greater value for your proposed solutions. Meanwhile, everyone else in your market will simply pull out their canned elevator pitches and spew forth with a litany of marketing hype and industry buzzwords.

Here's the fun part. As you near the end of your meeting with the customer, if they don't sign up with you right then and there (which could easily happen if they perceive high levels of value in you), you say, "Mr. Customer, I realize that you have to do your due diligence and possibly talk to other providers to be sure you are making the best decision for your business. Can I make a quick suggestion?"

"Sure," they will say.

"If you do happen to talk with another vendor about some these same decision issues, invite the other vendor to tell you about his company, and see what happens. If they jump right into an infomercial about their offerings, and they don't tell you straight up that there's a problem in the widget business, then you should run as fast as you can the other way."

The same customer who would call other vendors as part of their due diligence will absolutely ask competitors whatever you suggest they should ask. After all, what they're really trying to figure out is, which one of these vendors is giving me the straight scoop? At that point, the person who leverages the elephant in the room usually wins the business going away, and other vendors involved won't have the slightest idea why they lost.

2

Your Next Job Interview

....

Whether you are a person interviewing for a desirable position or you have ever evaluated potential candidates as a hiring manager, a job interview scenario is something that virtually everyone can relate to. It also provides the perfect metaphor for why it's important to sell yourself first.

As an applicant for employment, in addition to being solely responsible for selling yourself, you are also the product that's being sold. And even if you are the most qualified candidate applying for a position, you still have to say and do things during the interview process (or during a sales call) that will cause you to be perceived as such.

....

Make no mistake, an employment interview is definitely a sales situation. Even if you are not planning to change companies any time soon, you will still be competing internally with other qualified individuals within your current organization for advancement opportunities, bonus money, or for that future promotion.

Besides just meeting potential candidates in person, what do you suppose is the real value of an employment interview? Think about it. Why would a hiring manager or company even bother investing the time and money to meet with candidates in person as opposed to just hiring people after reviewing the paperwork they've submitted? Most of the candidate's work history and qualifications can be gleaned either from their résumé or by talking with references that have been provided.

Let's face it, everyone looks good on paper. While it's true that hiring managers can narrow the field of qualified candidates by culling through a stack of résumés, in most cases the final step in the decision process is to bring the strongest candidates in for a series of face-to-face interviews, in order to select the person who ultimately provides the best fit given the requirements of the position.

So besides just meeting each of the candidates in person, the question still stands: What's the real purpose of a face-to-face employment interview? The answer is actually quite simple. Once you bring human chemistry into the mix, individual candidates tend to separate themselves pretty quickly. Being face-to-face with someone in a real live interview scenario gives the hiring manager an opportunity to pick up on subtle but important character traits like the candidate's professionalism, preparedness, energy, passion, personality, commitment, assertiveness, helpfulness, communication skills, mutual respect, confidence, and humility.

The real purpose of a job interview, therefore, is twofold. First, a face-to-face meeting provides qualified candidates with an opportunity to sell themselves to the hiring manager, and second, it gives the hiring manager a chance to see, experience, and evaluate many important intangible qualities about the person that wouldn't otherwise show up as specific line items on the candidate's résumé.

> **Every job interview is a sales situation, and every sales situation is also a job interview. In either case, to succeed, you must sell yourself first.**

Not surprisingly, the purpose of a sales call is very similar. For customers, time spent with a salesperson either on the telephone or in person gives them a chance to evaluate the vendor's value proposition. Your probability of success and the customer's perception of your value will be significantly influenced by some key intangibles like professionalism, preparedness, energy, passion, personality, commitment, assertiveness, helpfulness, confidence, and mutual respect, and the extent to which they can be demonstrated by the salesperson during the call. Think of it this way. Every job interview is a sales situation, and every sales situation is also a job interview. In sales, if you want to have opportunities to position your product or service offerings to qualified decision makers, then you must be able to *sell yourself first*.

This concept of selling one's self has eluded sales organizations for many years. As a result, people have tended to attribute a salesperson's success to having a certain level of charm or charisma, and to their ability to either break into a wide-eyed toothy smile or come across as having a jovial personality. Projecting a pleasant disposition is nice, but it's no longer enough to differentiate yourself in a competitive selling environment, as many of your toughest competitors are likely to be just as pleasant and energetic as you.

The realization that your personal performance during a job interview or on a sales call will have a direct impact on the outcome of the hiring manager's (or customer's) final decision can be empowering and terrifying at the same time. If the conversation goes well, you will have every right to congratulate yourself for a good showing. A successful sales call or job interview can be a terrific confidence builder. On the other hand, knowing that a minor misstep in front of a key decision maker can cause you to miss out on an important opportunity can be somewhat intimidating. Nonetheless, your ability to position your company, educate the customer on the product, and sell yourself during an employment interview ultimately depends on how you are perceived by the decision maker.

You Are Constantly Selling Yourself

Why are we talking about how to handle yourself during your next job interview? Given the current economic climate, and the fact that we are in the midst of a Darwinian-style recalibration for businesses in all industries, as I mentioned earlier, it has never been more important for salespeople to be valuable in the eyes of their customers and their company, whether it's for the sake of career advancement or job security.

Frankly, an employment interview is the closest you will ever come to actually selling yourself. In these situations, the hiring manager becomes the customer, and you alone are responsible for conveying the value and benefits that you would bring to the position. Whether you are competing for your first career opportunity right out of school or you are hoping to secure a promotion within your current organization, applying sound logic and effective communication techniques to your next job interview can give you a significant advantage over other equally viable candidates. But, as with anything else, you must understand the underlying logic in order to leverage the strategic nuances that will enable you to be successful in making the sale.

The job interview itself quickly transforms into a classic Sales 101 scenario, where the host company is simply trying to fill a need, and your goal during the actual interview is to impress the hiring manager enough to convince him or her that your talent, experience, and abilities would best suit the open position.

Oddly enough, some of the most qualified candidates show up to their appointed interview, and within minutes, they verbally throw up on themselves by defaulting to the older-school approach of just telling about themselves until the customers either buys their product or kicks them out of the office. Even seasoned professionals with twenty-plus years of sales experience are quick to espouse the virtues of their personal experience, followed by a litany about their educational background and track record of success. Basically, when given the opportunity, qualified candidates default to reviewing and reiterating the key points listed on their résumés, hoping that a heavy dose of reiteration will tip the scales in their favor.

Out in the field of business, salespeople often gravitate to using this same strategy, barraging customers with an information dump in the hopes of impressing them with enough facts and figures about their product or service to earn the business. Put another way, sellers rely too heavily on product information, rattling off the preprinted bullet points that appear in their company's brochure, just as qualified candidates rely far too heavily on the notion that reviewing their résumé in excruciating detail will somehow increase their chances of success.

While information overload might work just fine when you are the only candidate or vendor being considered, if you are competing against a host of other similarly impressive candidates for a winner-take-all sales opportunity, then you're not likely to prevail just by describing and reiterating how great your product appears on paper.

The good news is, if you are able to think strategically in terms of how you position yourself in any sales situation, the same technique we talked about in chapter 1 (verbally acknowledging the "elephant in the room") can give you a significant advantage on your next sales call, or during your next job interview.

Perhaps you are familiar with the axiom "Everybody sells all the time!" Well, it's true. Most people sell themselves every day in some fashion. Whether you are in a traditional sales position or you provide support in a customer service role, if you interact with customers in any capacity, then the customer's perception of your company and products will likely be affected by the impression customers form about you. Thus, in my simple way of thinking, we are always selling ourselves. From there, it becomes an easy leap for me to conclude that we must take responsibility for our interactions with customers, partners, colleagues, our employer, and even with friends and family when we are not at work.

The logic behind this notion that you must *sell yourself first* is a culmination of the overall communication philosophy that I've been teaching for many years. My premise for this book, however, is relatively simple and pretty straightforward. As the subtitle indicates, selling yourself first is indeed the most critical element in every sales effort. This book was therefore written to be a direct commentary on what you (as a salesperson or potential candidate during a job interview) can do to give yourself an unfair advantage in those situations where key decision makers will be primarily forming their impressions about *you*.

Simply put, the single most important reason that someone should want to hire you, buy from you, or deal with you in any capacity is because of *you*! At the end of the day, you are the one who will invest the time to understand the customer's needs, and you will subsequently educate him as to how your offerings stack up against other options being considered. If all goes well, you can and should be in the best position to suggest solution alternatives that will help decision makers achieve both their business and personal objectives. No matter what job title you have in your current company, or what role you might be interviewing for, you want the unique blend of knowledge, experience, and insight that you bring to the table to make you an invaluable resource and an integral part of the customer's overall solution.

The fact that salespeople can directly contribute to their own success is a double-edged sword, however. When things go well, popping corks and congratulatory cheers can be heard for miles around—it's easy to take credit for sales success. Of course, there's a sobering flip side to this reality. If for some reason you are not winning business as often as you would like in this difficult economy, or you are not getting the results you desire in general, then it's possible you may need to look inward to identify the culprit.

I have been training sales professionals long enough to know that most people don't relish the idea of being on the receiving end of constructive feedback. Therefore, my goal here isn't to ruffle anyone's feathers, point fingers, or belittle your current sales process. Most of the sales organizations I've worked with over the years are staffed with honest, caring, hardworking people. But if you are truly motivated by success and you are willing to take an objective look at how you are being perceived through the eyes of your customers, you will soon discover that there are many upside opportunities to convey significantly more value by simply adjusting the way you position yourself.

First, ask yourself these questions: Are you the type of individual that people can trust? Do colleagues and customers solicit your input and listen to your opinions? Are you intelligent and street smart, beyond just being knowledgeable about your products or a particular industry? Do you have the customer's best interests at heart when offering recommendations and advice? Let's assume for a moment that your answer to all of these questions is a resounding yes. Terrific! But how is a customer who is meeting you for the very first time supposed to know that you possess these qualities?

I'm sure your closest friends and even some of your existing customers already recognize how much value you bring to the table. You have to recognize, however, that every seller who walks through the customer's door, along with every candidate who comes into the hiring manager's office for a job interview, will claim to offer the best solution. Unfortunately, all the chest pounding in the world doesn't change the fact that just because someone claims to be great doesn't necessarily make it so.

During an employment interview, for example, most candidates do whatever comes naturally. Usually they show up well prepared and enthusiastically ready tell about themselves and their backgrounds, the same way an eager salesperson is quick to tell all about their product features and benefits. But to prevail and ultimately get hired, perhaps you should ask yourself this question: How can I differentiate myself from the previous candidate who was ushered out of the hiring manager's office just a few minutes before I arrived? Or, prior to your next sales call, you might ask: What is going to separate me from the seven or eight other salespeople who previously called on this customer and delivered the same "we are the leader in our industry" pitch?

As I've said already, customers actually do depend on salespeople—as a source of information, creative ideas, a vision into the future, and for solutions. They just don't depend on all of them. So out of all the sellers who are calling the same list of target customers, some small fraction of those vendor representatives are going to be seen as a valuable resource. Likewise in an employment interview, out of all the candidates vying for a desirable position within the company, someone is going to prevail. The question is, how consistently are you being included in that small fraction of people who are perceived to be credible, intelligent, experienced, creative, honest, prepared, responsible, reasonable, and thought leaders in their respective fields? If we pose that question a different way perhaps we should ask: How consistently are you putting yourself in the customer's select group of valuable resources?

If you agree that a fair amount of skepticism exists in the marketplace, where customers have become increasingly standoffish toward salespeople they don't yet know or trust, then what sellers really need is a repeatable system—a formula that will enable them to consistently differentiate themselves and their products, one that can be easily implemented, managed, and will produce immediate positive results.

While I do agree that people tend to buy from people they like and respect, the extent to which someone recognizes the intangible value of your offerings, trusts you, and is willing to accept your advice has a lot to do with the approach you take in communicating with them. Hence, most of our attention throughout the rest of this book will focus on two things—how can you separate yourself from the rest of the "noise" in the marketplace by making a few simple adjustments with regard to how you approach customers in the future, and how you can use proven sales technique to increase customer receptivity and the customer's perception of your value.

The Biggest Differentiator Is You

The sales and marketing world has struggled for years to get its intellectual arms around the notion of perceived value. Millions of corporate dollars have been spent on initiatives to gain a competitive advantage with respect to product placement, promotional advertising, sponsorships, brand recognition, data mining, consumer buying habits, and leveraging demographics. As a result, a large investment of resources has been poured into analyzing consumers' behavior in an effort to understand what causes customers to either move forward with a favorable decision to buy from you, or to purchase a solution from someone else. Still, the number one issue facing most sales organizations today remains the same—how can we duplicate the success of our top performing salespeople. In every company, some salespeople are significantly more effective than others, even though they are basically offering the same menu of products and services to the same types of customers.

> **In every company, some salespeople are significantly more effective than others, even though they are offering the same menu of products and services to the same types of customers.**

One might wonder why cracking the code on this sales formula has eluded our strategic focus for so long. Back when I was a neophyte salesperson, I vividly remember wondering what top performers at my company were doing that I wasn't. Did they have a secret formula, more experience, or were they just lucky to have good accounts? What afforded them such a competitive advantage?

While I acknowledge that some people are naturally endowed with certain innate gifts and skills, if you attribute high performance to those things that are beyond your control, you will never reach your full potential, especially not in sales. As an example, during the 1980s, I fell short of my sales quota in my first few years in corporate sales. As time marched on and I got tired of beating my head against a wall, and I became increasingly frustrated with the idea of consistently not achieving my sales goal. Finally, I started looking in the mirror and made a few adjustments with regard to how I approached the sales process when dealing with prospective customers. Within a very short time after I started doing things differently, I dramatically exceeded my sales numbers, which enabled me to finish over 200 percent of my assigned corporate quota for multiple consecutive years. During that period, my DNA didn't change at all, and I was no more or less charming. But my approach to sales and how I chose to position myself to customers changed dramatically. So did my perspective on being successful in life.

In a competitive sales situation, the true differences between your proposal and a competitor's offering can be very small, if not negligible. If you have a unique offering that no one else in the world can provide, then you may not need to think strategically. But it's more likely that you sell in a highly competitive market where you don't enjoy total exclusivity, and other vendors are aggressively trying to convey to your same prospects and customers that they offer similar, if not more viable, solutions. I can assure you that you will have plenty of competition during your next job interview.

The Perfect Metaphor for Selling Yourself

The most effective way I have found to show individual sellers or entire sales teams how to significantly enhance their value in the eyes of their target customers is to examine in more depth what actually happens during an employment interview. Everyone is familiar with the job interview scenario, and it's the perfect metaphor for learning how to sell yourself first in a competitive marketplace. Be advised that the techniques I'm about to explain not only provide legitimate advice for someone who's currently in the job market or hunting for a new opportunity, but this metaphor is also an excellent way to show sellers how to increase their current sales volume.

In the case of your next job interview, chances are good that you will be competing against other qualified applicants who have résumés that are just as impressive as yours. After meeting with each of the applicants in person, hiring managers tend to be quick in forming their impressions, and they will generally gravitate toward a clear preference for one candidate over another. When pressed, these decision makers will cite various reasons to support their impressions, but if you listen carefully, there usually isn't a clear-cut differentiator between their top choice and the also-rans. Instead, you will hear a hiring manager say things like, "I just felt more comfortable with this person," or, "We just seemed to click." It wasn't the product, the company, or the résumé alone that created their comfort level; rather, it was the intangible qualities of the way the person was perceived that made all the difference. Knowing this, it follows that how you are likely to be perceived in your next job interview has everything to do with how you choose to position yourself.

If we agree that your current sales effectiveness and longer term success ultimately hinges on your ability to sell yourself, then pardon my candor as I drop a bombshell that may change your perspective on selling forever. What if we were to discover that how most people sell naturally is upside down from how most customers make decisions? Seriously, what if many of the things you have been taught over the years, or the way you have been conditioned by your environment, are exactly the opposite of what would otherwise give you the greatest advantage? Would you be open to the possibility of making a few adjustments in strategy, and in how you choose to position yourself moving forward? If so, I'm here to tell you that you have a huge upside opportunity. The good news is, once you recognize that a discrepancy exists between what you gravitate to naturally and what you could be doing, and you then replace it with a more effective approach that produces immediate results, a huge opportunity is created for those salespeople who are willing to leverage technique and strategy to separate themselves from the rest of the noise in the marketplace.

Let's play out the scenario and I'll show you what I mean.

Meeting the New Boss

Picture yourself walking into your next job interview. Suppose it's a great opportunity, and one that is aggressively being pursued by other legitimate candidates who, like you, have been screened and vetted down to a short list of finalists who are being considered for a desirable position with a leading company. Even though you are on time for your interview and you are very well prepared, you still feel an involuntary surge of nervous energy pumping through your veins. Let me assure you that this is quite natural, as I experience the same nervous energy whenever I take the stage for the first time in front of a new client.

As you wait patiently in the lobby, in walks the hiring manager to escort you back for your long-anticipated interview. With a somewhat clammy palm, you shake the outstretched hand of your potential new boss. "It's nice to meet you," you say, intentionally trying to speak clearly and confidently so as not to bumble the initial introduction.

Everyone knows that it's important to make a good first impression. Particularly in a business setting, you obviously want to start off on the right foot when meeting someone for the first time. If you are a decent judge of people or you have the presence of mind to scan the hiring manager's office for subtle clues, you might get a feel for his or her personality and style. You might also be able to assess his or her current mood or disposition. In most cases, it doesn't take a rocket scientist to tell whether the person you are interviewing with is having a tough day or feeling pushed for time. So you put on a happy face and walk into their office, keenly aware that they are also sizing you up and simultaneously forming their first impressions of you.

Personally, I am not a fan of interviewing gimmicks, like when a hiring manager makes the candidate sit in a chair that is intentionally positioned much lower than his to see if you are easily intimidated, or he asks invasive personal questions to see if timid candidates will crumble under pressure. Fortunately, most of these underhanded interviewing tactics have fallen out of vogue, having faded away with the previous generation of egotistical, chauvinistic bosses. Honestly, if you do happen to encounter someone who is outwardly disrespectful during a job interview, you might want to think twice about whether you would really want to work for that company. Fortunately, most hiring managers don't play games with potential new hires, so we won't waste a lot of time dealing with interviewing tricks.

The purpose of an employment interview is generally pretty clear. It is an opportunity for hiring managers, along with other people who could influence the decision, to meet with qualified candidates face-to-face, so they can evaluate and match the candidate's qualifications against the needs of an open position within the company. Since multiple candidates are usually being considered, hiring managers will analyze and dissect all of the information gleaned from the various interviews, assess their options, and ultimately select and offer the position to the person who presumably provides the best fit from the current pool of applicants.

As I have suggested already, the ultimate decision about whether to hire you or someone else is largely based on the impressions the decision maker forms during these face-to-face interviews. Can you see how this metaphor for selling yourself also applies to a typical sales situation? Mind you, the interviewer and candidate both play an important role in these meetings. As with any important transaction, an employment opportunity should be a mutually beneficial experience that meets the needs of both the hiring manager and the applicant who is being considered for the position.

Upon your initial arrival in the conference room or when you first sit down in the interviewer's office, a certain amount of casual chitchat usually ensues as a starting point for most job interviews. Hiring managers want qualified candidates to feel comfortable and relaxed so they can observe you at your best. So hiring managers will generally ask a few light-hearted questions like "How was your trip across town?" or "Were the directions helpful?" They might even inquire as to how your summer is going. After some brief small talk, however, the conversation will quickly transition to the purpose at hand—the actual job interview.

Let me back up for a moment. Just as any good salesperson would diligently prepare prior to meeting with an important prospect or customer, I will presume that you too would be similarly prepared in advance of your next job interview. Presumably, you would have done some research on the company, their product offerings, and their competitive position in the marketplace. You might have even typed the interviewer's name into your favorite search engine on the Internet to see what pops up. It's smart also to have a list of questions in mind that you would like to ask about the company and the specific job opportunity.

In anticipation of the meeting, candidates do their best to prepare and strategize, but they often worry about the type of questions that might get asked during the interview and how best to answer. There's no need to wonder what the first question will be during an employment interview because the opening salvo from virtually every interviewer will sound exactly the same. At the appropriate time in the discourse, the hiring manager will say something to the effect of "So, why don't you tell me a little about yourself?"

This common and predictable question officially kicks off the serious portion of the employment interview. This is where the rubber meets the road, and you had better be able to gain significant traction early in the conversation and answer more intelligently than the other qualified candidates who have been paraded through the company headquarters over the last few days.

Now it's just a matter of answering the question and telling the hiring manager about yourself, right? Perhaps, but let's not miss the target completely on your very first shot. Although there are many ways to respond to this initial question, I can tell you without a doubt that the standard answer most interviewees give is generally *not* the most effective response. In fact, if you answer the interviewer's question in a way that causes you to sound the same as everyone else, you immediately forfeit any competitive advantage. Let's continue with this metaphor to illustrate how you can avoid missing the target, and instead, learn how to instantly separate yourself from other similarly qualified counterparts.

What's Most Important to the Customer?

When this first softball question gets tossed out by the hiring manager, "Tell me a little about yourself," most people respond by doing just that—they tell about themselves. Hmm. Is that wrong? One wouldn't necessarily think so, since that's what the interviewer seems to be inviting the candidate to do in this scenario. The problem is, the standard way of responding (by just telling about yourself) instantly commoditizes your value, which significantly lessens your chances of a successful outcome—being selected as the preferred candidate.

Just like any salesperson who wants to win a sale, the typical job candidate wants to succeed in the job interview by successfully selling himself or herself to the hiring manager. These roles can sometimes be reversed if a hiring manager is trying to "sell" a top-notch recruit on coming on board with the company. But for all practical purposes, in your next job interview, you will definitely be trying to sell yourself to the hiring manager.

Once we have a firm grasp on who is selling to whom, we should realize that there is more than one way to skin a cat, and the best way to respond to the hiring manager's initial question ("Tell me about yourself . . .") might have less to do with you, and more to do with focusing on those things that are most important to the customer. Would you agree that the typical buyer is much more focused on their own goals and objectives than they are interested in hearing a standard product pitch?

To illustrate the difference between what the typical interviewee says and what a hiring manager really wants to hear, I often go around the room and facilitate pretend job interview scenarios during our QBS training seminars. In doing so, I will invite audience members to role-play with me (as interviewees) in order to get a feel for how they are currently positioning themselves to prospective customers. As it turns out, the way most people approach a job interview tends to mirror the approach they take when positioning products and services to real live prospects. Given our premise throughout the book that you are the biggest differentiator in the sales process, this exercise shows just how easy it is to reduce yourself to sounding like every other Tom, Dick, or Harriett who is competing for the same opportunity.

In these role plays, I start by asking for volunteers from the audience to play the interviewee. Then I will assume the role of the hiring manager. To emulate the initial exchange, I say, "Let's assume I've come out and greeted you in the lobby, offered you a cup of coffee, water, or a soft drink, and we then head back to my office to chat." Next I simulate the transition into the official portion of the employment interview by simply saying, "Tell me a little about yourself."

Here's a sample of the typical responses I get.

Candidate: Well, I have been with my current company for the past five years in a variety of roles, most recently as sales and marketing liaison for some of our largest customers in North America. Prior to that, I was an account manager in Chicago, and I also completed the management training program at our corporate headquarters in Philadelphia. While I was an account manager, I achieved my sales quota two out of three years, and made President's Club both times.

Upon graduating from the University of Michigan in 1997, I first went to work in the family business, which my father sold four years later. I had planned to go back to school to complete the MBA program, but that's about the same time when my wife and I decided to start a family. We now have two kids, a boy who just turned six and a new baby girl. Consequently, I was hoping to find a secure opportunity that would provide me with a reasonable income while allowing me to spend more time with my family.

I am willing to travel, but I would need some flexibility for choosing days off as we vacation every summer in northern Michigan with my wife's parents. My salary requirements are . . .

If we interrupt this exercise for a moment, you might notice that the person being interviewed is responding exactly as requested, by telling the hiring manager "a little" about himself. On the surface, the candidate seems like a decent enough person to me. But something is clearly missing from this sample dialogue.

In order to make the point during a QBS training, I will usually repeat this exercise by soliciting multiple participants from the audience to duplicate the exchange. Now we have a baseline for what the typical approach when responding to the hiring manager's initial question usually sounds like. Once everyone hears five or six people respond in pretty much the same manner, by recounting a brief history of their personal lives, education, and job experience, we quickly realize that using the standard approach would probably make you sound very similar to what every other candidate says during their respective job interviews.

Still, something is definitely missing.

What's missing from the dialogue is any mention of (or concern for) the hiring manager's goals and objectives. If you notice, the candidate in the sample dialogue above is totally focused on communicating his own work history, current goals and objectives, and other personal requirements. It's perfectly fine for a salesperson to have goals and want to express them at the appropriate time during an employment interview, but you must recognize that the hiring manager (i.e. the customer) also has goals and objectives, and to them, their issues and concerns are far more important than listening to yet another candidate drone on about their own work history and personal requirements.

Frankly, this scenario, where potential candidates all respond to the hiring manager's initial question by describing themselves ad nauseam, may be the perfect example of how *not* to begin a job interview, or how *not* to position yourself during a real live sales call. By the time the hiring manager has met with three or four qualified candidates, the responses from each interview sound so similar that any important details about your personal backgrounds tend to all mush together.

The same thing happens when prospective customers evaluate multiple vendors, which is one of the reasons that your next job interview provides such a great metaphor for selling in the real world. After a while, decision makers who invest the time to meet with multiple vendors start to forget whose solution does what, as all the claims of market leadership and product superiority start to blend together. At that point, a confused customer might just decide to delay their decision. An overwhelmed customer could choose to cancel the project altogether. A customer who doesn't fully understand the differences between competing vendors might just flip a coin, or select whichever company is willing to offer the lowest price.

To successfully sell yourself, you must do something that makes you stand out in the customer's mind, as opposed to sounding the same as everyone else. In a competitive sales situation or job interview scenario, let's assume for a moment that each of the finalists who are being considered have similarly strong educational backgrounds, and let's presume that they all have impressive work histories. Therefore, you must do something that sets you apart from the competition, or else your next job interview or sales opportunity will come down to a virtual coin toss at best.

Fortunately, there is another tack you can take that will not only set you apart from the masses, it will literally give you an unfair advantage when it comes time for the hiring manager to make a decision. Let me show you how it works.

What the Hiring Manager Really Wants

A hiring manager, by definition, is trying to accomplish some specific goals or objectives; otherwise there's no point in going through the exercise of scheduling a series of face-to-face interviews. Usually, an open position that needs to be filled has specific performance criteria, in addition to whatever needs, issues, concerns, wants, and desires happen to be rattling around in the hiring manager's head. Whether they are trying to replace an employee who recently left the company or the company has a need to staff up to address a new project or business opportunity, managers are absolutely looking to address their short- and long-term business objectives by hiring the right person.

During the actual employment interview, personal preference and interviewing style will almost certainly vary from one hiring manager to the next, and let's acknowledge upfront that qualified candidates are not always privy to the underlying nuances that may be driving the decision process. But one thing is for sure. Goal-oriented managers are looking for team players who will be instrumental in helping to achieve the company's goals, instead of people who are just focused on achieving their own personal success. That said, would you agree that during an employment interview, the candidate who comes across as being the most able to help a hiring manager accomplish his or her goals and objectives has the best shot at being offered the position? This is not a selfish play on the part of the interviewer. It's only logical that the customer would want to select the person or solution alternative that would seem to provide the best fit, and help *them* the most.

So let's suppose for a moment that you are truly the most qualified candidate who is applying for an exciting new position with a desirable company. Even if that's true and you are indeed the most capable, intelligent, experienced, and the most selfless person in the world, you still must be perceived as such during the actual interview—particularly early on when the customer (in this case, a hiring manager) is rapidly forming their initial impressions. The question now becomes, what impression do you want decision makers to form about you during your next formal job interview or sales call?

The best way to give yourself an unfair advantage during an employment interview (or in any sales situation) is to apply the strategy I introduced back in chapter 1. Rather than just delivering an elevator pitch diatribe of industry buzzwords and self-serving clichés, you literally pull back the proverbial curtains and verbally point at the elephant in the room. Here's what that might sound like in your next job interview:

Manager: Pat, thanks for your time today. Can you tell me a little about yourself?

Candidate: Sure. Do you have a copy of my résumé?

Manager: Yes, I've got it right here.

Candidate: Well, since you've already seen a snapshot of my work history, I'd like to think that I'm a good person with a decent track record of success, but I'll let you be the judge of that. I'm thinking that you might be looking for more than just a "good person" to fill this position, however. In fact, in researching this opportunity I'm guessing that you might be looking for some of the intangibles that wouldn't necessarily show up as specific line items on a résumé.

For example, I'm thinking that you might be looking for someone who can ramp up and become productive as quickly as possible, especially given the challenges posed by the current economy. You may also be looking for someone who can blend with the existing culture, but still bring a fresh perspective or new ideas from outside the company. You might also be looking for someone who can grow existing opportunities, while also being able to defuse potential hot spots that may exist within problem customer accounts. If so, those are the types of things that have enabled me to be successful thus far in my career.

Do you mind if I ask, what other specific goals would you want the perfect candidate for the position to be able to accomplish?

At this point in the conversation, the interviewer's decision process might as well be over, as the hiring manager would likely be jumping up and down in their chair if someone showed up and actually demonstrated that they were indeed interested in helping the interviewer (or company) accomplish their goals .

What's not to like? This person has clearly done their homework in advance of the interview, and instead of just reiterating all the stuff that's already printed on his résumé, he is proactively bringing up key business issues that would be important to any hiring manager. He has also succeeded in taking a humble but very direct approach to positioning his value, as opposed to all the other candidates who just rattle off a list of personal accomplishments followed by a litany of their own goals and objectives. Don't be surprised when the hiring manager's first (and lasting) impression is, "Wow, this person really understands the type of person I'm looking for!" You're hired!

The Secret to Being Customer-Focused

Though I alluded to it earlier, let's revisit a very important question that should guide you in these sales situations, which is: What is the real purpose of an employment interview? Like before, the answer is, hiring managers want to have an opportunity to look potential candidates in the eye as opposed to just hiring someone off a piece of paper. But have you ever thought about what (exactly) they are looking for? The purpose of a job interview is not just to review your work history, because they already read about that on your résumé. It's also not to find out where you went to college, or evaluate whether you have adequate work or industry experience. That's all listed on the paperwork you submitted well in advance of the face-to-face interview.

> **The real purpose of a job interview is to give the hiring manager an opportunity to evaluate the highly intangible qualities that don't show up as specific line items on a résumé.**

I'm just guessing, but I bet your résumé doesn't mention anything about your appearance, your professionalism, your confidence level, or your enthusiasm about the position. Can you be assertive without being pushy? Are you customer-centric, or do you focus on your own objectives first? Do you have a pleasant personality that would fit within the existing corporate culture? Other important character traits that probably aren't listed on your résumé include honesty, integrity, personal conviction, a strong work ethic, the ability to deal with pressure, a vision for the future, and a commitment to doing whatever it takes to get the job done right.

Thus, the "real" purpose of an employment interview is to give the hiring manager an opportunity to assess and evaluate all of the important yet highly intangible character traits that could affect your performance with the company, but aren't going to show up as specific line items on your résumé.

Let's now take a quick look back at the sample verbiage I suggested in our revised interview exchange, which always starts when the hiring manager says, "Tell me about yourself."

Candidate: Well, since you've already seen a snapshot of my work history, I'd like to think that I'm a good person with a decent track record of success, but I'll let you be the judge of that. I'm thinking that you might be looking for more than just a "good person" to fill this position, however. In fact, I'm guessing that you might be looking for some of the intangibles that wouldn't necessarily show up as specific line items on a résumé.

Again, you're hired! I can tell you right now that with the exception of other people who have read this book, you will be only candidate (or vendor) who actually points to the elephant in the room—in this case, by verbally acknowledging that the real reason we're here is to discuss and evaluate important intangible qualities that aren't listed on the typical résumé. Bingo!

Out of the four or five candidates who are invited in for a face-to-face interview, someone who positions themselves in this manner has an unfair advantage. It's that simple. Besides being the only candidate who demonstrated that you are indeed customer-focused—recognizing that the hiring manager probably wants to address specific business objectives— plus you were the only one who verbalized real purpose of the interview— to evaluate the intangible qualities you bring to the table. Let all the other candidates talk about themselves in terms of their own work history and personal goals. Why would you want to hire someone who demonstrates, by the very first thing that comes out of their mouth, that they are not customer-focused?

I'm not asking you to be clairvoyant. Rather, it's just a matter of shifting your focus, from jumping directly into a litany about yourself, to understanding what the customer's needs might be. To accomplish this, just ask yourself: What types of things might be important to you if you were the hiring manager? By taking just a few moments in advance to think about the goals of the interview from the customer's perspective, it's pretty easy to create a top-ten list of desirable attributes a hiring manager might be looking for in the perfect candidate. Those qualities might include:

Desirable Qualities of the Perfect Candidate

1. Knowledgeable, experienced, savvy.
2. Likable, easy to get along with.
3. Customer-focused versus self-serving.

4. Could easily blend with existing business culture.
5. Quick learner, short ramp-up time.
6. Offers a new perspective, with fresh ideas.
7. Independent, motivated, hard worker.
8. Track record of success, combined with a dose of humility.
9. Positive attitude and commitment to excellence.
10. Solid references.

If a candidate for employment possessed each of these qualities, and they could effectively demonstrate them during a job interview, can we agree that in addition to having a pretty good chance of being hired, they would also have the potential of being a valuable long-term asset for the company?

The challenge each candidate faces during an in-person job interview is figuring out how to convey that you indeed possess these desirable attributes without sounding inappropriate. Most people, in an attempt to try and sell themselves, will climb up on a verbal soapbox and start declaring their value—claiming to be a quick learner who is also smart, likable, independent, and self-motivated. Did I forget humble? Trying to articulate one's own strengths in any sales situation creates somewhat of an awkward situation because there's a fine line between seeming confident and credible and sounding pompous or arrogant.

Alas, we have arrived at yet another crossroads in your professional development. As a salesperson, whether you are representing a product, a company, or yourself, you must choose between sounding just like everyone else who uses a traditional elevator pitch in an attempt to convey value and employ a differentiation strategy that will truly separate you from the rest of the noise in the marketplace.

The first step toward implementation is actually quite simple. Just ask yourself this question: What's more important to the typical decision maker, their specific goals, objectives, issues, wants, needs, and concerns, or listening to a salesperson ramble on about their own personal agenda?

Be aware that your success in a formal job interview (or sales call) is not just about the initial impression that gets formed. During a thirty- or sixty-minute employment interview, there will be plenty of opportunities for you to talk about your educational background, your work experience, and your family situation. In fact, I will lay out an entire strategy for "Competitively Positioning Your Solutions" in chapter 9. For now, let's just acknowledge that the first impression someone forms about you or your offering is definitely important, as it sets the tone for the rest of the meeting. Put it this way. If you are consistently able to get your next job interview (or sales call) off to a solid start, there will be plenty of opportunities for you to facilitate more in-depth conversation about how your qualifications or your solutions match up to the opportunity that's being evaluated.

Making this one adjustment in strategy is relatively simple if you understand the logic behind the technique. Just remember that focusing on whatever is most important to your customers—their goals, objectives, needs, wants, desires, problems, issues, and concerns especially the intangible benefits that aren't listed on a résumé or in a product brochure—is more important than anything you could say in a standard sales pitch. Customers want us to focus on their needs *first*. That's why the ability to sell yourself first has become such a huge differentiator in competitive sales situations. If you earn the customer's confidence and you have invested the time to understand what's really important to the customer, then it's actually pretty easy to align your value proposition to convey the value you bring to the table.

Of course, the more goals, objectives, needs, problems, issues, and concerns you can identify in your discussions with potential customers, the more opportunities you will have to provide value. This raises another question. Knowing that different types of buyers have different priorities, hot buttons, and personal agendas, how can you know more specifically which things are most important to a prospect who you are meeting for the very first time?

That's what we'll talk about next.

3

Customers Won't Trust Just Anyone

....

Have you ever been "burned" by a salesperson? Most people have, some-where along the line. Whenever this happens, the decision maker tends to become even more cautious toward subsequent vendors, which makes the next salesperson's task of gaining credibility and earning trust an even bigger challenge.

Selling solutions is fine. But if you want to build strong relationships within target customer accounts, then you must address the decision maker's primary and most important concern, which is knowing who to trust.

....

Imagine this scenario: A handsome, well-dressed representative from ABC Corp. confidently steps up and says to a potential customer, "Buy from us, we're the industry leader!" A few hours later, a salesperson from a different vendor shows up saying, "Buy from us, we offer the highest level of service and our track record is undeniably the best!" Later that afternoon, a third vendor stops by and proclaims, "Choose us, we're number one!"

One could argue that customers have an easier decision when multiple vendors are competing for their business, especially when the products being offered are very similar. Just pick your favorite supplier, or whoever is willing to offer the lowest price, and place your order. If for some rea-son the chosen vendor stumbles or fails to meet expectations, the cus-tomer can easily switch horses and call someone else to provide basically the same thing.

But what happens when the options being considered are not func-tionally equivalent, and the customer must make a not-so-obvious choice between proposed solutions that aren't exactly the same? Whether a corporation is buying a database for a large-scale IT implementation

or an elderly couple sits down at the kitchen table to evaluate supple-
mental health insurance policies, customers often find themselves faced
with the daunting task of somehow sifting through all kinds of marketing literature and sales hype to select the best alternative. At that point,
customers are often left without a good way to compare apples and
oranges. Of course, these decisions are further complicated by the fact
that every vendor in the mix claims to offer the best solutions.

A sales representative from each vendor who submits a proposal for
consideration will predictably don a polished smile and be well versed
in exchanging pleasantries at the beginning of the conversation. From
the customer's perspective, however, knowing that the ramifications of
making a bad decision can be costly or irreversible, how are diligent
customers supposed to know which vendor to choose, especially in
those cases where a first-time buyer isn't even sure what questions to
ask? The answer, along with the outcome of the sale, will largely depend
on which salesperson is able to establish enough credibility to earn the
customer's trust.

Building Mutually Beneficial Relationships

If the intangible nature of perceived value is sometimes difficult for customers to quantify, try putting a fence around the notion of trust. Let
me pose this question: who is it that you trust? I bet it's not some cold
caller on the telephone who's offering a fantastic deal chosen "just for
you!" Cold callers are ostensibly trying to offer you an ideal solution, yet
they don't even know you. It's important to realize that prospective customers may be just as reticent to engage in an open-ended dialogue when
meeting a salesperson (i.e. you) for the first time.

There's no doubt that our business culture has grown increasingly
cautious toward vendors. And our society as a whole has become much
less trusting when it comes to engaging with a salesperson with whom
we don't already have an existing relationship. Thus, it stands to reason
that getting burned or being disappointed by one vendor's actions could
very easily erode a customer's faith in the system, making it that much
more difficult for the next salesperson who wants to build a strong

or trusting business relationship. Our cultural skepticism has evolved to the point where I recently saw a bumper sticker in a church parking lot that read, TRUST IN GOD, BUT LOCK YOUR CAR!

Understanding the dynamics of how mutual trust is created is particularly important for salespeople because trust serves as the foundation for building solid relationships, whether personal or professional. Especially these days, if someone is not willing to trust you, then it is unlikely that any attempts you make at offering potential solutions will produce a positive result. In fact, without some level of trust, or at least the benefit of the doubt, your conversation with new prospects may never even get off the ground.

Trust is also a critical element in maintaining existing relationships. At the point where someone decides they can no longer trust you, it is predictable that whatever relationship you may have had with them will abruptly come to an end.

Once we agree that trust is the foundation of every relationship, it's important to note that trust comes in different forms. In terms of interpersonal relations, trust can officially be defined as having a firm reliance on the integrity, ability, or character of a person or thing. For example, I trust my wife implicitly and my two daughters most of the time. I also trust that our clients will pay their invoices on time. I even trust that there will be a rental car and hotel room waiting for me when I arrive at my next destination, provided I booked a reservation in advance. Although the sentiment being conveyed by the word *trust* is context dependent, the actual emotion of trusting someone or something is another one of those highly intangible concepts. Trust is not something that you hold in your hand or distribute to a prospective customer. And though you cannot measure trust empirically, you can definitely sense whether someone trusts you or not.

What are the chances that customers will implicitly trust the very next salesperson who walks through their door or calls them on the telephone? If it's a vendor they are meeting for the first time, the chances are slim. To date, I haven't discovered any magic button that can be pushed to cause someone to instantaneously trust you. Some fraction of customers might be willing to give a sales professional some initial leeway, but let's not confuse common courtesy with an inherent level of trust. Trust is a long-term human emotion that grows out of the confidence one has developed from successive encounters, where the other person's expectations were either met or exceeded. As I'm sure most of us know, you can lose someone's trust in an instant, but it takes a series of positive affirmations to earn it over time.

> **Trust is a long-term human emotion that grows out of the confidence one has developed from successive encounters, where the other person's expectations were either met or exceeded.**

Contrary to what you might think, trust is not a good strategic target for salespeople to aim at when trying to forge new relationships with potential customers. Sure, every salesperson wants prospects and customers to trust them. And if you consistently meet and exceed their expectations, they will surely begin to trust you at some point. But just as you wouldn't wholeheartedly trust someone after spending a few minutes with them during a job interview, it's impossible to cause new prospects to implicitly trust you after a single telephone call. Instead, sellers are better served in today's business environment by focusing their efforts on the concept of building credibility.

While it can take some time to truly earn someone's trust, a savvy salesperson with the right approach can begin to establish credibility with prospective customers almost immediately. Fortunately for us sellers, the concepts of credibility and trust are closely interrelated. As you earn more and more credibility with customers over time, they will absolutely begin to trust you.

The key is to have a repeatable method that enables you to establish as much credibility as possible early in your sales conversations. Essentially, you want to gain maximum "traction" with potential customers when forging new relationships. Earning credibility quickly gives you an opportunity to convey more value throughout the sales process and ultimately gain an unfair advantage over the competition. The rest of this chapter is a lesson in how to accomplish exactly that.

Solution, Problem, Alternative (The SPA Approach)

Another question I like to ask sales professionals during a live QBS training course is: how do customers know you're smart? Surely, everyone is aware that some salespeople are more knowledgeable than others, or they may have more experience, or they are simply more capable. So how do *you* stack up when meeting prospective customers for the very first time? Do you simply pitch the value of your solutions, hoping that product features will sell themselves and differentiate you from other salespeople? Or, do you just announce to the various decision makers you meet that you are one of the smartest and most capable reps they will ever encounter, and just accept the risk that self-aggrandizing could come off sounding arrogant or presumptuous?

Unfortunately, it has become second-nature for many salespeople to rely on self-promotion—basically, telling about themselves and their products in the hopes of verbalizing enough value to hopefully touch a nerve or pique the interest of prospective buyers. Do you remember the job interview verbiage from chapter 2? It's amazing how quickly job applicants (and salespeople) will break into a litany about themselves or their offerings when given the opportunity. I suppose that's just a reflection of how our selling culture has evolved into a self-serving profession over the years.

I continue to be amazed when companies spend millions of dollars every year to try and craft more impactful, next-generation marketing messages that they can distribute to their field sales organizations in the hopes of gaining a competitive advantage. Of course, when those same companies hire me, one of the first things I do is inject a dose of reality. Did you realize that opening with a traditional elevator pitch, an introductory blurb about your company and products, actually puts a salesperson or sales team in an extremely weak position? As I mentioned earlier, using the same buzzwords as everyone else is the quickest way to commoditize your company's value proposition.

Back in the 1980s and early 1990s, a paradigm shift occurred in the marketplace, where sales leaders began to recognize that it was lucrative to focus on selling a total solution as opposed to just touting individual product features. As a result, sales conversations began to shift from being product-focused to focusing on total solutions, even though the company itself and the products being recommended hadn't really changed. Particularly in large accounts, proposing an entire suite of products and services offers the mutual benefit of providing fully integrated solutions for the customer and big commission checks for the seller. Solutions, solutions, solutions . . . it was all about selling solutions. Ever since, the word *solutions* has transformed into a favorite lingual condiment of marketers everywhere. Especially when it is preceded by the phrase "leading provider of," claiming to be the leading provider of solutions is regularly used to enrich the headlines on everything from corporate Web pages to product literature and press releases.

> **Opening with an elevator pitch about the company or product actually puts a salesperson or sales organization in an extremely weak position.**

Selling solutions continues to be a good business strategy in the current economic climate, although sellers must recognize that the playing field has changed with regard to the overuse of industry buzzwords. If you want to be seen as customer-focused, then the focus of the conversation should no longer revolve around your solutions. Instead customers in every industry are much more focused on addressing their problems, issues, and concerns than they are interested in hearing another high-level elevator pitch.

Even so, sellers tend to gravitate naturally to what I would characterize as an *SPA approach* when positioning their company and products. SPA is how most salespeople have been conditioned to sell themselves and their solutions. As we saw with the job interview metaphor, when a potential customer (i.e. hiring manager) says, "Tell me about yourself (i.e. your product)," we tend to do just that. We start telling about our solutions (S), in the hopes that the conversation will transition into a more in-depth discussion of the customer's problems (P). Then, later in the sales process or dialogue, we sellers end up fending off objections, which are usually just a reflection of the questions the decision maker has about how our product compares with other alternatives (A). Hence the acronym, SPA.

After much study and having worked with literally thousands of salespeople all over the world, I have come to believe that the reason salespeople gravitate to an SPA approach is because it's easier to talk about what we do know (our solutions) than what we don't necessarily know (the customer's problems). Maybe it's fortunate, however, that we have reached a point where the theory behind this notion of "selling solutions" can be called into question and more carefully examined. Let me show you a couple logic problems with the traditional SPA approach.

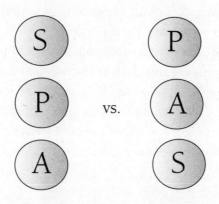

Let's start by asking, once again, what's more important to the typical customer when you first engage—their problems (P) or a salesperson's solutions (S)? From my vantage point, it's clear that the vast majority of customers are much more focused on their own problems, issues, goals, and objectives than they are interested in hearing a salesperson's pitch. Thus, it no longer makes sense for a customer-focused salesperson to open his or her presentation with a data dump of product information (S) rather than focusing on the customer's problems (P).

Nonetheless, salespeople are quick to do exactly this, as countless sales training seminars and courses are still being offered suggesting that sellers should open with a perfunctory elevator pitch about their products and services. I'm sure some of you will think to yourselves, "I don't do that." And maybe you don't. But to prove how prevalent SPA is among sellers today, try this experiment. Next time you deal with a salesperson of any kind, make it a point to ask them, "Can you please tell me about your product?" Then, time them on your watch to see how long they ramble on about themselves, their products, or their company, before they realize that they have absolutely no idea what you might need, or even why you asked the question.

What's the alternative to SPA? The answer will reveal itself if we simply apply some deductive reasoning. To even have an opportunity to provide solutions, one must first understand the customer's problems (P), right? To the extent that selling is about helping people accomplish their goals, objectives, issues, and concerns, then whatever advice and direction a salesperson ends up providing should be prescriptive in nature, as opposed to just a data dump. Do you agree?

We also agreed earlier that it's important to be customer-focused. Well, if we know customers are much more interested in their own problems (P) than a salesperson's solutions (S), and we know that sellers must identify a problem in order to provide valuable solutions, then it would seem to make more sense to adjust your sales strategy slightly in order to follow more of a *PAS approach*.

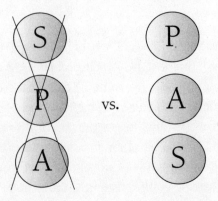

Ironically, PAS is not only a more effective positioning strategy, it also represents the logic most people use to make decisions every day. Case in point, in order for a customer to purchase your product or service, the decision maker at some point must think to themselves, "Because I have this problem (P), which the alternatives (A) don't solve as effectively, that's why I choose to purchase or implement this particular solution (S)." The thought process customers use when deciding whether or not to purchase your product or service is the same logic hiring managers use to assess and ultimately choose between multiple candidates who are interviewing for a desirable position.

For example, have you purchased a digital camera in the last few months or years? If so, let me take a guess at the decision process you used to make that purchase—and I don't even know you personally. Regarding the camera, at some point you said to yourself, "Because I have this problem (a need to take great pictures) (P), which the alternatives (my film camera, our movie camera, buying a disposable camera while on vacation, or taking no pictures at all) (A) don't solve as effectively, that's why I choose to buy this new digital camera (S)."

Essentially, every value-based decision that you or your customers make is arrived at using PAS logic. Whether you are considering the purchase of a new computer, car, house, or fancy outfit, the underlying decision process is essentially the same. Because you have a problem (P) that the alternatives don't solve as effectively (A), that's why you are going to choose this particular solution (S).

The underlying logic is universal. If a hospital administrator must choose between multiple suppliers from which to purchase medical equipment, the decision maker in the hospital will ultimately conclude the following: "Because we have certain goals, objectives, issues, concerns, wants, needs, desires, or problems (P), which the alternatives (other suppliers) don't solve as effectively (A), that's why we are going to procure these solutions from this particular vendor (S)."

The underlying logic of this new PAS positioning model comes with a hidden benefit. Simply put, you bond with people by focusing on what's most important to them (their goals, issues, needs, concerns, desires, and problems (P)), as opposed to whatever is most important to you—your solutions (S). This especially makes sense in the selling arena because in order to communicate the value of your product or service, you must first have something to build value against. Bonding with potential customers on what is most important to them is strategically significant because that's what allows them to begin to trust you. Your ability to solve problems is also the trigger that piques the customer's interest. Bingo, again!

Avoid Rhetorical Sales Questions

One of the most effective ways to earn the customer's trust is to demonstrate high levels of credibility and competence, particularly early in the sales conversation. Customers tend to connect with people they perceive as being capable, experienced, knowledgeable, relevant, purposeful, intelligent, and well prepared, particularly if you come across as being customer-focused. The best way to demonstrate this level of competence is by asking relevant and intelligent questions, which we will talk about in much more depth later when we focus on needs development. For now, I just want to recognize that it's important to avoid falling into the trap of asking overly rhetorical sales questions in an attempt to uncover customer needs.

The problem comes when a salesperson thinks to themselves, "I've been taught that it's important to uncover the customer's needs, so I'd better start by asking probing questions." Even though sales trainers have beaten the drum about the importance of uncovering needs for decades, there are some ineffective ways to ask questions that must be avoided at all cost. For example, you must do everything in your power to avoid the noticeable awkwardness that occurs when the questions being asked by an eager salesperson sound rhetorical.

Whether you are in a business that sells medical devices, high-tech equipment, or financial services, or you are a candidate interviewing for a position with a company in one of those fields, it's probably safe to assume you would have done some research prior to your actual conversation with the decision maker. As a by-product of doing your homework, I would argue that a capable and intelligent salesperson should know something about what customers might need before actually talking with them. Can we agree on this premise?

Prepping in advance for an important sales situation is a common practice for many of the people who are reading this book. That said, let me illustrate the downside of asking rhetorical questions by revisiting our previous interview scenario.

First impressions are very important, wouldn't you agree? I would go so far as to say that a bad first impression could cost you a sale, or at the very least, your opportunity to engage key decision makers. So what do you suppose would happen if a job applicant responded to the interviewer's initial question by countering with a few probative salvos to theoretically uncover the hiring manager's needs? Let's see.

Interviewer: Robert, thanks for coming to meet with us today. Can you tell me a little about yourself?
Candidate: What types of things are you looking for in an employee?
Interviewer: Uh, well, I suppose we would like to select someone who is self-motivated, qualified, and someone who can grow in this position, and hopefully, grow with the company. What would you say are your best attributes?
Candidate: Is having knowledge and experience important?
Interviewer: *(awkward silence)* Next!

While I appreciate that this applicant may just be wanting to better understand the opportunity, the beginning of a sales situation is no time for playing games. From my perspective, when a prospective customer asks you a question (in this case, the hiring manager), there is some obligation on the candidate's part to provide a meaningful response. Otherwise, you risk sounding like you're trying to dodge the interviewer's question. Don't worry, if the conversation gets off to a solid start, there will be plenty of chances for you to ask detailed questions about the opportunity, particularly if you demonstrate a level of competence early in the meeting that causes the other person to form a positive impression.

It's almost goofy that the candidate in this example responds to the interviewer's initial question by countering with a question of his own. If I were the hiring manager, I would be wondering, "Why is this person dodging my question? Is he unprepared, or is he just trying to manipulate the conversation? Seriously, what does this candidate hope to accomplish by asking me something so absurdly obvious, like if knowledge and experience are important? Of course knowledge and experience are important!"

If this candidate was hoping to impress the hiring manager or gather specific information about the opportunity, he has failed miserably on both counts. That's because asking rhetorical questions usually does not create a good first impression. Other than battling for control of the meeting, why would a capable job applicant or salesperson ask questions that are shallow and obvious?

Not only do rhetorical questions fail to breed confidence with potential buyers, they usually have the opposite effect. Picture the used-car salesman who walks up to a prospective customer and asks, "Sir, is value important to you?" What's the customer going to say? "No, I was actually hoping to get ripped off." Of course the customer wants a good value! Hence, asking a question that seems obvious or unnecessary is more likely to cause cautious customers to immediately doubt your intentions, which instantly erases any credibility you may have had with them or were hoping to build.

I'm not suggesting that you should refrain from asking questions during a sales call or your next job interview. The methodology I developed and have been teaching for the last decade is called Question Based Selling for a reason—because it has a lot to do with asking questions. But you must be smart about how you ask, because customers aren't always open to sharing information with someone they don't yet know or trust.

Striking a Chord of Connection

What you say (or ask) during a job interview, or in the midst of any sales situation, is definitely important. But in the eyes of your target audience, your value is ultimately defined by how you are perceived. With that in mind, let's revisit through the job interview metaphor to examine what actually happens when we put this new PAS positioning logic into practice. Besides creating a very different first impression from other candidates in the initial moments of the exchange, taking a PAS approach is a surefire way to strike a chord of connections with the hiring manager by raising issues that are important to them.

Manager: Pat, thanks for your time today. Can you tell me a little about yourself?

Candidate: Sure. Do you have a copy of my résumé?

Manager: Yes, I've got it right here.

Candidate: "Well, since you've already seen a snapshot of my work history, I'd like to think that I'm a good person with a decent track record of success, but I'll let you be the judge of that. I'm thinking that you might be looking for more than just a "good person" to fill this position, however. In fact, I'm guessing that you might be looking for some of the intangibles that wouldn't necessarily show up as specific line items on a résumé.

For example, based on the research I did prior to coming here today, I'm thinking that you might be looking for someone who can ramp up and become productive as quickly as possible, especially given the current economy. You may also be looking for someone who can blend with the existing culture, but still bring a fresh perspective or new ideas from outside the company. You might also be looking for someone who can grow existing opportunities, while also being able to defuse potential hot spots that may exist within problem customer accounts. If so, those are the types of things that have enabled me to be successful in the past.

Do you mind if I ask, what other specific goals would you want the candidate for the position to be able to accomplish?

When you're interviewing for a new job or selling a product, what sellers really want is a competitive advantage. Somehow you must find a way to separate yourself from the other people who are being considered, and in the process, you want customers to perceive that you bring superior value to the table. To accomplish this, you must demonstrate that you have some understanding of the types of issues that might be important to the decision maker.

How can you know what might be important to a customer before actually meeting them? That's actually the easy part. If you are indeed a serious candidate for the position, you would have researched the company on the Internet and you may have even reached out to your own network of contacts. Doing your homework in advance is fine, although you should be aware that other candidates will probably have visited the company's Web site as well. In addition to finding out some general information about the company, however, the real key to connecting with decision makers is to demonstrate an understanding of their specific goals, objectives, and concerns.

The operative word here is *demonstrate*. Don't worry, you don't have to dress in all black with face paint and crawl over the company's wall late at night to know what issues might be important to a prospective customer. All you really have to do is put yourself in their shoes for a couple minutes and think about if you were them, which decision issues would be most important to you?

Ask yourself, "What would I want a candidate to be capable of if I were the hiring manager?" You don't have to be clairvoyant to realize that attributes like knowledge, experience, quick ramp-up time, and high productivity are all desirable attributes, and would likely be on the mind of most hiring managers. Likewise, you don't have to adjust your personality to talk intelligently about blending with the current culture while bringing a fresh perspective from outside the company. These are some fundamental employee traits that are pertinent to virtually any job opportunity and would appeal to every hiring manager. The key to striking a chord of connection with decision makers is for the seller to proactively bring these relevant issues up to the customer, as opposed to hoping they just happen to come up naturally somewhere in the conversation. This is an intentional play to connect with the decision maker, in order to differentiate yourself, pique their interest, and establish enough credibility to cause the conversation to subsequently take off. This method of proactively raising key decision factors or business issues to gain traction with prospective buyers will pay huge dividends at the end of the day.

Also, did you notice in the sample dialogue that four out of the first five sentences that came out of the candidate's mouth were entirely customer-focused, as opposed to self-serving? That's excellent, because of what it conveys—a perception that you are focused on the hiring manager's goals more so than your own personal agenda. You might as well be perceived as someone who is customer-focused, because customers are more focused on their own goals than yours anyway.

Companies aren't just looking to hand out good jobs, or further someone's career path. What hiring managers are really trying to do is address a specific issue or business need, and a face-to-face employment interview provides them with an opportunity to evaluate whether or not you would provide the best possible solution. The same principle applies in any sales situation—customers in a typical sales call don't consider buying your product or service just so you can make a sale. Rather, the only reason to spend time with a salesperson is because the customer is trying to address a need of some kind, and they want to evaluate your product or service to see if it provides the best solution.

Making a good first impression doesn't replace the need for a solid performance during the rest of the decision process. If you completely bungle the rest of your next job interview, for example, whatever positive impressions that may have been initially formed will quickly dissipate. Still, much credibility can be earned by demonstrating that you do understand and care about the customer's needs. This gives the strategic salesperson a tremendous opportunity, if not an unfair advantage, to showcase the intangible qualities that differentiate you from other qualified candidates who just treat the interview like a Q & A session.

Priming the Pump

For centuries, wise men have wondered whether selling is more of a science or an art. Frankly, I believe that in order to become a consistent top performer in sales, you should be a master of both the art and the science.

The science of selling I would characterize more as standardizing the steps of the sales process and defining procedures. The art of selling has more to do with identifying best practices and applying your repertoire of communication skills to match the needs of a given sales situation.

The beauty of science is that it's predictable. The law of gravity, for example, never takes a day off, which enables us to assume that certain things will happen based on scientific fact, or at least we can have a high degree of confidence in their probability.

Oddly enough, the natural laws of physics provide some of the best guidance for dealing with customers, particularly when you're forging new relationships with prospective buyers, or if you are wanting to impress a potential employer. Since we know that people in general are often reluctant to share with someone they don't know or trust, let me suggest an idea that will enhance your ability to establish credibility and gain traction when kicking off your needs development conversations. Let's call this technique "priming the pump."

When I was fifteen years old, I was an active member of Troop 92— an enthusiastic group of Boy Scouts that met regularly at the American Legion post just outside my hometown of Spencerport, New York. In addition to attending the weekly meetings, my brother and I also participated in several scout jamborees and summer camps, which gave us an opportunity to get our hands dirty once in a while and transform the sterility of classroom learning into some neat real-life experiences.

On one such outing, our scoutmaster led a small group on a weekend road trip down to the southern tier of New York state. There we camped with several other scout troops on a fifty-acre wooded area situated next to a local farmer's corn field. That probably doesn't sound very glamorous, but it was still exciting to be out in the "wilderness" and on our own.

At some point on the trip, a fellow scout and I wandered a bit deeper into the woods to see what trouble we could find. A few hundred yards down the path, we happened upon a small ramshackle outbuilding that upon further investigation turned out to be a pump house for a freshwater well. Have you ever seen one of those vintage cast iron pumps set into a concrete block with a large curved handle? As curious fifteen-year-old boys, we felt an immediate urge to see if the rusty old pump still worked. So I grabbed the iron handle, and, using some muscle to get it started, strenuously pushed down to see if water would come out. After a few mighty pumps, we got nothing. My friend and I mustered some energy and pumped even harder. Still, nothing came out. I bet we pumped that thing for twenty minutes before deciding that the old well below the concrete base must be dry. Oh, well (yes, pun intended!).

When we got back to the campsite, we announced our discovery, and of course, the other boys all wanted to come see the pump house. "Wait," our scoutmaster said. "If you go back, you might try pouring a canteen full of water into the top of the pump and see if that does any good."

No one actually said it out loud, but I'm sure that more than one of us was thinking, "Mr. Martin . . . duh! We're trying to get water to come out of the well, not pour water into it." I'm sure he could tell by our facial expressions that we thought his idea was foolish, but he encouraged us to try it anyway. "What do adults know about pumping water?" we wondered as we wandered back into the forest.

Several boys took turns behind the large iron handle, pumping ferociously in an attempt to get something to come out. As before, the spigot on the end of the pump was bone dry. We pumped and pumped with no success. I don't recall who actually remembered Mr. Martin's sage advice, but one of the scouts who had a canteen on his belt offered it up as a last resort. It was worth trying, since the strong-arm approach was obviously not getting it done.

Carefully, we poured the canteen water into the top of the pump. I remember thinking, "This is the dumbest idea ever."

Then came the moment of truth. I grabbed the giant pump handle and heaved downward with all the might a spindly fifteen-year-old Boy Scout could muster. Nothing came out. Big surprise! So I gathered my strength and pumped again. This time, the spigot end of the pump started to bubble and spit, and by the third pump, buckets of water started gushing out onto the surrounding concrete block. I mean, water was splashing everywhere and most of us got soaked! We took turns drinking the fresh spring water and later reported back to camp, where Mr. Martin basked in the glow of being right.

The most valuable lesson I learned that day didn't actually register with me until many years later, when I was struggling to start a career in the sales profession. You see, when I first went into sales, I was taught the same way as everyone else—that I should ask probative questions to uncover the prospect's needs. When penetrating new prospect accounts, the act of probing for needs felt like I was pumping customers for information. Not surprisingly, the proverbial well (of information) was often bone dry. It quickly became apparent that prospective customers were reluctant to share information with a salesperson they didn't yet know or trust, and the more forcefully I pumped, the less information I got.

For decades, sellers have been taught to *probe* for needs by asking open-ended questions like, "Mr. Customer, what are your goals and objectives for the next five years?" A popular alternative is, "What's the biggest issue that you currently face?" Another perennial favorite is, "Ms. Customer, what keeps you up at night?"

The truth is, most people don't want to be "pumped" for information. Customers will share their goals, issues, and concerns, but only if they perceive you to be a valuable resource. No one wants to be probed by an aggressive salesperson. We sure don't want to be on the receiving end of rhetorical questions or something that feels like an interrogation from an eager vendor rep.

If you have appropriately prepared in advance and you are willing to invest a few moments to prime the pump of communication, the customer's reaction is likely to be "gushingly" different. In the context of your next job interview, I already showed you how to prime the pump for more in-depth conversation. You do this by proactively raising issues that will strike an immediate chord with the hiring manager and convey a perception that you are indeed a valuable, customer-focused person. Salespeople can just as easily prime the pump in their needs development conversations by raising relevant decision issues that contribute to the conversation rather than expecting customers to open up and share their needs with a salesperson they don't yet know or trust.

In chapters 4, 5, and 6, we will talk about needs development at length, in terms of conversational dynamics, "Decision Making 101," and how to be more strategic with your questions, so let's not worry about building a script full of specific questions just yet. However, I do want to make the point that a few well-placed strategic questions can give you a strategic advantage. For example, consider what happens in the customer's mind when you ask questions like:

"How many service calls do you handle per day?"
"Do you send out customer satisfaction surveys?"

"What percent of revenue comes from repeat business?"
"Have you experienced a decrease in customer traffic given the recent economic slowdown?"

In addition to gathering important data about the client, asking specific questions about business issues that might be important to the customer gives them the opportunity to form the impression that you are knowledgeable, intelligent, and customer-focused. These are just a few of the intangibles that will determine how successful you will be when selling yourself. In fact, raising relevant topics like number of service calls per day, satisfaction surveys, revenue, customer traffic, and recent economic conditions, is one of the most effective ways to bolster your own credibility. From there, it's a matter of simple physics. A salesperson who contributes nothing of substance to a conversation will most likely get very little substantive information in return. However, if you can demonstrate the ability to raise and discuss relevant decision issues that are important to customers, don't be surprised when buckets of valuable information begin to flow in your direction. Therein lies the magic of taking a PAS approach—you bond with customers on their problems (P), not your solutions (S).

Tips for the Hiring Manager

If you are in a role that is responsible for making hiring decisions, here are five "tells" that will help you determine whether a candidate would be a good hire. Applicants should pay attention, too, because understanding what hiring managers look for can provide useful insight into how you should conduct yourself in your next job interview or customer call.

1. Was the candidate interested enough to ask questions, or did they mostly respond to what was asked? If they were indeed shy about asking questions, was it because they felt intimidated, were overwhelmed, or simply did not appear to be interested in the opportunity?

2. Did the candidate demonstrate that they were prepared and had put some thought into the specific opportunity?
3. To what extent was the candidate aware of your specific hiring objectives? Were they focused on helping you accomplish your goals?
4. How much of the candidate's preinterview or follow-up was person-to-person as opposed to hiding behind the electronic veil of e-mail or the Internet?
5. What did the applicant do to differentiate themselves from other candidates interested in the position?

A good-looking, professional résumé is definitely a plus if you are seeking a new career opportunity. But any good salesperson will tell you that just having a nice product brochure is not enough to guarantee your success in making the sale. The candidate must also demonstrate a certain confidence in how to conduct a meeting, and a vision for how they plan to be successful in the position.

Tips for Qualified Candidates

Beyond the numerous strategies and techniques outlined in this book, here's an extra piece of advice I would offer active job searchers with regard to how to sell yourself. Make sure you are well prepared (in advance) to discuss your vision of how you plan to succeed in whatever you aspire to accomplish. Success rarely happens by accident, and if you were interviewing for a position within my company, the first thing I would want to know is, "Do you have a specific plan for being successful in this job, and can you share it with me right now?"

Successful people plan their work and work their plans. They have a vision of what it takes to succeed and they also have an ability to communicate that vision to others. Since even the best-laid plan doesn't always pan out as we originally envision them, your ability to make reasonable adjustments along the way is also critically important to hiring managers. Shooting from the hip is no longer a viable strategy in today's business environment.

If I were interviewing you for a sales position, I would also want to understand your philosophy on selling. More important, I would want to know that you had a specific sales philosophy. Which sales courses have you attended and what books have you read? Of all the candidates being considered, why should I hire you?

Make it your mission to be the one who stands out, even to the point of creating a strategy binder and bringing a specific business plan to the job interview. Present it as if you were already in charge of the division. It's perfectly acceptable to make assumptions that allow for flexibility during the implementation phases of your plan. You can even make "ongoing revisions as you acclimate to the position" an integral part of your plan.

Potential employers are just like prospective customers in the sense that they want to know that you are confident in your abilities and you have the foresight and fortitude necessary to make things happen in ways that will benefit them and you.

Even with a notable track record, we must recognize that in a competitive environment, you will rarely be the only candidate (or vendor) being considered. Other qualified candidates will also garner a serious look. Hence, the purpose of an employment interview is not just to review one's honors and accolades from the past. The real purpose of these evaluations is to give the hiring manager or prospective customers a glimpse into the future so they can evaluate which alternative (i.e., person) provides the best fit in helping them achieve their goals.

In the final analysis, especially in a highly competitive business environment, you become the differentiator between whether a customer chooses you or your closest rival. To the extent that you are able to demonstrate that your skills and perspective are indeed aligned with the customer's goals, you can expect to experience a great deal of success in your career going forward. On the other hand, if you put yourself in a position to sound just like everyone else, then your destiny lies in the hands of a virtual coin flip at best. It's that simple. Selling yourself during an interview (or with regard to a product sale) has everything to do with the customer's perception of you. Just know that first impressions tend to leave lasting impressions, and winning the sale or being offered the job is a whole lot more fun (and rewarding) than coming in second place.

4

Managing Conversational Dynamics

Ever wonder why some of the conversations you have with customers seem to flow along with inexplicable ease, while other times it feels like you're pulling teeth to initiate a dialogue or suggest possible next steps? Consistent with the overall theme of this book, the extent to which other people will respond to your questions, listen to your ideas, or be receptive to your advice is largely a reflection of how effectively you are able to communicate with them.

Reducing conversational tension is an area where superior technique can give the strategic salesperson a significant advantage. As you've probably heard many times, it's not just what you say (or ask) that's important, your success is also contingent on how those messages (or questions) are actually being delivered.

After twenty-one years of marriage, my wife Laura will sometimes say to me, "I agree in principle, but I don't like your tone." Sorry guys to let the cat out of the bag, but women are generally much more attuned to things like tone of voice and the nuances of other interpersonal communications than men are.

"What tone?" I will say, as if to deny any malice or intentional wrongdoing.

"That tone," she reiterates. "And, I don't appreciate your look either!"

"What look?" I inquire, as if I have been mysteriously beamed onto an alien planet where they interpret communications much differently than I am used to on Earth.

My wife, Laura, is a great person, along with being a very effective communicator. Like any husband of twenty-plus years, I have my moments where she feels the need to remind me that it's not just what I say, it's how I say it that's causing the problem. I couldn't agree more, which is an excellent segue into a discussion about managing conversational dynamics.

What if it was possible to remove the pressure and awkwardness sellers often feel when probing for needs, dealing with price objections, or when trying to secure the commitments necessary to close a sale?

Minimizing any conversational tension with the customer is where superior sales technique gives top performing salespeople a competitive advantage. In this regard, it's not just what you say (or ask) that's important; your effectiveness and resulting success are also contingent upon *how* your messages (or questions) are actually being interpreted.

Most of the QBS clients we train are hungry for new ideas, suggestions, or strategies that will give them a competitive edge. But there's not much upside in just reiterating to sellers what they already know—like that it's important to uncover the customer's needs, propose valuable solutions, and close sales, for example. What sellers really want is strategic insight and guidance on "how to execute more effectively" with regard to each of these common sales objectives. More specifically, they want to understand "how" to penetrate more new opportunities, especially given the challenges of the current business climate. Moreover they want to understand "how" to create a differentiable advantage in highly competitive markets, where everyone else claims to offer similarly great solutions, just like you. Many clients want to become more creative in order to secure more mind share with key decision makers in important target accounts. Other sales goals include increasing the customer's sense of urgency to move forward with a favorable decision, and then wrapping up a sales transaction without having to stress the customer relationships that you have worked so hard to build.

In sales, achieving trusted adviser status has become the Holy Grail in terms of placing yourself in the strongest possible position to earn the customer's trust, and close business. Why? Because customers usually do business with the person or company from whom they feel most comfortable taking advice. You have to assume that other vendors will also be competing as hard as ever to have a share of the decision maker's ear. The challenge in today's competitive marketplace is putting yourself in a position to be the vendor who ends up in the coveted role of trusted adviser.

To be an effective advice giver in the eyes of prospective clients, whoever is on the receiving end of your insight and guidance must be open to listening to, considering, and ultimately heeding your recommendations. Salespeople, managers, and sales trainers all agree that education plays a significant role in the decision-making process. Thus, your ability to educate customers on how your solution alternatives compare against other options, while clearly conveying the value of your product or service is a valuable sales skill. Effective communication is a two-way street however. In addition to positioning the value of your solutions, your probability of success is also contingent on your ability to make audiences more receptive to your ideas. Consequently, it's no longer enough for sellers to convey a strong message. You must also be able to cause customers to "want to" hear it.

This raises an interesting question. If the receptivity of your target audience greatly contributes to your success, perhaps we should ask, is there anything a salesperson can do to influence a customer's receptiveness, especially when they first encounter a salesperson who they don't yet know and trust?

I'm not a fan of manipulative sales tactics, nor do I believe your sales approach should be built on the premise of trying to control people. Decision makers are going to interpret your product's value proposition and form their own conclusions. A salesperson who tries to force their own agenda down the customer's throat, therefore, enters into dangerous territory. Most customers don't respond well to being pressured and they are only going to act on something if they believe it suits their objectives. How would you force prospective customers to become interested in your product anyway? Moreover, how do you force someone to recommend your proposal to their colleagues or boss? It turns out that subversive attempts to strong-arm or manipulate a customer's own judgment can actually hurt your sales efforts rather than help.

While trying to "control" other people is indeed a flawed strategy, we sellers do have the opportunity to control our own actions, especially if one recognizes that how you choose to deal with prospects and customers can directly influence the perceptions they form about you. And just as you can harm or damage a relationship by doing something inappropriate or out of context, you can help yourself by paying attention to the underlying dynamics of your sales conversations.

Conversational dynamics refers to the intangible subtleties that affect the flow of your customer interactions, and the rest of your everyday conversations for that matter. Understanding how the subtleties of your interactions with clients can influence the perceptions they form can empower a salesperson to facilitate more productive conversations. If the real purpose of a job interview, for example, is to get a feel for which candidate provides the best fit, then the true purpose of a sales conversation is for customers to form their impressions about the potential value of your proposed solutions, coupled with their impression of the value provided by the person representing that product or service.

Given that how you represent yourself influences the perceptions people form about your company and your solutions, one of the easiest ways to increase your value in the eyes of your target market is to proactively manage the dynamics of your sales conversations. That's why you need to *sell yourself first.*

The object of this chapter is not psychological—just logical. Personally, I'm averse to using covert sales tactics because most people (including me) don't want to be manipulated by a salesperson. Fortunately, causing potential customers to "want to" engage in productive conversation about their decision objectives and your corresponding value has nothing to do with being manipulative. Instead, it's about building and then nurturing mutually beneficial business relationships.

It has been said that sales would be a lot more fun if it were somehow possible to eliminate the risk of rejection and fear of failure that often accompany critical milestones in the sales process. In fact, Question Based Selling was originally developed as a risk reduction strategy, recognizing that a salesperson's success is directly related to his or her ability to help customers accomplish their goals. It just so happens that reducing your risk of failure is also the single most effective way to increase your probability of success. The good news is, communicating effectively doesn't have to feel awkward or be difficult if you are willing to pay attention to how you are being perceived.

Securing the Customer's Permission

Much of the awkwardness sellers feel when engaging potential customers occurs during the opening exchange, and then again at various points of transition throughout the conversation. Particularly if you deal with prospects who are used to holding salespeople at arm's length, it's important to get the timing right in order to easily transition from the introductory stage of your sales conversations into needs development, or from needs development into the product presentation, and on to securing a commitment. Most of the tension in that process comes from the inherent risk sellers face, knowing that cautious customers aren't always willing to yield to our desired objectives in the conversation. If you can just get the dialogue rolling, both parties in the conversation often relax to the point where buyers and sellers can then focus on the issues at hand.

One of the keys to being an effective communicator in sales is the ability to gain traction (credibility and perceived value) early in the dialogue. Accomplishing these things early helps you transition through the rest of the conversation with relative ease. Mind you, most customers are pretty smart, and they understand that to get valuable advice from vendors, they must be willing to provide some relevant information about their needs. When you go to a doctor, for example, a nurse comes into the room prior to the doctor, to ask you a series of specific diagnostic questions about the status of your health. With this information in hand, the doctor can easily facilitate a discussion about your symptoms or options, and then prescribe the appropriate treatment. The same principle applies when you meet with an accountant or attorney. You want these professionals to understand your specific needs before giving advice or recommending a solution.

The sales profession should be no different. At some point, customers must be willing to share some basic information about their situation if they want a salesperson to provide advice or recommend valuable solutions. By definition, helping people is, and should always be, prescriptive in nature. The catch is, decision makers aren't willing to engage in an exploratory dialogue with every vendor who happens to come calling. This creates a bit of a paradox, where customers want new ideas and sensible solutions, but they are still reluctant to share information with someone they don't yet know or trust.

> **Customers must be willing to share pertinent information if they want sellers to provide valuable advice and recommend the best solution.**

Suppose for a moment that it was possible to completely sidestep the standoffishness sellers often encounter from prospective customers, and instead, it was easy to engage potential buyers in a productive conversation about their needs and your solution options. In fact, wouldn't it be great if sellers could just push a button that would cause customers to say, "Sure, go ahead and ask me a series of specific questions so we can have a valuable exchange of information"? Or, suppose you could get prospective customers to say, "Ms. Salesperson, can you help me better understand the value of your products?" Either of these requests from a customer would provide a wonderful entrée for you to facilitate a needs development conversation, and then educate them on the value of your solutions.

I'll let you in on one of the most valuable secrets from Question Based Selling. When someone invites you to ask them questions, when you do, you get more information, in more depth, than if you had simply bulled ahead with your own probative agenda. Similarly, when someone invites you to educate them on your solutions, or they ask for your opinion, you get significantly more mind share with key decision makers to present your ideas. It's only logical that someone who invites you to engage would be more open to sharing information and receiving advice.

Unfortunately, there is no magic button sellers can push to enable this degree of cooperation. I do have some ideas for you, however, that will essentially produce the same result. Allow me to introduce you to the concept of mini-invitations, which is as close as you can come to magic when it comes to engaging standoffish prospective customers in more productive conversations.

Leveraging Mini-Invitations

If you study human interaction, you will notice that it's difficult to initiate a dialogue with someone, or navigate a sales conversation into greater depth, without some spark of "invitation" from the other person enabling you to do so. More simply stated, it's easier to advance a conversation if the person you are talking with invites you to proceed, as opposed to you just bulling forward with what might sound like a self-serving agenda. Rather than sitting back and hoping that customers will issue an unsolicited invitation, however, sellers can manufacture these mini-invitations by using a specific question-based technique that I call leveraging mini-invitations.

Back when I officially left the corporate world to develop the Question Based Selling methodology, one of the questions people kept asking me was, "Why did you decide to stop selling?"

It turns out that I am still very much in sales. Only now I'm responsible for selling myself and my company, in addition to the services we provide. What a novel concept! My company, QBS Research, Inc., offers a full spectrum of sales development courses and consulting, from on-site QBS Methodology Training, to QBS OnLine, QBS books and audio programs, in addition to the various speaking engagements I get asked to deliver. Accordingly, I spend a great deal of time talking with sales managers and executives about their goals and objectives, and about how our company might be able to provide value.

Sometimes, potential clients jump right in and ask, "How much does a QBS training class cost?" I don't mind if someone asks me about price. To me, that sounds like an invitation. If you think about it, what the client is really saying here is, "Tom, can you help me understand the value of your offering, relative to how much it costs, so I can make an informed decision?" If you represent a viable company that sells valuable products, you want prospective clients to invite you to share details that will help them make informed decisions.

Thirty minutes later, another potential client might say, "Can you tell me about Question Based Selling?" Sounds a little like a job interview, doesn't it? The hiring manager could just as well have said, "Tom, tell me about yourself."

Whether the client asks about cost or wants an overview of our training options, my response is basically the same.

Tom: I'm happy to provide you with details about the different QBS programs how they would impact your business, and the associated costs. Can I ask you a couple specifics about your sales organization in order to give you relevant, and more accurate, information?
VP of Sales: Sure, go right ahead.

Human nature is very predictable. The prospect's answer in this scenario is going to be yes. I mean, who wouldn't want relevant and accurate information about the program alternatives, along with the associated costs? In this simple example, notice that the dynamics of the conversation shifted dramatically from the customer's original request, which could have sent me down the path that focused only on price, to the customer actually inviting me to ask them a series of specific questions to better understand their needs. Notice it was "my" choice of words that created this invitation as well as a predictably more receptive audience. By first securing permission to proceed down a seemingly logical path, the conversation instantly shifts to a productive exchange that will end up benefitting the customer—so I can understand their needs and prescribe the best possible solution. It also benefits me by creating a much easier transition.

The secret is simply to know how to manufacture a mini-invitation. Because of the way I opted to respond to the client's inquiry, and specifically, the words I chose, the customer could either grant me permission to go ahead and ask "a couple specifics" or not. I tell clients to expect a 99.9 percent probability that when this question ("Can I ask you a couple specifics about_____") gets asked at the appropriate time, customers will absolutely say "Yes," "Sure," "Go ahead," or "No problem!" If your customer had been willing to respond to any other question you could have asked, they will definitely respond affirmatively to this one.

Why are potential customers so willing to grant their permission? It's because of the way my opening question was framed. By them responding in an affirmative way, and inviting me to "ask a couple specifics about . . . ," my words have positioned the conversation in a way that allows customers to accomplish their own objective of getting relevant and accurate information, on the way to making a more informed decision. That's what customers really want anyway—a salesperson who is forthright and willing to provide details, yet customer-focused enough to realize that some specific information is needed in order to offer valuable recommendations.

Make it a point to practice this technique next time you visit your favorite restaurant. After the server reviews the menu, you simply say, "Can I ask you a couple specifics about the Cobb salad?" Instantly, their face will light up on the way to answering your question as completely as humanly possible. There's nothing magical here. People enjoy helping other people. In sales, you just have to break down the barrier of standoffish reluctance before customers will be willing to engage. After all, the only way you can be effective as a salesperson moving forward is if the customer chooses to help you help them.

> **The simple technique of manufacturing a mini-invitation causes an instantaneous reduction of a client's natural defense mechanisms.**

Customers who would otherwise be reserved and standoffish toward salespeople will suddenly open up and share tons of information once they have invited you to ask. This simple technique of manufacturing a mini-invitation causes an instantaneous reduction of a client's natural defense mechanisms. Because the other person is essentially granting me permission to ask questions, I am virtually guaranteed to receive a more valuable response.

Like many of the softer skills in selling, the significance of this mini-invitation strategy can easily be lost in its subtlety. By securing a customer's permission to ask questions, the dynamics of the conversation suddenly shift out of "spew mode" and into discovery. This is not a strategy for dodging the customer's request. On the contrary, I'm happy to tell potential clients about programs we offer and how much they cost. But, like most things, recommending the best alternative usually requires that I know a few basic facts about the nature of the customer's request, such as: Is the client more interested in QBS methodology training or a speaking engagement? Where will their event be held? How many people are expected to attend? Are they targeting a specific date?

Notice that the client's mini-invitation materializes as the result of good communication technique on the salesperson's part. This is important because it puts you in control of your own destiny, to foster more productive conversations and also to repeat your success moving forward. The logic behind conversational dynamics is simple—by asking permission, and thus, being respectful of the other person's right *not* to share with you, you lower the customer's defenses in a way that assures you will get much more information. Who knew that being respectful and responsive to customers could also be extremely productive?

Perfecting the Technique

The best example of where this strategy (of manufacturing mini-invitations) can help a salesperson is when you want to seamlessly transition your initial interactions with potential customers into a more in-depth needs development conversation. This is the one time in Question Based Selling when I recommend exact words. At the appropriate time in the dialogue, the salesperson simply says, "Mr. Smith, can I ask you a couple specifics about _____ ?"

Let's go back to the interview analogy from chapters 2 and 3 for a moment, and see what happens when we apply this idea of manufacturing a mini-invitation to the first part of the job interview.

Manager: Tom, thanks for coming in to meet with us today. Can you tell me a little about yourself?

Candidate: Sure. Well, since you have my résumé already, I would add that I'd like to think I am a hard worker and a good person, but my guess is you may be looking for more than just a "good person" to fill this position. In fact, I'm thinking that you might be looking for some of the intangibles that don't show up as specific line items on a résumé. For example, based on the research I did in preparation for this meeting, I'm thinking that you might be looking for someone who can ramp up to become productive as quickly as possible, especially given the current economy. You might also want a person who can blend well with the existing culture, yet still bring new ideas and a fresh perspective from the outside world. You may also be looking for someone who can grow existing opportunities, but also diffuse hot spots that may exist in some problem accounts. If so, those are the types of things that have enabled me to be successful in the past. Am I close in terms of some of the skills that might help me here?

Manager: You're right on the money.

Candidate: Well, can I ask you a couple specifics about the job description so I can get a better sense of the opportunity?

Manager: Sure, go right ahead.

Selling yourself in today's competitive marketplace requires more than just answering whatever questions the customer happens to ask. You must also be able to manage the dynamics of your conversations to keep the dialogue on track and make the best use of your time with important customers. Don't worry—the interviewer (or customer) won't know or even think that you are using a specific QBS technique. Hiring managers want qualified candidates to show interest in the position being offered, and there's no better way to demonstrate your interest than by asking "a couple specifics" about the opportunity.

This strategy of manufacturing mini-invitations is not limited to the beginning of a sales conversation, however. Mini-invitations can also be valuable conversational tools when transitioning your dialogue from needs development into your product presentation, or when it's time to close and suggest possible next steps.

For example, once you've exhausted the needs development portion of your conversation, and it's time to educate the customer on your potential solutions, you can use this same technique to manufacture a mini-invitation that would seamlessly transition you right into your presentation. Just say:

Seller: Mr. Customer, thanks for giving me an overview of your organization and your current business goals. Would it be valuable for me to explain the different solution alternatives we offer and how they would impact your organization's sales effectiveness and resulting productivity?

If the customer is even the slightest bit interested in hearing about your offerings, they will intuitively say, "Sure, go ahead." Perfect!

Using Mini-Invitations in Everyday Life

Even though I've been leveraging mini-invitations in my business dealings for quite a long time, I didn't really start thinking about why this technique was so valuable until I started using it in my everyday life. So whether you are socializing at a neighborhood dinner party, chaperoning a teenage youth group, or serving on a charitable committee at your kids' school or church, you will find that there are countless opportunities in your daily experiences where this technique works to energize conversations with just about anyone.

Part of my epiphany came as the result of serving on various church committees over the years. Essentially, I found these experiences enlightening and frustrating at the same time. You see, my style in business is to size up a situation, understand the options for moving forward, and then make a decision. Thus, I have a tendency to share ideas as they pop into my head, rather than being patient (or strategic) and waiting for just the right moment. Granted, I don't share every idea that happens to pop into my brain, but when I think of something really good, I tend to get excited and want to share it—right now!

The trouble is, particularly when you are dealing with a team of volunteers, such as on a church committee, not everyone moves or thinks at the same pace. So after enough of my best ideas got shut down or simply fell on deaf ears, it started to occur to me that just blurting out my thoughts on a particular subject wasn't working very well. The truth is, if Delores is still pondering the color of the napkins needed for the church-wide fall picnic, then she may not yet be ready to talk about who will bring the potato salad or what type of punch should be served.

I wish this revelation about using mini-invitations had come to me much earlier in my life, because it would have saved me a lot of time and grief. Once I realized people were not going to change their nature, I decided to adjust my own approach to see if I could cause people to become more receptive. Now, whenever I want to share an idea at a church meeting or during a neighborhood homeowner's meeting, I am much more inclined to say, "You know, I just thought of something that could save us a bunch of time and money."

Invariably, someone in the gathering will respond by saying, "What's your idea?" It's particularly fun and rewarding to share ideas when your audience is eager and ultrareceptive. If you give people a chance to decide and acknowledge that they are indeed interested in what you have to say, they are much more likely to actually listen to your ideas. Thus, they are more likely to actually consider the information or advice being offered.

This same technique works just as well when dealing with teenagers. My fourth book is a variation on the "sales" theme called *The Question Based Parent*. From experience, it's clear to me that kids (just like adults) need to buy into your ideas if you want your guidance to actually have an impact. In that vein, we are always selling. Ever notice how young people aren't always eager to take advice from adults, especially from their parents? Next time you want to offer a budding teen some advice, try manufacturing a mini-invitation first. You simply say, "Can I make a suggestion that might spare you some time and hassle next time this happens?" You may have to give them a minute to exhale dramatically and roll their eyes up into their skulls, but if you can be patient for a few seconds, your teen will ultimately say (or grunt) something to the effect of, "Sure, go ahead."

In my book, *Secrets of Question Based Selling*, I noted that "Spending a few minutes to make someone feel special is more important than spending hours to make them feel average." People who feel respected by a salesperson are quick to invite you to ask questions, and they are generally much more open to heeding your advice. It's human nature.

Understanding Question-Based Logic

People are sometimes surprised when they discover that Question Based Selling isn't just about asking questions. Frankly, it's a shame that traditional sales training courses have placed so much emphasis on the desire to gather information, uncover needs, and qualify opportunities, without regard to the fact that customers are often reluctant to share with a salesperson they don't yet know or trust. Call me crazy, but I would argue that if someone doesn't want to share with you, then it doesn't matter what questions you ask—the conversation will end right there. Hence, the real skill with regard to selling yourself first is causing customers to *want to* open up, and engage in a more productive conversation about their needs and your potential solutions.

We sellers totally have an agenda. We want to understand the customer's needs in order to provide them with valuable solutions. It's okay to have goals. After all, identifying opportunities is ultimately what drives every company's bottom line. But customers have agendas, too. They're dealing with problems, issues, and concerns, in addition to wanting to satisfy certain wants and desires. Only if a product or service seems to provide a good fit might they be willing to listen, and then only to the extent that the salesperson makes a valuable use of their time. This is where Question Based Selling comes in—using logic, not just asking a bunch of questions.

Personally, I like the idea of securing the customer's permission prior to asking questions. Do you think customers today would rather deal with someone who is polite and respectful, or would they rather sellers just bull forward with their own self-serving agendas? Knowing that a mini-invitation from the customer instantly opens the door to a more productive conversation, it is very easy for me to think in terms of saying, "Ms. Customer, I'd be happy to give you all the details. Can I ask you a couple specifics about your upcoming project?"

Asked at the appropriate time, customers will surely say yes. This is not about fooling people into answering questions a certain way. It's about being customer-focused, respectful, and demonstrating that you want to make the best use of the decision maker's time. In fact, the word *specifics* is usually music to a decision maker's ears, because they either want to get specific, or they would rather not be dealing with you at all. Customers are tired of all the marketing hype, and they're even less excited about sitting though another generic sales pitch.

Getting Your Foot in the Door

Mini-invitations are particularly valuable early in the sales process when you're trying to break into a competitive marketplace. When I think of the insurance business, real estate, or selling manufactured goods, in these highly competitive businesses, one vendor's value proposition is often very similar to the rest of the field. It's to the point where customers who are satisfied with their current supplier may not even bother to entertain conversations with other vendors. In those cases, sellers must find some way to pique the customer's interest and lower their defenses at the same time.

My friend Bart Burton and his brother, Bill, started a business in Little Rock, Arkansas, selling print supplies. Since we are well into the electronic age, Bart correctly assumed that most of his target customers probably had a supplier already, from whom they purchase print supplies and toner cartridges. Penetrating new accounts was sure to be a challenge, especially if Bart and his brother sounded just like every other cold caller trying to get the customer's attention.

Now, whenever the Burton brothers get in front of a potential buyer, their strategy focuses on piquing the office manager's interest and creating a mini-invitation that will then pave the way into a more in-depth conversation. Check it out.

Salesperson: Hi, Ms. Jones, my name is Bart Burton with Integrity Office Solutions here in Little Rock. I realize that you may have a source for office equipment already, which is perfectly fine. We specialize in print supplies. But the value we offer to customers is unique because we basically solve problems that the traditional toner vendors have created, and we can save customers a significant amount of time and money in the process.

Office Manager: What problems do you solve?

What the customer is really saying here is, "Can you give me more information so I can know how you might be able to help us?" Doesn't that sound like a nice invitation from an otherwise standoffish prospect? If the office manager is at all curious about what problem(s) Bart is referring to, she will absolutely invite him to educate her on his value proposition. Perfect! What happens next is pretty straightforward, especially if you implement the PAS strategy from chapter 3. Remember that your greatest opportunity to provide value starts with a discussion about the customer's problems, issues, and concerns (P).

Salesperson: Well, there are a number of sales tricks that get pulled on customers by vendors in the toner business. Things like overstocking the customer's supply cabinet, substituting lesser quality products, or not keeping enough inventory on hand such that customers run out of product at the least opportune time. We eliminate these issues because of how our service is set up. Would it make sense for me to give you a quick overview of how we can do that?

Asking, "Would it make sense to . . ." is a particularly effective phrase from a conversational dynamics perspective. Instead of sounding hopeful that you might earn a sales commission, you bring logic and sensibility into the equation. If you are recommending the next logical next step in the decision process, it probably does "make sense" for the customer to have more information about your solutions, which creates another invitation. By the way, the reason your suggested next step does "make sense" is because it gives customers the products, and any other insight they might need to make a decision that addresses their business issues.

For a company that sells via the telephone, a telesales person could easily say, "Would it make sense for us to schedule a time where one of our representatives could come out and show you how our solutions would impact your business?"

This same technique also works as a trial close. At the appropriate time in the sales process, you can easily say, "Mr. Customer, would it make sense for us to move forward with some portion of your desired quantity in order to prove the product on-site?"

"How Familiar Are You With . . . ?"

You can use a variation on this technique to manufacture additional mini-invitations when kicking off your product presentations. Basically, this approach takes the guesswork and any awkwardness out of your transition into the education phase of the sales process. This approach eliminates the risk of offending a knowledgeable buyer by talking too generically. On the other hand, you don't want to presume some level of knowledge and confuse a neophyte customer. Since clairvoyance is not one of my strengths, I would rather just ask, "Mr. Customer, how familiar are you with the different types of training programs we offer?"

If the customer says, "I've been to your Web site and that's about all," their response tells me exactly where to begin my presentation—at the beginning. In the next opportunity, the decision maker might say, "I attended one of your courses a couple months ago, so I'm pretty familiar with the methodology." For them, I would start my presentation in a very different place. In either case, the customer's response tells me where to begin, as they are essentially saying, "Go ahead and present your solutions . . . but please start here." By knowing up front how familiar a customer is with your solutions, your job as a salesperson becomes much easier.

Not surprisingly, the way in which the question is delivered is just as important as the question itself. For example, I recommend against asking, "Are you familiar with . . . ?" Sounds similar, doesn't it? It's not. Asking someone if they "are familiar" with something tends to generate a yes/no response, which doesn't provide enough feedback to tell you how best to proceed. You will also encounter some prospects who will say yes just because they don't want to seem ignorant or uninformed. Lastly, if a customer does respond by saying, "Yes, I am already familiar with your products," your opportunity to educate them shrinks significantly— because of your words. Instead, make it a point to ask, "How familiar are you with . . . ?", because this way of asking causes customers to quantify their answer. Here's a simple example.

Seller: Mr. Customer, I would be happy to review the different solution alternatives with you. Can I ask you a couple specifics about the project in order to give you more accurate information?
Buyer: Sure, go ahead.
Seller: How familiar are you with the various secondary insurance coverages that are currently being offered to seniors?

Even if a potential buyer claims to be an expert on your product or service, you can easily say, "Well, there have been a number of updates or new announcements in recent weeks. Would it be valuable for me to bring you up to speed?" Predictably, customers will wonder, "What recent updates?" Exactly!

A Certain Precision Is Required

In addition to having trained thousands of salespeople over the years, I have also coached my fair share of sales managers. That said, here's a quick coaching tip with regard to selling yourself first. *Almost* doing it right is not close enough in today's competitive marketplace. Your team will need a certain amount of precision to execute consistently.

For example, oftentimes when I deliver an Advanced QBS Training as a follow-up to the original training, it's not unusual for someone in the audience to say, "Tom, I tried one of your techniques but it didn't work."

"Really, what happened?" I ask, interested in the nuances that may have affected the specific sales situation.

They proceed to tell me that they said to the customer, "I would like to ask you a couple specifics about . . ."

Can you spot the problem? A tiny change in wording can cause a HUGE difference in results. It's possible that this particular salesperson encountered a rogue customer who was in a foul mood that particular day. Granted, there are going to be some situations where nothing works. But it's usually pretty easy to identify the culprit when something's not right.

In this case, let's start with punctuation. "I would like to ask you a couple specifics about . . ." is not a question. As the founder of Question Based Selling, I teach people to be question-based, not statement-based. Whenever a salesperson announces, "I would like to do (anything)," that sounds self-serving to potential customers. In fact, almost any sentence that begins with "I would like to . . ." tends to automatically increase a customer's natural defense mechanisms, making them even more standoffish.

> **Almost doing it right is not close enough in today's competitive marketplace. When communicating with customers, you need a certain amount of precision to execute consistently.**

"But, Tom, what I said was close to what you suggested," they sometimes assert. Again, there is only one time in all of Question Based Selling where I recommend exact words. At the appropriate time in the conversation, usually when you are in a suitable position to kick off the needs development conversation, you simply say, "Mr. Customer, can I ask you a couple specifics about _____ ?" Their response will undoubtedly be yes. If you recognize that a certain amount of precision is required to be successful at anything, it's not that hard to execute this phrase exactly as planned.

Sometimes, even the most loyal advocates of QBS will comment about this technique, saying, "It feels different," or "That's just not my style." Since I'm not a believer in verbatim sales scripts, I have no problem when a salesperson uses his or her own judgment to take the context of the conversation into consideration. But for the record, let me say that the need to adapt everything to your own personal style is overrated. If something in this book seems logical or at least makes enough sense to give it a try, and it works over and over again, I can assure you that it will very quickly become part of your style. Granted, you may have to step outside your comfort zone in order to try something for the first time. But I can assure you that these techniques and strategies have been time tested and proven thousands of times over, in many different cultures, so there's no need to reinvent the wheel just because you're uncomfortable with a new idea.

Don't Treat Price as an Objection

In pretty much every type of selling, price becomes the number one objection on the way to making a sale. Most sellers know it's going to come up at some point. Not only do customers need to cost-justify the purchase, some buyers will try to beat you up on price simply because it's part of the sport of negotiation.

Sellers often dread these conversations about price. I don't, because asking about the cost of a product or service is a legitimate request and an important element in any decision. Later in the book, I dedicate an entire chapter to "Selling Intangibles and Cost Justification" (chapter 7). The problem comes when decision makers focus on price first, such that your product or service gets commoditized and the advantages of your solution often go unnoticed. That's why sellers usually cringe when the first question out of a prospect's mouth is "How much does it cost?"

In terms of conversational dynamics, when customers ask about price, they're usually not just trying to find out how much something costs. You might wonder, "How can you say that, Tom? I get asked about price all the time!" I am keenly aware that sellers are getting continually "beaten up" on the issue of price. I myself encounter a steady stream of clients every week asking me to help them deal with the price issue in their respective businesses. Fortunately, I can show you a very effective way to sidestep the traditional risks associated with these early price requests.

I'm guessing that you would be very happy to talk with potential customers about the price of your product or service, but just not as the initial focus of the conversation. So, rather than dreading the cost issue and worrying about when it will come up, what if it was possible to reframe the customer's request in a way that sparked a more in-depth conversation about their needs and your corresponding value? Watch. Wouldn't it be cool if a customer asked you the following question:

Customer: Mr. Seller, can you please help me understand the cost of your product and how it compares with other alternatives so I can make a smart decision?

If you could get customers to actually say these words, that would be music to a salesperson's ears: Besides just being a polite and reasonable request, the customer would clearly be asking for the salesperson's help, which is good because the subsequent pricing discussion should revolve around how your proposed solutions match up to their needs. Since customers will ultimately base their purchase decision on your product's cost effectiveness, helping customers understand how your product or service compares with other options is what most decision makers really want to know when they ask about price, anyway.

Let me show you how it all flows together.

Buyer: How much will this cost? [The real request is: "Can you help me understand the cost of your product and how it compares with other alternatives so I can make an informed decision?"]

Seller: Sure, I'd be happy to give you all the details about our training programs, and their associated costs. Can I ask you a couple specifics about your sales organization (or project) in order to provide you with relevant and accurate information?

Buyer: Sure, go ahead.

While I am eager and willing to share cost with qualified customers, it's important to shift the focus of the conversation long enough to understand what the customer is really wanting to accomplish. Once you understand what someone needs, then it's relatively easy to educate them on whichever options would be the most cost-effective way to satisfy their objectives.

Deflection Is a Strategic No-no

While it is reasonable for sellers to understand a customer's objectives before just spewing out prices, sellers must avoid the trap of sounding like they are trying to dodge the customer's question. Here's a classic example of what *not* to say.

Customer: How much would you charge to implement the entire system?
Salesman: Before I tell you the price, first I would like to ask you a bunch of questions.

This salesperson here might have noble intentions, and he might even recognize the importance of understanding a customer's needs before diving headfirst into a price discussion. The problem lies in the words he uses and the perception that creates. Honestly, most customers are not really interested in changing their focus away from knowing about cost just because a salesperson "would like" to ask some questions first.

If you examine more closely what just occurred, you might notice that when the customer asked about cost, the salesperson essentially responds by saying, "Instead of talking about what *you* would like to discuss, Mr. Customer, I'd like to take you down a different path in the conversation." This is a classic example of deflection, which most customers simply won't stand for. While this particular salesperson may think he's trying to help the customer by not tossing out random prices, the skeptical or standoffish customer is more likely to think, "I asked about cost. Why can't you just give me a price?"

Good Technique Becomes the Differentiator

I encourage you not to engage in an emotional battle of wills with prospective customers. Furthermore, there's no guarantee you will win a sale just because of a few neatly worded sentences. The goal of leveraging mini-invitations is simply to increase a salesperson's probability of success for having more productive conversations about the customer's needs. This technique also paves the way for you to provide them with enough information for them to be able to make sound decisions.

Almost immediately after I adjusted my own approach as a territory salesperson, I started blowing out my sales goals year after year. People who went on calls with me would say afterward, "There doesn't seem to be anything magical about what you do." That's true. I'm just a regular guy, trying to help my customers, just like you. "But," they would quickly add, "it's amazing how eager customers are to share account details and other information with you." That was true as well.

My DNA is no better than my competitors'. In many cases throughout my career, I ended up competing against vendors whose products were just as solid as mine. My advantage was really in my approach to dealing with customers. I believe most customers are going to share their thoughts, feelings, and concerns with somebody—I just wanted to make sure they felt more comfortable sharing with *me*, as opposed to the competition. Of course, once key decision makers started sharing tons of information with me, while they naturally held my competitors at arm's length, life was good.

Before I started writing books, no one had ever heard of a mini-invitation, and sellers were much more focused on telling than selling. Frankly, lots of salespeople are still in that mode today. However, you now have the opportunity to adjust your approach, and in the process, change the way you are being perceived in the marketplace. But don't delay. If your customers are not "inviting" you to ask them questions, or inviting you to educate them about your offerings, chances are good they are inviting someone else to help them—perhaps your closest rival.

5

Establishing the Customer's Buying Criteria

Have you ever noticed that your local hardware store sells drills and drill bits? But if you think about it, no one actually wants the drill itself. What they really want are holes. Isn't that odd? Hardware stores don't sell what the customer really wants—holes. Instead, they sell drills and drill bits as a means to accomplish the customer's true objective.

In the same manner, the decision to purchase your product or service usually is a way to accomplish other more specific goals or objectives. Knowing the customer's true motivations, therefore, is very important. Identifying multiple reasons for customers to buy from you can also boost your sales while significantly benefiting the customer.

Customers make decisions to purchase products and services for a variety of different reasons. That's actually a good thing, since the needs of individual decision makers can span a wide range of priorities, agendas, and hot buttons, not to mention the fact that personal preference, personality, and previous buying experiences all affect a customer's decision-making tendencies. One thing is for certain, however. Something in the sales process will either motivate potential buyers to move forward with a decision to purchase, or cause them to respectfully decline.

While some buyers are comfortable and ready to move forward with a purchase, others hesitate or turn away from what seems to be a worthy transaction. Why do you suppose that is? It's because the decision to purchase ultimately comes down to the customer's perception of your value—more specifically, whether the value of your proposed solution is great enough to justify the expenditure.

There's that word again—*value*. One of the things that makes selling a challenge these days is the realization that the actual value of your product or service is less important than how it is perceived by prospective customers. In fact, I would argue that there is no such thing as actual value. While your product or service might seem extremely valuable to one prospect, that doesn't necessarily mean it will be perceived the same way by the next. Like physical beauty, the perception of your company's value proposition is in the eye of the beholder.

> **The actual value of your product or service is less important than how it is perceived by prospective customers.**

Let me put this in perspective by using a simple analogy I often demonstrate when delivering QBS training to live audiences.

During these events, when we arrive at the point where it's time to talk about perceived value, I will reach down inside my computer bag and pull out a crisp $100 bill. Everyone's eyes instantly light up. Usually, I ask someone in the front row to verify that I am holding a bona fide $100 bill, rather than play money or some sleight-of-hand magic trick prop. Then I pick someone in the audience and ask them, "Would you be willing to trade twenty dollars in exchange for this one-hundred-dollar bill that I'm holding in my hand?"

There's no deception or trick involved. The person I have called on is either willing to trade their $20 for my $100, or they aren't. Most people jump at the offer, reaching for their wallet or purse as if I were holding a winning lottery ticket. Why wouldn't you want to take advantage of such a lucrative deal? Of course, everyone has a quick chuckle when I qualify this scenario as being only "hypothetical."

The point is, it's an easy decision. Agreeing to move forward with my proposed trade would net the lucky person a quick 500 percent return on their initial $20 investment.

With that image fresh in the audience's mind, I reach down and put the $100 bill back into my computer bag. In the same motion, I come back up with my hands cupped together to conceal what's inside. Next, holding my hands out to the audience, I say, "Ladies and gentlemen, I am holding something in my hands. This is not a joke. I am definitely holding something of value, and I believe it's something you would like very much if you were willing to trade for it."

People sometimes surmise that my cupped hands are filled with air, thinking that there must be a catch, and air is indeed valuable. But I quickly let the audience know that it's definitely an item of some sort.

Turning to the audience, I ask, "Who would be willing to give me twenty dollars in exchange for the concealed item that I am now holding in my hands?" Strangely, no one reaches for their wallet this time. I even walk up to individuals and directly ask them, "Do you have twenty dollars in your wallet?" Most people do. "Can I see it?" Out comes their twenty to prove that they're not completely broke. "Would you be willing to trade your twenty dollars for the item I am holding [still concealed] in my hands?"

"No, thanks" is always the answer.

"How about you, sir? Do you have twenty dollars?" I ask, turning to another unsuspecting person in the next row.

"Can you tell me more about the item in your hands?" someone might ask.

"Sure," I say with a big smile. "It is a VERY valuable item that you will definitely like a lot. In fact, I guarantee it!"

Sometimes they pause for a moment, but still the answer is "No, thanks." One person after another politely declines as I wander around the room with cupped hands.

Once it's clear that no one is willing to pay $20 for whatever I am holding in my hands, I reveal the item. It's the same crisp $100 bill that I held up earlier. Imagine that! I was offering to trade $100 for $20, but no one in the room was willing to take the risk.

What's the lesson in all of this? In the first scenario, where I was offering to trade $100 for a significantly lesser amount, people could clearly see the value of the deal. And when it was obvious that I was offering such a good deal, people were more than willing to make a decision on the spot. They didn't have to check with their business partner, spouse, or put it into the budget for the following year. When the proposed value of a product or service clearly exceeds the cost to procure it, it's easy for people to pull the trigger and make a buying decision.

> **When the proposed value of a product or service clearly exceeds the cost to procure it, it's easy for people to pull the trigger and make a buying decision.**

On the other hand, when the value of the deal being offered is ambiguous or unclear, as with the item concealed in my hands, decision makers tend to hesitate or retreat rather than move forward. With the exception of a few riverboat gambler types, customers today are very reluctant to act on a salesperson's promise that the value of an item will "definitely" justify the expenditure.

That's Decision Making 101. When the perceived value of a product or service clearly exceeds the cost required to purchase it, it's easy for decision makers to move forward. But when the value being offered is ambiguous or doesn't clearly justify the transaction, the answer will most likely be "No, thanks."

Customers Don't Want the Cheapest

I cut my teeth as a salesperson selling big-ticket software solutions in the high-tech marketplace. Potential buyers always complained that our price was too high. Come to find out, complaining about price is just one of the things customers do during a price negotiation. One day it occurred to me that the same decision makers who were groaning about cost were surrounded by many other products and service options that were not the "cheapest." Technology giants like Oracle and Microsoft do not offer the cheapest software applications. IBM became a hundred-billion-dollar company, but not by offering the absolute cheapest technology. The Fortune 500 list of top performing companies is chock-full of businesses that aren't selling the cheapest products.

As I mentioned back in chapter 1, most customers aren't looking to buy the absolute cheapest alternative. I bet you don't use the cheapest computer or live in the cheapest house. You don't eat the cheapest food or wear the cheapest clothes, right? You probably don't always choose the most expensive options, either. Instead, I find that most consumers gravitate to whichever solution gives them the biggest "bang for their buck." Especially in a tight economy, it's all about perceived value.

The cost effectiveness of a proposed solution is critically important in terms of consumer behavior. But much like value, cost effectiveness is another area that is highly subjective. Something that seems like a good deal to one decision maker may not be perceived as cost effective by the next. That's because customers have different priorities and circumstances that affect their perception of your offerings.

If you do happen to offer the cheapest alternative in a competitive situation, then your sales strategy may just be to try and convince customers that your solutions will do the same as other products, for less money. The more likely scenario is that your company's sales success depends largely on a salesperson's ability to differentiate the value of your products and services from competitive offerings.

Alas, we're back to the idea of having enough perceived value to justify the cost. Remember my earlier illustration, where I cupped my hands to conceal an item that I claimed was valuable? If I had offered to reduce the price by 10 percent, do you think people would have jumped at the chance to trade $18 for something that was still unknown? I bet they wouldn't have. Would an even further reduction in price have made a difference?

Granted, there are times in business when it's smart to offer discounts or incentives to spur sales. But lowering your price to create differentiation usually isn't a great sales strategy because you end up giving away profit margin without actually increasing the perceived value of your product or service. Closing low-margin deals is of little value if your company can't turn a profit.

If you want deals to hinge on more than just price, then the focus of the sale must somehow shift to the other variable that will ultimately affect the decision—the customer's perception of your value. That becomes a function of your product or service's ability to accomplish specific decision objectives for the customer.

How Many Reasons Do Customers Have to Buy from You?

A customer's perception of value is not some binary switch that gets flipped on or off. As we discussed earlier, the value you offer is an intangible commodity that can increase or decrease based on how customers perceive your products, your company, and perhaps most important, you. Hence, the best sales strategy in any competitive market is the one that accumulates value throughout the sales process by addressing multiple facets of the customer's need.

Think about it like this. If it were completely up to you, how many reasons would you want customers to have to buy from you? Similarly, how many reasons do you want customers to have to meet with you, or to recommend your offerings to their boss or to colleagues within the organization? When I pose these questions to live training audiences, the most common response people say is, "One." Sometimes people say, "At least one." I suppose that makes sense, because if a customer doesn't have at least one reason to buy your product or service, you probably won't make a sale. Regrettably, giving customers just one reason to buy from (or meet with) you is no longer enough in a competitive environment.

For years, traditional sales approaches promoted the idea that in order to provide valuable solutions, you must first uncover a need. Salespeople were accordingly sent out into their respective territories to probe for needs. We have since discovered that customers don't always know (exactly) what they need. And, even if they do recognize their own needs, they aren't always willing to share this information with a salesperson they don't yet know or trust. Consequently, the strategy of probing for needs is flawed because it's not as easy as it sounds.

Even if you are able to successfully uncover a need, what then? Conventional wisdom would suggest that you should address the customer's need by proposing one of your company's solutions. Ironically, that's where the train slides off the tracks.

One of my favorite parables that I have been using to train salespeople since the mid-1990s is the now-infamous water pump analogy. For training purposes, it's important for people to think outside the scope of their normal daily routines, in order to focus on two things: strategy and technique. So for the next couple minutes, whether you sell technology solutions, medical supplies, financial services, real estate, or manufactured goods, I want to divert your attention away from thinking about your usual selling environment. Instead, let's imagine a scenario where you are employed as a salesperson for a fictitious company that sells water pumps.

Depending on where you are geographically located and the time of year, flooding can be a real problem. During the rainy season, for example, the foundation of a home can settle to the point where water starts seeping into the basement. Another unlucky scenario for a homeowner is to have a pipe burst because of subzero temperatures have frozen an unprotected pipe in the dead of winter. A rapid springtime thaw can be equally problematic, causing headaches for even the most diligent homeowners.

Suppose a lead were to come into our hypothetical water pump company, and you and I were selected to go on a joint sales call tomorrow to meet with a potential customer who has a flooded basement due to heavy rain over the weekend. Today, prior to meeting with the customer, suppose that you and I carved out a few minutes to strategize in advance. Do you ever strategize with a colleague or partner, or perhaps with your boss, before calling on real live prospects?

During this strategy session, the first thing we should ask is: What problem or issue is the homeowner trying to address? That's easy—they want to remove the water from their flooded basement. Done! We're ready to head out and meet with the customer, right? Not so fast. To understand why we are not yet prepared, let's fast-forward out of our strategy session to anticipate what could happen during the actual sales call.

Seller: (Knock . . . knock) Hello, Mr. Customer, my name is Tom Freese with XYZ Pumps and this is my colleague, *[insert your name here]*. We are responding to your inquiry about water removal. How can we help?
Homeowner: Thanks for coming. We have a flooded basement.
Seller: Great, let me tell you about our pumps!

For decades, sellers have had the notion drilled into our heads that we must first understand the customer's need. So we go out into our respective territories and try to understand the customer needs, usually by asking them. In this case, the customer was quick to share their problem—they have a flooded basement. Doesn't that sound like a need? Once uncovered, sellers have been taught to believe that the identification of a need is our cue to jump in and provide "solutions."

Here's the problem with basing your current sales approach on outdated logic. After completing this initial dialogue, how many reasons does the customer have to buy a water pump? The answer is, just one. And the reason? They have a flooded basement. But if it were totally up to you, let me ask again: How many reasons would you want customers to have to purchase your product or service?

I can tell you with total confidence that I would much rather my customers had three reasons to buy from me, instead of only one. For that matter, I would like customers to have six or seven reasons to buy my product over the competition, instead of only three. And, if it were totally up to me, I would just as soon customers had twelve, fifteen, or even twenty reasons to move forward with the purchase of my proposed solution.

Why do I want customers to have more reasons? Well, in QBS it's a three-pronged strategy. Giving customers more reasons to buy your product or service usually translates into a greater sense of urgency on their part to move forward with a favorable purchase decision. Giving customers more reasons to buy from you also tends to create competitive separation. Case in point: if there are seven or eight reasons to buy from you, but only two or three to stay with a competitor, then you will be in a strong position to win the business. Note that the opposite is also true, where having more reasons to stay with a competitor quickly forfeits any advantages you might have. Last, giving customers more reasons to buy your product or service makes it easier for them to justify the expenditure, especially if your product is not the cheapest.

Now, let's jump back into our precall strategy session in order to put this idea of expanding the customer's needs into practice. Once we understand that the customer is dealing with a water leak, it's easy to expand the scope of the problem by asking ourselves the next logical question, which is: "Why might water in the basement be a problem for this homeowner?" Unless you are a mind reader, there's no way to know what the customer's specific hot buttons are prior to actually talking with them. But since you and I would presumably be knowledgeable about our industry, we should be able to hypothesize in advance about how a flooded basement might affect a customer.

Frankly, the issue of flooding has numerous implications for potential customers. A simple water leak in the basement, for example, could impact a homeowner in any number of ways, including causing:

1. structural damage
2. damage to personal property
3. mold or mildew
4. damage to furnace or electrical system
5. unsanitary conditions or health hazard
6. safety risk for children and pets
7. unwanted pests or insects
8. inability to use the space
9. damage irreplaceable heirlooms
10. increased stress in the household
11. insurance issues
12. cost to clean up
13. time/hassle factor
14. decrease resale value of home
15. unpleasant odor

Can you see how talking about the broader issue of having a "flooded basement" only scratches the surface of the customer's real challenges? What customers really want is to prevent structural damage, protect their personal property, eliminate mold and mildew, avoid damaging their furnace or electrical systems, and so forth. In fact, while some customers might be concerned about potential health risks, other homeowners will focus more on the insurance issue or the cost to clean up the mess.

The fact that customers have different priorities is perfectly fine. As I said, people buy for different reasons. Nonetheless, recognizing that the underlying implication(s) of an issue are what ultimately drives the customer's decision puts you in a stronger position to increase the customer's perception of the value you offer.

Watch what happens when we plug this thought back into our sample dialogue.

Seller: (Knock . . . knock) Hello, Mr. Customer, my name is Tom Freese with XYZ Pumps and this is my colleague, *[you again!]*. We are responding to your inquiry about water removal. How can we help?

Homeowner: Thanks for coming. Our basement is flooded.

Seller: Yes, we're getting lots of calls because of the recent storm. Could I ask, besides the obvious goal of getting the water out of your basement, what specifically are you most concerned about?

Homeowner: Two things—I'm concerned about cost and possible structural damage to the foundation of my house.

Asking "Besides the obvious goal of _____ ?" is a brilliant way to open the floodgates of conversation (pardon the pun). It eliminates any risk of sounding rhetorical because the salesperson directly acknowledges the obvious problem as part of the question itself. It is absolutely fair and reasonable for a salesperson to ask beyond "the obvious goal" to understand the full context of the customer's true concerns. Just asking a rhetorical question like "Why is flooding in the basement a problem for you?" could make you sound naïve, inexperienced, or just plain stupid. If you are at all knowledgeable about your business, then you should already have a pretty good idea about why flooding might be a problem for homeowners. Hence, by asking "Besides the obvious goal of _____ , what specifically are you most concerned about?" it's predictable that most homeowners will mention one or more of the implications on your list. Perfect!

If the customer in the sample dialogue responds by saying, "I'm concerned about cost and possible structural damage," this information is absolutely valuable for the seller, and it also paves the way for you to expand the discussion and identify other implications that are on the customer's mind.

What are the chances that customers will name all fifteen of the implications on our sample list? Very slim. But human nature is fairly predictable, so how many implications do you think most customers will bring up on their own? The answer is usually only one or two, and once in a while, three. So who is going to bring up all the other implications that might also be important to a prospective customer? If not you, then the door is left wide open for a competitor to be perceived as a more valuable resource.

At the end of the day, I want customers to have multiple reasons to buy from me, and I want them to have a sense of urgency to move forward with a decision. I also want to make it as easy as possible for them to cost-justify the purchase decision to their boss, peers, or spouse. Bearing all of this in mind, it's fairly easy to expand the customer's needs and facilitate a more in-depth conversation simply by raising additional implications, such as:

"Have you had flooding problems before or is this a one-time occurrence?"
"Is your basement used for storage only or is the water damaging personal property or encroaching on your family's living space?"
"Have you ever had a mold or mildew problem in the house?"
"Where is the water level in relation to the electrical box?"
"Are you sensing any unpleasant odors coming from that affected area?"
"Does your homeowner's insurance cover this type of claim?"

With a few well-placed questions to kick off the needs development conversation, the seller can easily raise any number of potential implications (e.g., recurrence, personal property, inconvenience to the family, mold, mildew, safety, unpleasant odors, insurance) in the conversation that the customer may not have otherwise mentioned. Suddenly, the tally of important decision factors has increased from the initial two the customer brought up (cost and structural damage), to as many as fifteen implications that could affect the homeowner's decisions.

Herein lies one of the main differences between Question Based Selling and traditional sales approaches. Probing for needs too often reduces a capable salesperson to sounding like they are reading from a script. Frankly, you can teach minimum wage employees to ask survey questions. QBS, on the other hand, is a true facilitation, where the salesperson actually participates in the needs development process by raising issues and implications that customers might not think to bring up.

Frankly, if you are an expert in dealing with flooded basements, then you should absolutely be ready to ask questions about an array of possible implications. Should you barrage customers with a litany of questions, by bringing up all fifteen implications while standing on the homeowner's doorstep? Of course not. But once the conversation starts rolling, you can be sure that there will be plenty of opportunities to expand the dialogue.

Your Recipe for Success

Certain things in this chapter might be starting to sound familiar. Like any good recipe, in addition to identifying the right ingredients, you must also be able to blend an array of different ingredients together into just the right mixture in order to be consistently successful.

For example, in preparation for your next job interview (or sales call), you will already know that the official start of the sale begins when the hiring manager or customer says some version of, "Tell me about yourself (or your product)." At that moment in an interview, you have two choices—either to provide a dump of information about your work history, educational background, and family situation (SPA), or you can talk about those issues that are likely to be most important to the hiring manager (PAS).

Though the hiring manager's primary goal may be somewhat obvious (wanting to hire the best person for the job), you can be sure there are several underlying and more specific implications that the interviewer is also hoping to satisfy by making a good choice. Let me show you what I mean in a quick revisit of the earlier interview dialogue.

Interviewer: Can you tell me a little about yourself?

Candidate: Sure. Do you have a copy of my résumé?

Manager: Yes, I've got it right here.

Candidate: Well, since you've already seen a snapshot of my work history, I'd like to think that I'm a good person with a decent track record of success, but I'll let you be the judge of that. I'm thinking that you might be looking for more than just a "good person" to fill this position, however. In fact, I'm guessing that you might be looking for some of the intangibles that wouldn't necessarily show up as specific line items on a résumé.

For example, based on the research I did prior to this meeting, I'm thinking that you might be looking for someone who can ramp up and become productive as quickly as possible, especially given the current economy. You may also be looking for someone who can blend with the existing culture, but still bring a fresh perspective or new ideas from outside the company. You might also be looking for someone who can grow existing opportunities, while also being able to defuse potential hot spots that may exist within a problem customer account. If so, those are the types of things that have enabled me to be successful in the past.

Do you mind if I ask, what specific goals would you want the perfect candidate for this position to be able to accomplish?

If the issues you raise are indeed important to the hiring manager, you are "in like Flynn." The candidate in this dialogue brings up a host of decision factors including knowledge, experience, the learning curve, productivity, blending with an existing culture, and bringing a fresh perspective to the team. Certainly these "reasons to buy" would strike a chord with any manager who wanted to hire the right person. As I said earlier, a salesperson who *demonstrates* that he or she is customer-focused is much more valuable during a job interview (or sales call) than someone who just claims to be.

Don't be surprised when you are the only candidate or salesperson who takes the conversation down a customer-focused path. Most sellers, when given the opportunity, jump immediately at the chance to delve into a self-indulgent diatribe about themselves and their capabilities, thinking that they are doing well because they are answering the question the interviewer asked.

Depending on customers to fully articulate their needs is a bad strategy in today's business environment, and into the foreseeable future. Most customers share fractionally, by mentioning only some portion of the implications that will influence their decision. This is because a.) they're not engrossed in the nuances of your product or service on a day-to-day basis, as you are, and b.) human nature dictates that people are naturally reluctant to share information with someone they don't yet know and fully trust. That's okay; facilitating conversations that help customers identify and understand their needs is one of the greatest opportunities we sellers have to provide value.

Some people resist this notion of proactive participation in needs development, arguing that guessing what the customers' needs are could put a salesperson at risk of sounding presumptuous. Granted, there's no way to know the customer's needs (exactly) until you actually talk with them, but we're not exactly guessing here. If you specialize in a business that deals with similar issues every day, and if you use your industry knowledge with a dash of common sense, couldn't you hypothesize in advance as to what a customer's needs might be?

Even though I've never actually sold water pumps, it would be easy for me to come up with a top-ten list of implications for how a flooded basement could potentially affect a customer. The same logic applies to any value-based sale. If you sell financial services, for example, besides the obvious goal of making good investment decisions, what specifically are your customers trying to accomplish? Go ahead and ask about their specific goals. Don't be surprised, however, when customers only bring up some fraction of the implications on your list.

Once again, who's going to bring up the rest?

If you are well prepared (in advance) to facilitate the discussions by raising additional implications, be ready for the floodgates of conversation to burst wide open. This is what I referred to earlier when I talked about priming the pump. The underlying lesson is simple: When a salesperson raises important decision factors that a customer wouldn't necessarily have brought up, or even thought about, on their own, decision makers start to perceive you as an extremely valuable resource, which is very different from just rattling off a series of canned survey questions.

It's a credibility play. Once customers begin to form the impression that you might be able to help them, they are usually willing to share tons of information with a salesperson they believe to be a valuable resource. The customer's perception of the value you bring is, therefore, largely in your own hands, and establishing credibility is a direct function to your ability to *sell yourself first*.

Do You Own an Umbrella?

Getting your arms around the customer's decision criteria is complicated by the fact that customers often speak in generic or general terms, as opposed to articulating what they really need. This natural vagueness creates another good opportunity for sellers who are prepared to facilitate more in-depth conversations.

To illustrate, here's a simple exercise you can try for yourself. I often demonstrate this to audiences during live QBS training programs, and the scenario plays out the same way every time.

Basically, I pick out a face in the crowd and ask, "Do you own an umbrella?" Most people do. This is hardly an attempt to catch someone off-guard, as it's just a simple question. With few exceptions over the years, the typical response is yes.

Out of curiosity, I then ask a follow-up question: "Why do you own an umbrella?" Again, there's no trick. I'm just asking *why* they own an umbrella.

"In case it rains" is the standard response.

This is where things get interesting. Watch what happens when I take the conversation to the next level by asking, "What is it about the rain that you are trying to avoid?"

"I don't want to get wet," the person will say. Fair enough. It makes total sense to me that someone would use an umbrella to protect them-selves from getting wet when it's raining outside.

But what do you suppose happens to the value of the conversation when we start exploring the customer's aspirations even further, this time by asking, "What is it exactly about getting wet that is undesirable to you?"

"I don't want to ruin my clothes."

Finally, we're getting somewhere. One of the reasons people own umbrellas is to protect their clothes (a nice silk scarf or leather jacket, for example) from getting ruined if they happen to get caught in a down-pour.

Other times, someone might say, "I don't want to catch a cold." That makes sense, too. Without an umbrella that protects you from getting soaked, you could easily get sick. By the way, if you do get sick, you could end up missing work. And if you miss work, you might lose an important sale and miss out on the commission. Can you see how the simple issue of "getting wet" begets a whole trail of related implications?

Besides protecting your clothes and your health, there are plenty of other reasons to own an umbrella. A businessperson who wants to pre-serve a professional image, for example, probably would want to fend off inclement weather. For others, preventing the possibility of having to sit around all day in damp clothes is another big motivator. Still, other people use umbrellas to protect themselves from the sun, wanting to minimize the possible links between ultraviolet rays and skin cancer.

If you notice, the first response I always receive when I ask someone why they own an umbrella is, "In case it rains." Upon further analysis, we discover they were really trying to "avoid getting wet." But when we peel back the onion, we found out that what people really wanted was to:

1. look their best
2. feel comfortable
3. protect their clothes
4. preserve a professional image
5. protect electronic devices

6. stay healthy
7. avoid sick days from work
8. not lose money
9. limit exposure to ultraviolet rays
10. move around freely during inclement weather

In this umbrella analogy, it's not until the third layer of depth that we discover the true motivations behind why someone might want to own an umbrella. People don't buy umbrellas to "avoid getting wet." You don't take an umbrella into the shower, do you? Of course not. You are not averse to the idea of being wet. You just want to avoid getting soaked at certain inopportune times. Therefore, the value of an umbrella is more than just protecting against wetness, it's a whole list of potential motivators (i.e. implications).

One lesson to take away from this exercise is the realization that "depth of conversation" is a salesperson's best friend. I'm not suggesting you should interrogate potential umbrella buyers. If you worked at a kiosk selling umbrellas in the mall, for example, and you asked, "Why do you want an umbrella?" we know how most customers would answer—they would say, "In case it rains." If you probed further, "Why, what happens if it rains?" you'd probably get some funny looks. If you pressed the issue by asking, "What are the real reasons you don't want to get wet?" rather than sharing their thoughts, customers would likely be turned off by your invasiveness. That's because most people don't want to be probed for needs.

Some old-schoolers still defend this notion of probing for needs, saying that sellers must "drill down" to find out what is really driving the customer's decision. Frankly, this brings us to a crossroads in your professional development as a salesperson. If I sold umbrellas at a kiosk in the mall, I would probably ask potential customers this question: "Besides the obvious goal of staying dry, what specifically are you most concerned about?" I'd be willing to bet the farm that most customers would respond by mentioning one of the implications noted earlier. What's the likelihood they will bring up all ten? Again, it's very slim.

Predictably, most customers will mention one or two, but I would be more than ready to facilitate a more valuable dialogue by raising additional implications that would not have otherwise come up.

The actual value of your product or service doesn't change whether you have a detailed conversation with potential buyers or a superficial one. But if the solutions you offer are capable of addressing multiple issues and implications, and you know customers are not going to fully articulate their own needs, then your success is closely linked to your ability to facilitate more in-depth conversations, which is very different than just probing and having customers reluctantly share some fraction of their needs.

Applying Your New Decision Logic

This new participative philosophy on needs development has dramatically shifted the older-school paradigm away from the idea that customers will openly share all their needs with a salesperson they don't yet know and trust. Instead, mutually beneficial sales conversations will only occur as a result of a proactive facilitation where you are able to gain credibility and focus on which issues are most important to the customer. In QBS, my vision includes having salespeople convey more value by actually helping customers recognize possible implications that potentially otherwise wouldn't even have been considered.

This depth of conversation is essentially what happens in other professions. Whether you consult with a doctor, an attorney, an accountant, an engineer, or an architect, if you are the customer, you want these professionals to ask you a series of intelligent questions in order to then provide you with the best possible advice. Why should the sales profession be any different? As I mentioned previously, the profession of selling should be prescriptive in nature, where your recommendations and advice should be derived from and based on what the customer is specifically trying to accomplish.

Fortunately, the implementation of this approach comes with a price. I say "fortunately" because if I were in your shoes, it would motivate me to know that most of my competitors aren't focused on these strategic nuances, and even if they were, many wouldn't be willing to invest the time or effort required to enhance their credibility when dealing with customers. For me, the difference between success and failure often boils down to a simple formula—starting with putting in the necessary time and effort to give yourself an unfair advantage.

> **The difference between success and failure often boils down to a simple formula—which starts with putting in the time and effort necessary to give yourself an unfair advantage.**

It was great fun to win top salesman honors for multiple consecutive years. Success can be very rewarding and motivating at the same time, as many of you know. In addition to producing lots of revenue for my company, however, I was equally proud of my ability to ramp up quickly and become productive in a fraction of the time it took other people. There's no magic to doing this; it just requires some time and effort up front, and a little strategic thinking.

If you would like to have a similar advantage, let me encourage you to complete the same exercise I would challenge myself with during my first week on the job if I accepted a position with your company. I would create a physical document to serve as a "repository" that reflects a list of possible issues that might be important to prospective customers. I would also document the underlying implications of why each of those issues might be important. I would try to come up with a list of ten potential implications per issue. Push yourself past the standard top two or three. You want to be the rep who is able to bring up nuances that otherwise wouldn't come up in the conversation.

Knowing that decision makers buy for a variety of reasons, there is no better way to prepare yourself in advance than by burning these issues and implications into your "top of mind" memory. Making a physical list also gives you a reference document to refer to before your next sales conversation or customer meeting.

FINANCIAL SERVICES	MANUFACTURING	REAL ESTATE
Return on Investment	*Materials Management*	*Location*
Safety of Principal	*Inventory Turns*	*Traffic Volume*
Growth of Capital	*Growth*	*Aesthetics*
Risk	*Fixed Costs*	*View*
Diversification	*Shipping and Logistics*	*Noise*
Reporting	*Innovation*	*School Districts*
Market Updates	*Sales and Marketing*	*Proximity to Health Care*
Estate Planning	*Strategic Planning*	*Local Job Market*
Cash/Liquidity	*Customer Satisfaction*	*Retail Options*
Trust in Adviser	*Security*	*Construction vs. Remodel*
Access to Information	*Maintenance*	*Broker Reputation*
Inflation	*Multiple Locations*	*Time Frame for Decision*
Retirement Planning	*Profitability*	*Contingencies*
Income Stream	*Labor Unions*	*Size of Family*
Cost of Services	*Staffing*	*Amenities*
Confidentiality	*Quality Control*	*Financing Options*
Prompt Service	*Communication*	*Prequalification*
Integrity of Company	*Information Technology*	*Liquidity*
Consistent Performance	*Global Markets*	*Driving Distance to Work*
Tax Planning	*Research and Development*	*Residential vs. Commercial*

Building a Repository of Issues and Implications

Are you willing to make a one-time investment (of two hours) to kick-start the rest of your sales career? That is approximately how much time it will take to complete this exercise. Honestly, nothing in my experience will pay bigger dividends, or give sellers a greater competitive advantage, when facilitating needs development conversations with potential customers. If you are willing to invest in yourself, building a repository list of possible decision issues and implications will change the way you interact with prospective customers. More important, it will change the way they perceive and interact with you.

If priming the pump can initiate the flow of information between buyers and sellers, and you see the value of taking a leadership role when facilitating your needs development conversations with prospective customers, then you must prepare yourself in advance—much like the

TECHNOLOGY	PHARMACEUTICAL	CONSULTING
Availability	Clinical Efficacy	Expertise
Performance	Trials/Studies	Available Resources
Scalability	Exclusions	Time Frame for Decision
Cost Effectiveness	Possible Side Effects	Quality
Disaster Recovery	Contraindications	Experience
Manageability	Precaution Warnings	Job Security
Ease of Use	Drug Interactions	Cost
Interoperability	Multiple Indications	Justification
Customer Satisfaction	Cost Effectiveness	Proximity
Upgradability	Alternative Generics	Location/Travel
Reliability	On Formulary	Competitive Positioning
Maintenance	Paperwork Required	Employee Morale
Support/Services	Managed Care	Learning Curve
Time to Market	Ease of Use	Legal Liability
Company Viability	Samples Available	Return on Investment
Industry Leadership	Continuous Learning	Project Scope
Data Integrity	Company Image	Requirements Definition
Education/Training	Rep. Availability	Future Needs
Implementation	Patient Satisfaction	Peace of Mind
Remote Locations	Legal Liability	Time to Market

leader of a college debate team. How can you accomplish this in two hours?

Start by making an inventory of possible business issues (or decision factors) that might be important to customers in your target market. (*Repository* is a just fancy word for database.) Be sure to print out a hard copy and keep an updatable version on your computer, as you will build onto this list as the next step. The table above shows examples of common issues from select industries.

Once you've constructed a list of possible decision issues your customers might face, the next step is to enhance your potential value to prospective customers by creating a subordinate list of possible implications for each decision issue.

Just ask yourself, "Why might (*issue*) be important to a prospective customer?" If you work in the financial services industry, for example, you might ask, "Why might return on investment or tax planning be important to my customers?" You can ask customers, too. But the magic of this technique is "arming" yourself in advance so that you can proactively bring these implications up in a conversation, as opposed to always trying to coax or cajole it out of potential customers.

Make it your goal to create a list of ten implications for each decision issue. Push yourself to get to ten implications. It's like physical exercise, where the six, seventh, eighth, ninth, and tenth repetitions are far more important than the most obvious first two or three that your competitors will also be focusing most of their attention on.

For example, return on investment might be important to a prospective customer because of:

1. Cash flow
2. Tax planning
3. Adviser confidence
4. Investment buy/sell decisions
5. College savings
6. Retirement planning
7. Liquidity
8. Budgeting expenses
9. Peace of mind
10. Net worth

Note to sales managers: some QBS clients will attempt to save time by assigning this task of building a repository of issues and implications to a single person, with the idea that they could then forward the completed repository to everyone else. This is a big mistake, however, if you want to raise the effectiveness of entire sales team. If the goal is to create top-of-mind awareness for which issues might be important to a customer, and why those issues could be important, individual salespeople must create this thought process for themselves. Just reviewing an e-mail with an attached list of issues and implications will not cause a salesperson to be perceived as a better resource by potential decision makers.

You must also resist the temptation to cop out of this exercise by making a list of issues and implications in your head. Instead, invest the time to actually write it down, create a spreadsheet on your computer, or I've even seen salespeople make flash cards. Making a permanent copy allows you to update the information over time as your product changes or your industry evolves. It also gives you a resource to glance at in preparation for important meetings, or even as a reminder during live telephone conversations. I can promise you this: if you complete this exercise, you will find that you won't refer to the actual document you created very often. As a by-product of building your own physical list, you will also be burning these issues and implications into your top-of-mind memory.

I have been assigning this exercise as homework for many years now, and I have yet to meet a salesperson who completed the task and didn't rave about their newfound success afterward when dealing with customers. If you do the math on this, a repository of twenty decision issues that has ten implications linked to every issue suddenly creates two hundred opportunities for a salesperson to provide value, which is very different from just randomly running around probing for needs.

While building your repository list, you may notice that there is some definite overlap between the customer's issues and their corresponding implications. This is good. Back in our earlier water pump analogy, for example, structural damage to the foundation can affect the resale value of a home. Damage to personal property can also affect the overall cost of the customer's loss for insurance purposes. Odor or mildew issues can similarly impact the livability of the home. The fact that these issues and implications are closely interrelated makes it easier for the strategic salesperson to navigate deeper, wider, and more strategic needs development conversations.

Again, how many reasons do you want customers to have to buy from you? Many sellers spend countless hours chasing unqualified opportunities or deals that disappear off the sales forecast because there was little or no differentiation. Therefore, I say, why not invest two hours up front to put yourself in the strongest possible competitive position that will pay significant dividends for the rest of your sales career?

6

How to Be More Strategic with Your Sales Questions

Sellers have been taught to ask lots of questions. But as I've said several times now, just because a salesperson wants to ask a bunch of questions doesn't mean potential customers will share information with a salesperson they don't yet know or trust.

In today's competitive business environment, if it is possible to ask questions in a way that could be considered to be highly ineffective, then it must also be possible to ask effective questions, in a way that causes people to "want to" share lots of valuable information. The difference between these two outcomes is generally dictated by the logic behind the questions you ask.

Some people are smooth talkers, and thus, they just have a knack for navigating the flow of their sales conversations. You could say these individuals are born with the gift of gab. Fortunately for the rest of us, there is a methodology that enables sellers to engage more people in more productive conversations. Not only is it possible to teach people how to facilitate more valuable interactions with customers, you teach them how to repeat their success.

If we invest the time to understand the theory behind the questions you ask, a salesperson's goal shouldn't just be to interrogate potential buyers, or to pepper them with probative questions. To be effective, you must also do something that will cause your audience to be receptive to the questions you ask, to the point where they feel comfortable and "want to" share information with you. Managing the types of questions you ask requires a proactive thought process, however, one that will ultimately enable you to be more effective with your questions and cause prospects to be more forthcoming with their responses.

From a sales perspective, the most common reason sellers ask questions is simply to gather information. Everyone knows that in order to provide valuable solutions, sellers must first understand the customer's needs, goals, objectives, and concerns, in addition to knowing their time frame for making a decision. Somewhere along the way, we also want to qualify potential opportunities to ensure that we are making a good use of the customer's time, and our own. Some level of reconnaissance might also be needed if you are the primary contact on a named account and are responsible for communicating details to other members of the sales team.

When it comes to needs development, the desire to collect information from the customer has always taken center stage. "Go out and probe for needs!" has become a familiar battle cry coming from corporate sales managers for many years. The problem is, consuming yourself with the inwardly focused desire to gather information about the opportunity has unfortunately become a classic example of how a self-serving sales approach can inhibit your selling efforts. As it turns out, "gathering information" is only one of many facets of an effective questioning strategy.

This idea of being more strategic with your sales questions is important because besides just collecting information, asking questions strategically can benefit a salesperson in numerous ways throughout the sales process. For example, a well-placed strategic question is one of the best ways to pique the customer's interest, particularly early in the sales cycle when prospects are forming their initial impression. Asking relevant and intelligent questions also provides one of your best opportunities to establish credibility with prospective buyers. Your ability to deliver the right question at the right time can also differentiate you from the competition, as well as increase the customer's sense of urgency to move forward with a decision. Questions can even be used to help cost-justify the purchase and overcome obstacles that pop up throughout the decision cycle. Therefore, I say, if the only thing you do with questions is gather information about the opportunity, then there is a huge upside opportunity for you to increase your sales effectiveness by simply adjusting the strategy behind the questions you ask.

Information Gathering Is Underrated

Understanding the customer's needs, qualifying opportunities, and communicating with others who may need to be in the loop are an important part of many sales roles. To fulfill these objectives, sellers obviously must be able to gather some perfunctory information from potential buyers. There's just one catch. Soliciting information often feels (to the customer) like a self-serving act on the part of the salesperson. Sure, you're trying to make a sale, but what's in it for them? They're thinking, "Why should I share information with you as opposed to the dozens of other salespeople who are calling me every day?"

I am not suggesting that sellers should refrain from gathering information about their respective sales opportunities. But, what if we can identify specific questioning techniques that would allow you to ask questions in a way that lowered the decision maker's natural defenses, thus enabling you to engage them in a more productive conversation. You accomplish this by asking questions more strategically, in a manner that causes customers to recognize that sharing information with the salesperson actually gets them closer to achieving their own objectives.

The truth is, if someone doesn't want to share with you, then it doesn't matter what you choose to ask. Predictably, the conversation will come to an abrupt and immediate end. Fortunately for a salesperson, the opposite is true. At the very moment a potential customer begins to form the impression that you may indeed be a credible resource, the dynamics of the conversation will shift and the customer will start helping you help them. The challenge for sellers is getting over this initial hump in the conversation, so that customers who would otherwise be standoffish suddenly have a personal incentive to open up.

The Downside of Open-Ended Questions

Are you familiar with the traditional labeling of questions as being "open-" or "closed-ended"? A closed-ended question is one that can be answered with a single word or phrase. For example, "Mr. Customer, do you currently own a home?" This question can be answered with a simple yes or no, although closed-ended questions are not limited to yes/no responses. A salesperson could just as easily ask, "How many employees are in your company?" While the customer could choose to elaborate with a more detailed response, this still qualifies as a closed-ended question that can be appropriately answered with a single word or phrase, like "Seventy-three."

An open-ended question, on the other hand, is one that cannot be appropriately answered with a single word or phrase.

The very first sales course I ever attended was the old Xerox course, called Professional Selling Skills (PSS). One of the main themes that was drilled into our heads during the training was, "If you want to open a dialogue with prospective customers, then you need to ask open-ended questions."

Xerox pretty much wrote the book on sales training back then. Consequently, kicking your sales conversations off with open-ended questions has been the default advice most sales training courses have offered for the last thirty years.

At first glance, the strategy appears valid—beginning customer conversations with open-ended questions seems logical enough. What salesperson doesn't want to "open" a dialogue with potential buyers? Hence, the Xerox training, along with countless other sales training courses, have taught sellers to open their sales conversations with open-ended questions such as:

"Mr. Customer, what's the biggest issue you currently face?"
"What are your goals and objectives for the next five years?"
"What keeps you awake at night?"

These are classic examples of open probes. Since my initial Xerox training experience, I have attended many other sales courses and read dozens of books that tout the same philosophy—if you want to open a dialogue with potential customers, start with open-ended questions. I diligently stuck to this approach during my early years in sales. Kicking my conversations off with open-ended questions never seemed to make sense, however. In hindsight, asking open-ended questions at the wrong time was one of the reasons I struggled so much early in my selling career.

The problem is, prospects today are reluctant to open up and share information with someone they don't yet know or trust.

Next time you receive a cold call at home, and the salesperson on the other end of the telephone opens the dialogue by saying, "This is Joe Smith with Equitable Real Estate Life Insurance Mortgage Company, what are your financial goals and objectives for the next five years?" are you likely to open up and share your long-term financial goals with a total stranger? I doubt it.

As our society has grown increasingly more cautious and skeptical of strangers, sellers can no longer assume prospects will open up just because you want to ask broad, sweeping sales questions. In fact, asking for too much too soon is one of the quickest ways to shut down a budding conversation. In fact, this is more likely to make you seem invasive and inconsiderate. Customers are likely to think, "You don't have enough credibility to ask me that question." Or, "Why would I share that information with someone I don't know?"

Sellers Start with Near-Zero Credibility

As a skeptical buyer myself, I've always believed that sellers start with near-zero credibility when talking with real live prospects. Although customers don't despise salespeople, we sellers inherit the negative baggage from all the other salespeople who previously called on the customer, but didn't necessarily provide value. And unless you do something to separate yourself from the typical stereotype customers tend to harbor toward salespeople in general, until you do something to show them otherwise, prospects will assume you offer little or no value. That's what I mean by starting with near-zero credibility.

The current level of standoffishness from decision makers creates an interesting paradox: prospective buyers are reluctant to share their needs with a salesperson who hasn't yet established credibility, but the only way to establish credibility is to somehow engage potential customers in a productive conversation about their needs.

So how can you break this cycle and establish your credibility early enough to engage potential buyers in the sales process? There are basically three options a salesperson has to try and establish credibility with prospective customers. One is to leverage references or an existing relationship. If you know someone who can introduce you to key people within important target accounts, that could roll out a red carpet directly into the decision maker's office. Leveraging your current Rolodex is especially good when it comes to getting deeper, wider, and more strategic within existing customer accounts. The bigger challenge, however, is finding a way to establish credibility where no relationship currently exists.

The second, and the most common, way sellers attempt to gain credibility is simply by trying to claim it—generally in the form of an elevator pitch. When a customer or hiring manager says, "Tell me about yourself (or product)," most sellers do exactly that—they spew out bullet-point information about their company, their products, or themselves in the hopes of conveying enough credibility to engage the prospect in a mutually beneficial business conversation.

I talked about the pitfalls of trying to claim your own credibility back in chapter 2. Remember, talking about themselves is what most people do during a job interview. Given that propping yourself up runs the risk of sounding presumptuous, trying to claim credibility also tends to cause cautious customers to retreat even further. As a consumer yourself, when a salesperson brags about their offerings does this build credibility with you?

The third option for establishing credibility is to earn it. Real-life experiences have led me to believe that credibility isn't something that can just be claimed. In today's business climate, where buyers are cautious and more standoffish than ever before, I would argue that sellers have to "earn their own stripes" in every account. It's worth noting that credibility must also be demonstrated on an individual basis, which requires a proactive effort on your part to say and do things that will cause decision makers to perceive you as a valuable resource.

If we agree that credibility must be earned, the question now is: What can sellers do to establish more credibility with prospective customers, particularly early in the sales process?

Use Diagnostic Questions to Establish Credibility

Back when I was a rookie salesperson, it didn't take long to realize that prospects weren't eager to share information with a salesperson they didn't know. This created a huge problem for me since I was new to the company and territory. While the prevailing philosophy at the time revolved around this idea that open-ended questions would somehow open the dialogue, it quickly became apparent that asking invasive or probative questions was causing prospects to shut down rather than open up. Trying to impress people with an elevator pitch about my product or company wasn't helping either. Now what?

Under normal sales conditions, time is of the essence. When making cold calls, for example, sellers usually have a brief window of time during which they had better pique the customer's interest and establish some credibility, or whatever window of opportunity there is will quickly close. Therein lies the challenge: figuring out some method for piquing the customer's interest and establishing your own credibility within a relatively small amount of time.

Logic finally triumphed over tradition, and I decided to stop approaching customers with the traditional, open-ended questions that were essentially turning them off. Instead, I thought, if asking for too much too soon was causing a problem, what would happen if I tried taking a few baby steps on the way to accomplishing the larger objective? Are you familiar with the adage "You must first learn to crawl before you can walk, or walk before you can run"?

After experimenting with different types of questions, I began to notice that customers responded much more openly when I took a softer, more considerate approach, versus aiming for the jugular and asking something like "What's the biggest issue you currently face?" This idea of earning the right to engage has since evolved into one of the foundational philosophies within the QBS methodology. As a result, we now spend a fair amount of time "deprogramming" the mind-set of an entire generation of salespeople and replacing it with more contemporary logic that will enable more productive needs development conversations. The specific technique is called asking "diagnostic questions."

Scope, Focus, and Disposition

In Question Based Selling, I don't think of questions as being open- or closed-ended, because those labels fail to capture the true strategic value of a well-designed sales strategy. I'll say it again—if the only thing you are trying to accomplish with questions is to gather information, then you have a huge upside opportunity. From my perspective, I want to leverage questions in order to generate more initial interest, create competitive separation, increase the customer's sense of urgency to move forward, and cost-justify the decision—not to mention establish significant amounts of credibility with potential new clients. That's why, in QBS, we focus more on the conversational dynamics aspect of using specific question based techniques to invoke more predictable and productive response from the customers we call on.

Who's in control of the questions you ask? You are, right? Then I can tell you right now that your ability to manage the *Scope, Focus*, and *Disposition* of your questions will have a direct impact on how productively people respond. Of course, being aware of what types of questions you ask, and how these questions are actually being delivered, is very different from just bulling ahead with an agenda that could sound (to the customer) more like an interrogation.

Our study of the logic behind strategic questioning begins with the concept of *scope*. Specifically, let's zero in on the idea of narrowing the scope of your questions to establish more credibility sooner.

The scope of a question refers to its broadness, or narrowness. Like closed-ended questions, questions that are narrow in scope can easily be answered with a single word or phrase. These questions tend to be less invasive because you are asking about specific data points, that makes them easy for salespeople to ask, and easy for customers to answer.

Narrowing the scope of your questions essentially serves as a stepping-stone strategy for kicking off the broader needs development conversation. Asking a series of short-answer diagnostic questions is a simple technique that enables sellers to earn the right to get into more depth. Once you have earned some initial credibility, you can easily broaden the scope of your questions and probe more deeply into the customer's issues and concerns.

Managing the Scope of Your Questions

Let me put this technique of managing the scope of your questions in the appropriate context. Frankly, in today's selling environment, you shouldn't just pick up the telephone and barrage prospects with questions of any kind. Especially on your initial call, the first thing customers want to know is who you are and why you're calling. These conversations need to have a sense of purpose, where you are presumably calling for some reason that is relevant and valuable to the customer. I will talk about how to initiate more purposeful sales calls later. For now, let's agree that in most sales conversations, there will be an opportunity to ask questions at some point in the call. The opportunity could come at the fifteen-second mark in your conversation or after a few minutes, but at some point in the call, there will be an opportunity for discovery, where it will be appropriate for you to inquire about the customer's situation and potential needs.

My first needs development question is almost always the same. At the appropriate time in the conversation, I simply say, "Mr. Customer, can I ask you a couple specifics about (_____)?" Simply fill in the blank with something that is relevant to them, and this question will almost surely generate a mini-invitation.

In golf terms, this question is an absolute gimme. Unless you are dealing with someone who isn't going to talk with you no matter what, if you are calling for a purposeful reason, securing the customer's permission to proceed instantly makes a salesperson's job easier because it lowers the customer's natural defenses. This technique also paves the way for you to ask "a couple specifics" to essentially diagnose their situation.

The best way to show you how mini-invitations actually work is to give you a real-life scenario. If you were an independent life insurance agent, for example, opportunities for needs development would arise at some point during your client conversations right? Once you have secured the customer's permission to proceed, you would simply ask a series of specific questions that are narrow in scope (i.e. diagnostic questions) to better understand the customer's situation. For example, you might ask:

....

INDUSTRY: LIFE INSURANCE

Ms. Customer, can I ask you a couple specifics about your
current insurance coverage?
    Do you currently maintain any life insurance coverage?
    Is your existing life insurance whole life or term?
    Was it provided by your employer or purchased separately?
    And, how long have your current policies been in force?
    How many people are in your immediate family?
    When did you last review your specific insurance needs?

See the figures below for additional industry examples.

....

INDUSTRY: SOFTWARE

Mr. Customer, can I ask you a couple specifics about your
current IT platform?
    Is your current environment centralized or distributed?
    What's your primary operating system for applications?
    Are your applications developed in-house or do you buy
       packaged software?
    How much of your programming effort is object oriented?
    How many users do you support?
    In how many locations?

INDUSTRY: REAL ESTATE

Mrs. Customer, can I ask you a couple specifics about what you are looking for in the perfect house?

Are you interested in purchasing an existing home or building?

Do you need to sell your current home?

How long have you lived there?

How many people in your family?

When was the last time your home was appraised?

Can I ask what business you are in?

INDUSTRY: MANUFACTURING

Can I ask you a couple specifics about your plant operations?

How much of your production occurs at the headquarters location?

Do you use prefab materials or fabricate your own components?

Approximately how many suppliers are involved?

Where is the product warehoused once completed?

What inventory system do you currently have in place?

Supporting how many SKU numbers?

INDUSTRY: HEALTH CARE

Dr. Smith, can I ask you a couple specifics about your current patient services?

How many clinics do you currently support?

Are they automated with handheld devices?

Does patient data update in real time or at end-of-day?

Approximately how many patients do you see per month?

What's the mix of long term care versus short term?

Do you use a third-party billing service or handle those functions in-house?

INDUSTRY: OFFICE FURNITURE

Ms. Customer, can I ask you a couple specifics about your current facilities environment?

> How much of your furnishings are cubicles versus freestanding desks and chairs?
> Is your office decor traditional or contemporary?
> Do you prefer steel or a wood-grain finish?
> How many employees in your company?
> Working at how many locations?
> Do you own the office space or lease it?

DIAGNOSTIC QUESTIONS A CANDIDATE MIGHT ASK
DURING AN EMPLOYMENT INTERVIEW

Can I ask you a couple specifics about the open position?

> Is this a new position or are you replacing someone?
> To whom does the position report?
> How many people are on that team?
> How many other candidates are you considering?
> What percentage of the role is business development versus an account management position?

There's no need to shy away from being respectful or polite, as we definitely want to make good use of the customer's time. In most cases, you will find that this approach of taking a few baby steps on the way to the larger objective is a refreshing change from all the other sellers who are out there aggressively probing for needs. Especially in today's climate, buyers are no longer willing to endure the traditional grilling from a parade of overeager salespeople.

Notice that each of the diagnostic questions in these sample narratives is intentionally narrow in scope. This enables you to quickly and easily gather a series of relevant data points about the opportunity within a small window of time (less than sixty seconds). The timing is significant, because the first minute of your needs development conversation represents your single best opportunity to establish credibility with potential customers. Granted, this initial window is not your only chance to establish credibility, but it is an excellent opportunity to make a favorable first impression, especially when you're attempting to sell yourself first.

Buyers are always forming impressions, right? Do people form impressions based on statements a salesperson might make? Sure they do. But customers also base their impressions on the questions you ask. With that in mind, let me offer a quick lesson in human nature: if you can demonstrate an ability to ask a series of relevant and intelligent questions, customers will automatically form the impression that you are knowledgeable in each of the areas you asked about.

Our goal isn't to win the sale in less than sixty seconds. I just want potential buyers to give me the benefit of the doubt as they begin to form a positive first impression that will separate me from other sellers the customer may have previously dismissed. My goal is simply to gain traction early enough in the conversation to demonstrate that I might actually be a valuable resource instead of just another cold caller.

Asking about specific data points keeps your questions short, which is good initially, because that minimizes your risk of sounding overly invasive. The information you gather helps to guide the conversation and ultimately transition into more depth. The best part is, there is no downside when using this technique—starting off with a series of specific diagnostic questions. If you were selling life insurance, for example, you would need to know a few specific facts about the customer in order to make recommendations that would help them. This might entail knowing if the prospect currently owns one or more policies, whether it is provided as part of their employee benefits package, and whether the policies they own are term insurance or whole life.

Sometimes a student in one of my classes will ask, "Can't you just cut to the chase and ask people about their life insurance goals?" Sure, you can ask prospective customers whatever you like. And if your customer is the type of person who is willing to share information with a perfect stranger, you're all set. But that scenario is becoming rarer and rarer. Consequently, asking for too much information, too early in your sales conversations, has become one of the quickest ways to cause potential buyers to close up and not share, which is the opposite of our objective in needs development.

> **Asking for too much information, too early in your sales conversations, is one of the quickest ways to cause prospective buyers to close up and not share.**

In addition to boosting your credibility, asking diagnostic questions also helps to pique the prospect's interest. Within a short time window, asking a series of relevant questions about the customer's current situation causes potential buyers to start thinking about details. Has their family situation changed, such that their insurance needs might now be different? Especially if they haven't reviewed their existing coverages in a while, getting customers to think about "specifics" creates all kinds of opportunities to expand your needs development conversations.

Again, using diagnostic questions at the beginning of your needs development conversations is simply a stepping-stone strategy to get into more depth. If you succeed in kicking your conversations off in a nonthreatening manner, and you are able to gather valuable information that guides the dialogue, plus you establish your own credibility as a valuable resource and earn the right to expand the conversation, it then becomes very easy to broaden the scope of your questions in order to understand the customer's true goals and objectives.

Create a Bank of Possible Diagnostic Questions

People are sometimes surprised to hear me say I'm not a fan of precall planning. Don't get me wrong; you should absolutely be well prepared before making customer calls. It's just not realistic for a salesperson to sit down and document a verbatim script prior to each and every customer conversation.

My advice to salespeople is to prepare yourself once (in advance), by completing a simple one-time exercise where you create a bank of possible diagnostic questions that could be used to kick off your needs development conversations. There must be twenty or thirty possible data points you would want to know about a customer if you were given carte blanche to ask whatever you wanted.

The goal of this exercise is to be totally prepared before you actually contact the customer. After twenty minutes of dedicated typing, along with a little research if necessary, you then have a bank of possible diagnostic questions you can use on a continuing basis. To me, this exercise isn't really optional. If you want customers to perceive you as a valuable resource, then you should have a clear understanding of the specific details you need to know in order to provide valuable advice. Your investment on the front end will create an ongoing asset (bank of possible diagnostic questions) that will pay ongoing dividends in future sales situations.

Escalate the Focus of Your Questions

Once you understand how to narrow the scope of your questions to initiate a more productive needs development conversation, it's time to escalate the *Focus* of your questions to get into more depth. Every question a salesperson asks has a strategic focus, where you are either asking about the status of an opportunity, issues that a customer might be facing, the implications of those issues, or possible solutions for moving forward. Hence, the second strategic attribute that sellers have an

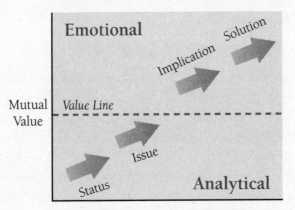

Escalating the "Focus" of Questions

opportunity to manage is the strategic focus of their needs development questions.

In the lower left of the diagram, you will notice that *status questions*, which are lowest in mutual value, are still valuable conversational tools used to gather (or verify) pertinent facts about the customer—relevant data points that will help to guide the conversation. These status questions should seem familiar, as we just talked about the strategy of kicking off your needs development conversations with a series of short-answer diagnostic questions that focus on the status of the opportunity. To sell yourself first, status questions are intentionally narrow in scope, which provides sellers with a nonthreatening way to establish credibility and a starting point for needs development.

It's important to recognize that status questions like "How many people are in your company?" or "Was your existing software purchased or developed in-house?" are low in mutual value because the customer isn't receiving any benefit. They already know the answers to these questions. Sellers must, therefore, accomplish the initial objective of kicking the conversation off, but then escalate to more valuable questions that focus on the customer's decision criteria.

Every purchase decision is ultimately driven by whatever issues are most important to the customer. Are they wanting to increase revenues, motivate employees, meet new compliance standards, or possibly reduce maintenance costs? The only way to provide valuable solutions is to identify and address a customer's concerns. That's where *issue questions* come in.

Issue questions are more valuable than status questions because they represent the first real stage of problem solving. Once you have successfully narrowed the scope of your questions to kick the conversation off in a nonthreatening manner, gathered valuable information, established your own credibility, and earned the right to get into more depth, it's time to broaden the scope of your questions and focus on the customer's true goals and objectives. You can literally watch customers perk up and lean forward in their chairs when you escalate the conversation from your initial status questions to more valuable issue questions.

The transition to issue questions is relatively simple. In fact, we touched on this briefly back in chapter 5. Let's play out the dialogue so you can see how the conversation actually flows.

Salesperson: Can I ask you a couple specifics about your current insurance coverage?
Customer: Sure.
Salesperson: Do you currently own a life insurance policy?
Was it provided by employer or purchased separately?
Is your existing insurance whole life or term?
How long has your current policy been in force?
How many people are in your immediate family?
When did you last review your insurance needs?
Well, let me ask you this—besides the obvious goal of protecting your family in the event of an untimely death, what specifically are you wanting to accomplish by owning life insurance?

Once you earn the right to get into more depth, it's easy for the salesperson to tee up an appropriate issue for discussion by asking, "To what extent is (issue) important?" That's the essence of an issue question—to raise relevant topics for further discussion.

The syntax of your question is particularly important. In addition to raising a valid issue for discussion, asking "To what extent . . ." also broadens the scope of your questions, which essentially signals to customers that it's time for them to respond with full sentences and paragraphs, as opposed to just specific data points.

If you are wondering which issue to start with, try asking, "To what extent is your (current environment) growing or changing?" The issue of "growth and change" is an easy starting point in most sales situations because it is always a relevant topic with virtually anyone you call on. Simply fill in the blank with something you know would be relevant to them. For example, executives might focus on how growth or change is affecting the budget, while a department head might be fully absorbed with how certain changes are affecting their production line. Even when selling to individuals, it's perfectly acceptable to ask, "To what extent are your family insurance needs growing or changing?"

Escalate Further to Identify Implications

When exploring issues that might be important to the customer, it's important to understand that just identifying key issues is not enough. To really understand what's driving the customer's need, you must further escalate your conversations to focus on why those issues are important. Without knowing the implications of why a certain decision is important to the customer, the issues you raise in the conversation don't really mean anything.

For example, if you just said to a doctor, "I feel sick," that doctor would not yet have enough information to properly diagnose your problem. When someone says they feel sick, they could mean anything from emotional heartache to experiencing flulike symptoms. Likewise, if a customer says they are growing by 10 percent year-over-year, that doesn't tell you whether growth means increased revenue, geographic expansion, new product lines, widening distribution channels, or something else.

To offer solutions, sellers must be prescriptive. This includes understanding how a given issue actually affects or impacts the customer. The implications of the problem or issue are ultimately what motivates and gives them the justification needed to move forward with a purchase. Again, how many reasons do you want customers to have to buy from you? I want buyers and influencers of any kind to recognize as much value as possible with regard to the solutions I offer. Therefore, my goal in needs development is to broaden the conversation in a way that expands the customer's decision criteria to include implications they wouldn't necessarily have brought up on their own. This can easily be accomplished via *implication questions*.

For example, when you ask, "To what extent is your business growing or changing?" the customer might respond by saying, "We expect to grow about five percent this year." To really understand how growth is affecting their business, I could ask any number of implication questions, such as:

"How will that affect your overall market share?"
"Do you plan to open any new stores?"
"Are you wanting to enter new markets?"
"What does your pipeline look for new product development?"
"How could that affect current staffing levels?"
"Will your supply chain be impacted by any of your changes?"
"Do you expect to need more physical space?"
"How does this compare with your closest competitors?"
"How will expansion change your role in the company?"
"Do any of these changes affect you personally?"

In chapter 5, I suggested an exercise where you should build a repository list of potential business issues, and under each issue, create a list of possible implications. The sample above shows how ten possible implications could easily be used to expand the conversation, or at least, better understand the customer's perspective on the issue of "growth and change." Is it possible that customers may raise some portion of these implications on their own? Sure, but who's going to bring up the rest? If not you, then you leave the door wide open for a competitor to identify opportunities you may not be addressing.

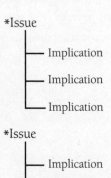

In a real-life sales situation, would I rattle off ten implication questions for every issue that came up in a conversation? Of course not. But I would absolutely be prepared and ready to bring up a host of potential implications that might be important based on how the conversation was flowing. Once you work through the issue of growth and change, using this escalation model, you can supply transition to the next important issue.

QBS' escalation strategy is pretty straightforward. Simply raise an issue for discussion, and then expand the needs development conversation by asking about various implications. Raise another issue, and then explore implication, implication, implication. Issue . . . implication, implication, implication . . . and so on. Each time a new issue is raised, you simply facilitate a more in-depth conversation about potential implications of that issue to better understand the prospect's true thoughts, feelings, and concerns regarding that particular topic.

How many issues and implications should you raise? That will depend on the customer and the natural flow of the conversation. The most important part of this strategy is preparation. If you have armed yourself (in advance) with a clear picture of which issues might be important to your customers, and you are ready to facilitate a conversation about why those issues are important, this escalation strategy will change the way you interact with customers. It will also change the way potential customers perceive and deal with you.

Global Questions Are Another Valuable Tool

Question Based Selling is essentially a philosophical toolbox, filled with techniques and strategies designed to engage more prospects in more productive conversations. In your toolkit, one of the conversation techniques at your disposal is asking *global questions*.

Global questions are another technique you can use to escalate your needs development conversations further without sounding invasive. Even when prospective customers do share information with you, most people tend to share only some fraction of what's really going on. If you're talking with your best friend in the world, and you want them to share more openly, all you have to do is say, "Tell me more." When forging new relationships with customers, however, commanding decision maker to provide more information can sound presumptuous. Thus, a global question is a question-based alternative that allows you to say, "Tell me more," without sounding like you are doling out a command.

Notice that a global question contains no subject. Instead, it simply builds on the context of the existing conversation. Examples of global questions include:

"Like what?"

"What else?"

"How do you mean?"

"Where do we go from here?"

"How would that work?"

Here's an experiment you can try in your next sales situation or just in your day-to-day interactions. The next time someone says something to you (or asks you a question), try responding with a global question—for example, by saying, "How do you mean?" You will be shocked at how easy it is to solicit tons of information that takes the conversation into much greater depth.

Do people like it when you show interest in what they are trying to communicate? The answer is, yes, absolutely! Global questions are intended (and taken) as subtle compliments. They demonstrate that you are indeed interested in what the other person is saying, as you are inviting them to please continue. In terms of conversational dynamics, global questions act like a reverse mini-invitation, where you are now inviting the customer to share more

Global questions are not only easy to deliver, they are also some of the most productive questions you can ask—especially when you are trying to encourage prospects to open up and talk about their issues or the underlying aspects of a problem.

Use Solution Questions to Secure Next Steps

Early in the sales process, a needs development conversation can be short-lived, lasting only a couple minutes. Later on, a more in-depth review of the customer's needs can span several hours. Mostly it depends on the type of sale and the particular customer situation. However, once you understand what a customer is trying to accomplish, it's time to escalate your questions one last time, to focus on the desired results that will come from procuring the right solution. This is where *solution questions* become valuable closing tools, to secure the next appropriate step in the sales process (see page 144).

Solution questions help to balance out your needs development conversations. We want prospects to have a sense of urgency to move forward, but we aren't trying to overwhelm them with the magnitude of a potential problem. Instead, we want customers to become excited and enthusiastic about actually solving the problem, as they realize that positive emotions like satisfaction and relief are just around the corner from their current pain, frustration, or concern.

Escalating your questions to focus on possible solutions is just as simple and straightforward as the other transitions. Basically, you summarize the customer's requirements and then suggest the next appropriate step in the decision process. Here's a quick hypothetical.

Salesperson: Mr. Customer, if (issue), (issue), and (issue) are all important to your business because of (implication) and (implication), would it make sense for us to (insert appropriate next step)?

What should you suggest as the next step in your sales process? That depends on what you are selling. The appropriate next step could be anything from a technical meeting to an executive briefing, or if you are selling to individuals, the next step in the decision could be to schedule a follow-up meeting with the prospect's spouse. The appropriate next step might even be to move forward with a purchase right now.

Another way to use solution questions is to ask the customer to visualize the perfect solution. If you are aware of the customer's perception of Utopia, that may give you a much better sense of what you're working toward. Here's how that could sound.

Salesperson: Mr. Prospect, in your mind, what would the ideal solution to this problem look like?

As potential buyers start to perceive you as a valuable resource, they will absolutely begin to confide in you regarding their problems, issues, and concerns. They will also want you to recommend the appropriate next step in the decision process. After all, you're the expert. That's why it is critical to have a strategy that escalates the focus of your needs development questions—first earning the right to engage, then identifying multiple opportunities to provide value, and finally, closing on potential next steps. If you can consistently accomplish these goals, you will differentiate yourself from all the other salespeople who are stuck in the mindset of asking highly invasive and probative questions.

7

Cost-Justifying Your
Intangible Value Proposition

The actual value of any product or service is highly intangible. Even if you sell tangible goods, the benefits of your offerings must still be recognized by potential buyers as being valuable, enough so to justify the cost of your proposed solution.

What if it were possible to increase your probability of success in making a sale, merely by causing customers to perceive more benefits? In addition to separating yourself from the competition, selling the intangible aspects of your solution is the best way to tip pending purchase decisions in your favor.

In order to close a sale, the value of a product or service must be great enough to justify its cost. Back in chapter 5, however, I made the point that there is no such thing as actual value. Why not? Because the value of your solution is ultimately enhanced or diminished by the customer's perception of how much it will help them, as compared with what they feel is needed. Causing customers to perceive greater value from your offerings than a competitor's, and enough value to justify a purchase decision, therefore becomes an important sales skill and one that must be developed.

Are the solutions you offer tangible or intangible? If we use product specifications as our definition of tangibility, the answer might boil down to whether or not someone can physically touch your product. If so, one could easily say that you're selling tangible goods. Someone who represents a computer manufacturer, for example, could rightly assume that a laptop computer is indeed a tangible product. Not only can you touch it, you can place it on your lap and tap your fingers on the keys. A salesperson who reps medical supplies can reach the same conclusion regarding their new line of IV pumps. If you can physically bring one of your pumps into an operating room and hand it to a doctor, then it must be a tangible item.

Selling services is a different story. You can't physically touch a dozen hours of consulting time or pull them out of a briefcase to show a customer during a sales call. Yet expert consulting is still a valuable offering. Insurance products are similarly intangible. Lots of people buy life, auto, and homeowner's insurance, but besides a hard copy of the contract with all its terms and conditions, you cannot hold the actual insurance in your hand.

Some people believe that selling intangibles is more difficult than selling tangible goods, mostly because customers can't touch or see the actual product. I'll grant you that selling intangibles is definitely a conceptual sale, where benefits of your product or service must be perceived by customers in order to register value. The fact that a salesperson or company believes their product is wonderful is not enough to convey value, however. Somehow, this perception of value must be transferred to the customer, enough so to justify a purchase.

Here's the tricky part for a salesperson who wants to perform at the top of their game. Even if the product you sell is indeed tangible or touchable, the value proposition of that item must still be conceptualized. This creates an interesting paradox. Even though you can hold tangible items in your hand, the real value that comes from purchasing a tangible product is still highly intangible.

For example, we agreed that a laptop computer is a tangible item, right? But while you can definitely hold a laptop in your hands (or on your lap), you can't actually touch the true value of a laptop computer. Think about it. Why are laptop computers valuable? Different users have different hot buttons, but speaking for myself, my laptop is valuable because it is convenient, it enables me to be more productive, and it allows me to stay connected while I'm away from the office. Have you ever stopped to consider that you can't actually touch convenience, productivity, or the value of staying connected with your business? You might be able to measure the degree to which your productivity has increased, but you still cannot hold increased productivity in your hand. Other intangible benefits of a laptop computer like increased mobility, reliability, ease of use, or the ability to play computer games on long flights, may also be valuable, but you can't hold any of those things in your hand either.

This same principle applies in most sales, whether you sell real estate, manufactured goods, telecommunications, or medical supplies. Take residential real estate. Real estate is a tangible item, right? You certainly can see and touch the house, the yard, and other physical characteristics of the property. But it's important to realize that most people who buy residential real estate aren't looking at physical characteristics alone. They're usually just as interested in intangibles such as location, usefulness, aesthetic beauty, spaciousness, growth potential, return on investment, quality of schools, and the view of the backyard from the kitchen window.

The value proposition for a more sophisticated product like a clinical IV pump (in medical sales) is just as intangible. Although medical devices are certainly tangible items, physicians don't care that much about product specifications. What they really care about are things like ease of use, clinical efficacy, patient comfort, availability, cost effectiveness, possible complications, reimbursement, liability, and seamless integration with other devices.

Everyday products like toothbrushes, breakfast cereal, automobile tires, or a nice pair of Italian loafers have similarly intangible value propositions. You can't actually touch the value of fresh breath, a healthy diet, keeping your family safe while driving in the rain, or feeling stylish from head to toe. Hence, even if you sell tangible goods, the true value proposition of those items comes from an array of intangible benefits that must be perceived by interested buyers.

> **Even if you sell tangible goods, the true value proposition of those items comes from an array of intangible benefits that must be perceived by interested buyers.**

If you think about it, the whole concept of selling yourself, especially in today's competitive marketplace, is extremely intangible.

Intangible Qualities Serve as Tiebreakers

You know what's weird? Companies invest millions of dollars to position their products, and salespeople work extremely hard to differentiate their respective value propositions, but most customers, even after they've made the purchase, can't articulate exactly why they preferred one solution over another. After considering the alternatives, the decision maker for some reason just felt more comfortable with the chosen solution as compared to the other alternatives.

The vendor of choice in a competitive situation may not have a distinct advantage in terms of product differentiation. I've been involved in numerous sales scenarios where either of the proposed solutions from different vendors could have done the job. In cases where multiple competitive options could suffice, your opportunity to win the sale is more likely to come from the manner in which your product is being positioned to the customer, rather than from the value of the solution itself. That's where intangible qualities like the salesperson's credibility, integrity, knowledge, strategic vision, and advice become important tiebreakers.

What is the value of working with a knowledgeable and trustworthy salesperson instead of a vendor whose methods are somewhat questionable? The difference can be huge from the customer's perspective, even if the products being offered are virtually identical. In competitive sales situations, the customer's perception of your value is equal to the benefits of your product or service plus the intangibles you bring to the table.

> **In competitive sales situations, the customer's perception of your value is equal to the benefits of your product or service plus the intangibles you bring to the table.**

From my point of view, it's no longer enough to be friendly and polite. There are plenty of nice salespeople in the world who are now struggling to make a living. The concept of selling yourself is more about accruing enough value to tip the scales in your favor, whether you are up against a competitive proposal, or the customer is considering the option of holding off altogether. Sellers also must accumulate enough value to overcome any concerns that may arise when dealing with objections.

Whether a salesperson is born with natural character traits like credibility, integrity, helpfulness, candor, or respect is debatable. What we are really talking about then is the ability to convey these intangible qualities throughout the sales process. That's where your overall strategy, along with specific QBS techniques, becomes very important. As I said earlier, even if you are the most valuable salesperson in your industry, you still must say and do things that will cause you to be perceived as such.

How to Gain Instant Traction with Prospects

Salespeople are always looking to put their best foot forward. As a result, the tendency among sellers is to look for opportunities to point out all of the valuable features of their products and services. Some people reading this book might think, "I don't do that." And maybe you don't. But during your last job interview, when the hiring manager said, "Tell me about yourself," did you launch into a synopsis of your background to try and convey that you would be a good hire?

The inclination to highlight key selling points may be rooted in good intentions, but focusing on yourself or your products doesn't necessarily speak to the customer's needs or their specific buying motivations. Let me give you a real-life example of how doing the opposite and being truly customer-focused can instantly change the customer's perception of you, your products, and your overall value.

Back in the mid-1980s, I finally got tired of paying monthly rent for a two-bedroom apartment, so one day, I pulled into the Merrill Lynch Realty office on my way home from work. Because it was late in the afternoon, there were only a few cars left in the parking lot. So I walked through the front entrance into the small lobby and stood in front of an empty reception desk. Then I noticed the customer service bell sitting on the counter, so I rang it. *Ding, Ding.*

A well-dressed gentleman suddenly appeared in the doorway, saying, "Can I help you?"

"Yes. My name is Tom Freese," I said, "and I am tired of paying rent to an apartment complex. Since I pass your office every day on my drive home from work, I thought I would stop in and find out what it would take to buy a house."

"I'm Jerry Saunders," the man said, greeting me with an outstretched hand. "Come on back to my office and we can look at a few different options."

We sat down in his cubicle area and I explained my situation. At the time, I was not married but had a decent job, and, with the exception of paying off my student loan, I had no debt to speak of. Jerry inquired what type of house I wanted, but honestly, I hadn't even made it that far in my exploratory thought process.

To get the ball rolling, Jerry suggested that we set aside an afternoon or two to ride around and look at homes, so I could get a sense of what was on the market.

The following Tuesday, I arrived back at the Merrill Lynch office promptly at three o'clock. Jerry was waiting for me with a stack of MLS listings he had printed prior to my arrival. At the time, only licensed agents could print "specs pages" for properties registered with the Multiple Listing Service.

"Why don't you cull through the stack and pick a dozen or so listings that look interesting," Jerry said, "and then we'll hit the road." I did just that, and we were off.

On the way to the first listing, we exchanged pleasantries while cruising along in Jerry's brand-new Cadillac DeVille. When we arrived at the first house, Jerry got the key out of the lockbox and opened the front door. As soon as I set foot in the house, I remember having an emotional moment—thinking, "This house could someday be mine." I was about to purchase my very first home. Momma's boy was growing up!

A voice from over my shoulder snapped me out of my short-lived daydream. "You don't want this house," Jerry said dismissively. A bit surprised, I turned around to hear the rest of the story.

"Tom, do you see this hairline crack in the tile?" he said pointing to the foyer floor. "If you look closely, the crack goes up the wall and then across the ceiling. I think this house has a structural problem," he said.

Jerry suggested that we look around anyway to see what ideas we could glean from the floor plan and design features. Sure enough, when we went down into the basement, there was a three-quarter-inch crack in the foundation. Jerry was right, I didn't want this house.

What do you suppose happened to Jerry's credibility at that moment? As an adviser, his value to me skyrocketed instantly. It was suddenly very apparent that this guy wasn't just trying to sell me a house. Instead, he was acting as my advocate to help match my needs against the product options that were available. Like Toto in *The Wizard of Oz*, he was pulling back the curtain in an effort to help me buy the right house.

By the time we walked through the front door of the third listing, my confidence as a potential buyer had increased significantly. "I don't want this house," I announced to Jerry.

"Why not?" he asked.

I pointed to the shag carpet, which was three or four shades more obnoxious than Pepto-Bismol pink. Combined with the peach-colored walls and light blue trim, the place was poorly decorated, on par with a low-budget bordello.

"Uggg-ly," Jerry agreed. But as the voice of experience, Jerry pointed out that the carpet in any of these "starter" homes would need to be replaced anyway, and the walls would probably get a fresh coat of paint. "If you can look beyond the carpet and paint color," he suggested, "you should focus on finding a house that is structurally sound and has a desirable floor plan, because those are the things that are not easily changeable."

We looked at several more houses that day and a bunch more the following week. Guess which house I ended up buying? Yep, the one with the pink carpeting. With a fresh coat of neutral-colored paint on the walls and newly installed wall-to-wall carpet, the house looked fantastic— completely different from what I originally saw when it was on the market.

Honestly, the idea of looking for houses while being flanked by an overeager real estate agent trying to "sell" me on the benefits of each listing would have been nauseating, to say the least. Like most buyers, I didn't want to be "sold to," especially not by a commission-hungry real estate salesperson. What I wanted (and needed) was someone I could trust, to not only provide insight about what features to look for, but also to help me know what to avoid when buying a home. I have since bought four homes from Jerry Saunders, now of RE/MAX North Atlanta, largely as the result of the way he solidified his credibility in my eyes as a candid and competent real estate professional.

Help Your Customers Make Smart Decisions

The temptation for sellers to always be "selling" unfortunately translates into a mode where the salesperson is always putting their best foot forward in an attempt to impress potential buyers. Rather than just promoting all the wonderful benefits that would come from purchasing your product or service, however, sellers must learn to convey value from the customer's perspective. The specific benefits you provide are only wonderful (and valuable) to the extent that they address a specific need, and that customers recognize the existence of that need.

Take the product I sell, for example—sales training. The value proposition of my company, QBS Research, Inc., is highly intangible. Although Question Based Selling is one of the most acclaimed sales courses available, and I have published five books (including this one) on the methodology to prove it, you still can't actually touch the QBS methodology or hold specific QBS sales strategies in your hand. Therefore, the only way for me to develop business opportunities is to somehow cause decision makers within potential client accounts to perceive large amounts of value when they evaluate our programs.

I have noticed over the years, however, that sales managers and executives are much more interested in knowing how QBS will address their goals, objectives, and specific problems (P) than they are interested in hearing a bunch of hype about how wonderful our training solutions (S) are. Whether the client is trying to bring more deals into the pipeline, create differentiation, protect profit margins, ramp up new salespeople, better qualify forecasted accounts, or close more deals sooner, the need to accomplish each of these goals is what creates a sense of urgency to move forward with QBS.

If we agree that customers are more interested in addressing their own problems, issues, and concerns than they are in hearing a standard sales pitch, then it stands to reason that your value proposition should revolve around the customer's issues, as seen from their point of view. Consequently, I focus most of my energy on talking with potential client managers, executives, and salespeople about the challenges posed by the current selling environment and economic conditions, rather than just rattling off a litany of our courseware's benefits. Essentially, I pull back the curtains and address the elephant in the room—customer skepticism. Here's an example of how this may sound to a potential QBS client. I would explain:

> *There is a problem in the world of sales training, which is why Question Based Selling is very different from traditional approaches. If you sell in a competitive market, teaching your salespeople to sound the same as everyone else is the quickest way to forfeit your competitive advantage. That said, most of the traditional sales courses focus on defining the sales process, which is fine. But just identifying the steps of the sales process is no longer a strategic differentiator for most sales organizations. Your competitors have a sales process in place, too, and it's a pretty safe bet that their process is probably very similar to yours.*

Defining the steps of the sales process isn't the problem most organizations face, anyway. You don't need to hire me to come in and tell your salespeople that the first step in the process is to "identify new opportunities," the second step is "uncovering needs," and so on. The problem sellers face on a daily basis isn't knowing *what* to do, rather it's understanding *how* to execute more effectively, especially within a highly competitive business environment. Ultimately, the goal of most sales executive is to produce a higher return on their invested sales efforts.

> *Mr. VP of Sales, as I'm sure you are well aware, today's selling environment has changed over the last several months, if not the last few years, such that potential buyers are more cautious and standoffish toward vendors than ever before. As a result, customers who are overwhelmed with more responsibility are being targeted by vendors, and they no*

longer have the patience or inclination to spend time with every sales-person who comes calling. . . .

Did you notice that in this snippet that I didn't just dive into a litany about our training programs, or our track record of success? Once you recognize that customers are evaluating you from the moment the conversation begins, first and foremost, they want to know that you understand their problems, issues, and concerns. This doesn't happen by the salesperson just spewing out the features and benefits of your product offerings. Do you remember our discussion about PAS positioning from chapter 3? What I'm really doing in the sample dialogue above is pulling back the curtains and pointing at the metaphorical "crack on the foyer tile." My intention is simply to gain instant credibility with customers by being more forthright and insightful than other sales trainers they have talked with previously. I do this by proactively raising issues and concerns that aren't always obvious to people who are wanting to make a good decision.

During conference calls with potential clients, for example, I am happy to explain the various QBS training options, how they would impact the customer's business, and the associated costs. But my value proposition for QBS (like yours) must be explained against the backdrop of a realistic acknowledgment of the competitive challenges the organization currently faces and why continuing with a traditional approach may no longer be a viable alternative. To sell yourself first, you must consistently demonstrate that you understand the customer's goals, interests, and concerns—just as we talked about earlier in the job interview scenario.

The moment a potential client begins to form the impression that "Hey, this guy actually understands our situation and I think he can help us!" you have a competitive advantage. That's also when you begin to gain serious traction in the conversation and establish your credibility as a potentially valuable resource.

Here's the cool part. Once you have demonstrated that you do understand the customer's challenges, your company's value proposition can basically be summed up in a few words by saying, "Those are exactly the issues we help clients solve." The next thing the customer will ask is, "How do you do that?" Doesn't that sound like a nice mini-invitation?

Talking about the problems (P) customers face is one of the quickest and easiest ways to pique their interest. Predictably, an interested customer will want to know more about how you might be able to help address specific challenges. From there, it's easy to suggest a face-to-face meeting, a conference call, or some other appropriate next step. Either way, the net result of taking a PAS approach is very different from what would have happened had I gone down the typical path of trying to claim credibility by touting the benefits of Question Based Selling.

This same principle applies to virtually any type of intangible sale. Take financial services, for example. With the roller-coaster ride people experienced in the 1990s, and then again just recently, customers have developed a fair amount of skepticism toward brokers, agents, bankers, and financial advisers. Nowadays, if you are a financial adviser and your role includes calling prospective clients, jumping headfirst into a speech about your track record probably isn't going to be enough to earn the customer's trust. A better way to demonstrate your knowledge of the industry and bond with prospective clients in the process might be to point at some of the "cracks in the tile," just as Jerry Saunders did. Go ahead and talk with people about some of the fundamental shifts that have occurred in the market and the challenges customers now face in terms of managing their investments.

Here are some other examples of positioning statements sellers can use from a variety of value-based industries:

Financial Services: "Mr. Customer, though our business is offering financial products and services, just making recommendations to buy or sell is no longer good enough for clients given the recent turmoil in the markets. Most of the people I deal with don't want to hear the latest hot stock pick, and they don't want to be pressured by a commission-hungry broker. Instead, clients want sound financial advice from an integrity-based partner who will help maximize their return on investment and manage risk. Customers also want someone who will invest the time to consider their current financial situation, as well as their

long-term investment goals. Mr. Customer, that's basically what we do
for the clients we serve."

Real Estate: "Ms. Customer, I understand you are thinking about listing
your home and are currently in the process of selecting an agent. The
way I see it, most of the value homeowners get from a licensed realtor
comes after the listing agreement is signed. In the current real estate market, however, selling a house is no longer as simple as taking a few pho-
tos and then listing it with a friendly neighborhood broker. If you want
to get quality offers on your property, your home must be proactively
marketed—to other real estate agents and to the buying public. Leads
have to be monitored and followed up on, and feedback should be used
to help us deal with any issues that arise once the home has been marketed to prospective buyers. If you want results, you need to choose an
agent who will put forth the same effort they would when selling their
own home, which is precisely what we do!"

Medical: "Dr. Smith, there are several medicines you can choose from
when prescribing a solution for patients with these type of symptoms or
a chronic condition. The problem is, patients generally aren't looking for
a temporary solution. They want permanent relief. Consequently, the
ultimate goal for these patients is for their doctor to prescribe a treatment
plan that will eradicate the underlying medical condition after a few
weeks of consistent usage. That's exactly what this new product does."

Notice that the first thing the seller does in each of these scenarios is
pull back the curtain and expose the real challenges that customers currently face. Earlier in chapter 1, we called this technique "pointing at
the elephant in the room." What a novel idea—partnering with a salesperson who talks directly to the customer's issues in order to help them
make good decisions!

You have to figure that decision makers often have to deal with a
multitude of issues. Getting these issues to come up in your conversations with potential customers is a challenge for sellers who are trying
to break into new opportunities. This is where one hand washes the

other. To be seen as a valuable resource, you must somehow demonstrate that you understand their current problems, issues, and concerns. Of course, if the issues you raise resonate with potential clients and you are able to position yourself as a valuable resource, the perception that you can help them will undoubtedly expand the conversation into a more in-depth discussion about the their goals and your solutions.

What's the Cost of Not Buying Your Solution?

When it comes to topics that are potentially important to customers, the issue of price often tops that list. Talking with customers about price is not only acceptable, it's vitally important. Customers won't move forward with a purchase without understanding how much your product or service costs. Thus, we want customers to have a clear picture of all the cost implications, which may include more than just an up-front price comparison.

In chapter 4, when we talked about conversational dynamics, I showed you how to redirect a customer's request for pricing into a more in-depth needs development conversation. At some point, however, the issue of cost will come to the forefront and customers will have to decide whether the solution being proposed is worth the price.

If you are an experienced salesperson already, then you understand that cost justification is a critical part of every sale. Whether or not something is "worth the money" is totally subjective, based on the customer's perception of your solutions plus whatever additional value you bring to the table.

Customers will ask, "How much does it cost?" It's a valid question and you should at some point provide all the relevant details for their consideration. But in addition to talking about your pricing, the question that someone should really be asking is, "What's the cost of not buying the proposed product or service?" While the customer may not ask this directly, the answer to this question may actually be the easiest way for customers to justify the value of an intangible purchase.

When we talked about the principle of being more strategic with your sales questions (in chapter 6), I made the point that the value of a proposed solution must exceed its cost for decision makers to move forward on a purchase decision. But comparing prices isn't necessarily the whole story, especially if you sell strategic solutions.

For example, suppose a salesperson is trying to convince you to purchase $100,000 in new computer equipment for your company, on the premise that it would end up saving the company $100,000 in ongoing maintenance costs. Would you consider that a good deal?

One could argue that since the amount saved covers the cost of the solution, this would be a sound business decision. Well, that's how the salesperson might feel, but I can tell you that there's going to be a logic problem with this from the CFO's perspective. Asking a customer to pay a substantial sum for the promise of simply getting their money back doesn't seem like a good return on investment (ROI). Would you invest $100,000 of your own money in the hopes of getting a 0 percent return on your investment? I bet you wouldn't.

When clients bring me in to train their salespeople, they're not just hoping to recoup the cost of the training course. You would be crazy to take your entire sales team out of the field for two days unless you believed that the return on investment from the training would far exceed the cost. The justification for my services, therefore, is pretty simple. People who bring QBS in to train their salespeople expect their return on investment to pay them back many times over.

I understand that customers have budgets and they need to be judicious with their expenditures these days. But what if we thought outside the box for a moment and asked: What's the cost of *not* doing a QBS training course? Well, if the cost of the training would be offset by selling one new account, one could argue that QBS is no longer an expense to the company, rather it's a money maker. In fact, if you trained twenty-five or thirty reps on a sales team, and you realized an upside of one new account per person (per month), suddenly the QBS training becomes a huge money maker, one that would be a no-brainer to justify. At that point, the cost of the training course becomes insignificant compared with the cost of not empowering your people and missing out on all of these lost opportunities.

Going back to the water pump metaphor for a moment, how much does it cost to pump water out of a flooded basement? I suppose that would depend on the cost of the pump and the size of your basement. But consider for a moment the opposite question. What's the cost of not getting the water out of the basement in a timely manner? That's a whole different story. Now, all kinds of issues are brought into play, like the possibility of significant structural damage to the foundation of the home, damage to personal property, mold or mildew, permanently damaging the furnace or electrical systems, not to mention potential health risks, safety hazards, infestation, displacement of the family, damage to irreplaceable heirlooms, ongoing stress, insurance hassle, cleanup time, declining resale value, and long-term odor issues.

What's the likelihood that customers will consider every one of these implications in their cost analysis? Slim. They might focus on one or two implications, possibly three or four, but certainly not all of them. So I ask you, who's going to bring up the rest? If not you, then you're leaving the door wide open for a competitor to be seen as a more valuable resource, and also to be in a stronger position to justify their solutions.

Think about this. Given the recent turbulence in the economy, what's the cost of not having a good financial adviser? Besides potentially missing out on positive upward trends when the market is showing strength, you could also incur unnecessary downside risk if the financial markets take another substantial hit.

What's the cost of not having the appropriate amount of life insurance in the event of an untimely death? The answer to that partly depends on the person. A billionaire probably doesn't need to think about life insurance. For the rest of us, what's the cost of your family not being able to count on your income, or the longer-term cost of your kids not being able to go to college?

In terms of justifying a purchase decision, it's impossible to calculate the exact cost of not buying a product or service. The calculation itself would be totally subjective, based on many intangible implications that cannot be measured empirically. But that does not mean those costs aren't real. For example, what's the cost of having a mildew problem in your home caused by excessive moisture? Who knows how to calculate that, but the desire to avoid the problem can provide significant motivation for homeowners to purchase a water pump. The same is true with regard to estimating the cost of your kids not going to college. It may not even be feasible to approximate these costs in actual dollars. But I can tell you that the long-term security of my family was the primary justification that caused me to purchase my first life insurance policy from Northwestern Mutual Life in July 1994.

Translating Capabilities into Benefits

By now, some of the pieces of the sales puzzle should be starting to fit together. Knowing that most customers aren't going to fully articulate their needs, one of the greatest ways a seller can provide value is to help identify latent needs that decision makers wouldn't have otherwise considered. Helping customers identify needs is an excellent way to cause them to perceive substantially more value from you than from a competitor's offerings.

Earlier, I suggested that you should arm yourself with a repository of potential issues and implications that could potentially affect the customer's decision. Each time you identify another facet of the customer's need that your solution addresses, you make it easier for customers to cost-justify the purchase of your product or service. Hence, giving customers multiple reasons to buy from you is one of the easiest ways to create separation between yourself and other competitive offerings. If a decision maker has seven or eight reasons to purchase your product, but only three reasons to stay with a competitor, you will be in a strong position to win the business. Of course, if the opposite is true and there are more reasons to stay with the incumbent than to switch vendors, your chances of losing the deal go way up.

This in mind, your ability to translate the capabilities of your solutions into perceived value for the customer, enough so for them to justify a favorable purchase decision, will always be one of the keys to being successful in a competitive sale.

Gold Medals and German Shepherds

Since we're talking about motivating potential customers to pull the trigger on a purchase, let's spend a few moments exploring the concept of Gold Medals and German Shepherds.

When I first developed Question Based Selling, it was clear to me that decision makers have a wide range of priorities, perspectives, hot buttons, and personal agendas that ultimately influence their buying preferences. However, at the end of the day, we find that customers are ultimately motivated in two ways—by positive reward and negative aversion. Hence, I created the metaphor in my first book (*Secrets of Question Based Selling*) that says *while some people are motivated to run fast toward Gold Medals, many others run even faster from German Shepherds.*

Does your product offer positive benefits like high performance, cost effectiveness, customer satisfaction, and increased productivity? Positive benefits like these will often register a great deal of value with customers who are motivated by positive rewards (i.e. Gold Medal benefits). But somewhere in your company's value proposition, I bet your solutions are also able to protect customers against certain downside risks, whether it's protecting computer data, not exceeding their maintenance budget, or avoiding customer complaints. This ability to prevent or protect against problems also represents real value to customers, especially for those customers who are motivated by German Shepherds.

Positioning positive benefits to Gold Medal buyers is a great way to accumulate value. But positioning the German Shepherd aspects of your solutions can be just as valuable to someone who wants to protect themselves or their company against potential downside risks. The vast majority of customers, however, are motivated by a combination of Gold Medal and German Shepherd benefits. Thus, I have been making the point for many years that sellers get maximum perceived value by positioning their solutions both ways. Doing so doesn't change your product's capabilities or the customer's requirements. The only thing that changes is the customer's perception of your value—it doubles when you position the Gold Medal and German Shepherd aspects of your offering.

This technique isn't new to marketers and advertisers. If you look closely, this strategy is already being used with everyday products. For example, why do people choose Johnson's Baby Shampoo? Some people buy it because it is gentle on the hair (Gold Medal), while other people choose Johnson's Baby Shampoo because it won't sting their baby's eyes (German Shepherd). Remember Johnson & Johnson's familiar slogan, "no more tears"? Frankly, the positive and the negative justifications are both valuable, because it's gentle on the hair and also because it won't sting their baby's eyes.

As another example, why do people buy Volvo automobiles? Some people like their elegant and stylish luxury automobiles. Other people feel Volvo stands for safety, and protecting themselves and their family in the event of an automobile accident is imperative. Once again, you register maximum value with customers by combining the best of both worlds, and talking with prospective buyers about the Gold Medal aspects of owning a Volvo, and also the German Shepherd benefits.

Note that it's natural for sellers to gravitate toward one or the other, based on their own personal preferences. But rather than focusing on whatever motivates *us*, we must remember that the goal is ultimately to convey maximum perceived value to the customer. Thus, the best way to maximize the customer's perception of your value and increase your probability of success for winning the business, is to position your solutions in terms of Gold Medals and German Shepherds, both. It's particularly exciting when such a small adjustment in strategy can double your perceived value in the eyes of your target audience.

Cost Justification: The Final Hurdle

In sales cost justification is often the final hurdle that must be cleared before customers are willing to pull the trigger on a purchase. When selling to individuals, cost justification might be as simple as buyers weighing the different options in their head before making a decision on the spot. In the corporate environment, a detailed cost analysis can sometimes drag on for weeks, weaving a tangled web that involves multiple levels of authority and a fair amount of political wrangling. Either way, to succeed in securing commitments to purchase your product or service, the perceived value of your proposed solution must justify the cost.

Here's a little-known secret about cost justification—depth of conversation is a salesperson's best friend. As we discussed earlier, people don't just buy umbrellas in case it rains, or even to avoid getting wet. People buy umbrellas because of the underlying implications—like wanting to preserve a professional image if they're on their way to an important business meeting, or to be comfortable during the day, to protect their clothes, to avoid catching a cold, or to limit exposure to ultraviolet rays.

Can you differentiate the Gold Medal benefits on this list from the German Shepherds? Whatever value is perceived from each of these points accumulates into a total sense of worth that, again, cannot be measured empirically. While a customer might be able to calculate the cost of a leather jacket damaged by rain, there is no way to calculate exactly what it's worth for someone to avoid getting sick, or the value of a businessperson's looking their best when they show up for an important meeting.

Therefore, it's debatable whether one can ever calculate the true value of any product or service. I say you can't. You can estimate the value of a proposed solution all day long, including making projections about a variety of hypothetical scenarios. The problem is, if you ask five different people to calculate the exact value of something that is up for interpretation or dependent on someone's personal perspective, you will get five different projections. At that point, we must deduce that valuation is highly subjective, and is significantly influenced by a decision maker's perception.

In sales we see this all the time, where someone who likes your product or service can make it look good on paper, while someone else in the same account who doesn't like your solution will almost certainly calculate a value that is significantly lower. For buyers, it's a simple matter of perspective. Different strokes for different folks, as they say.

For sellers, cost justification is more about expanding the buyer's perspective. Since buyers tend to focus on a few specific hot buttons, sellers can accrue more value by causing customers to recognize additional needs or facets of your solution that would have otherwise gone unnoticed.

That's where your newfound needs development skills come in. If you have done the homework assignment I recommended by constructing a repository of issues and implications, there are easily ten or more implications relating to any particular issue that could affect your customers. For example, if you asked me to coach you and I listened in on one of your sales calls, I would make a tiny tick mark every time I heard the customer say something like "Good point," or "That's right," or "Yes, that's definitely important." Every time you raised an important issue or implication that the customer would not have brought up on their own, you broaden the conversation along with your opportunity to provide value. After we did this in few times, you would start to listen for these same cues during subsequent calls. Let's call this self-coaching, which is the best kind. Put it this way: If you are subconsciously accumulating tick marks in your mind, chances are good that you will be accumulating value with your customer as well.

If you are subconsciously accumulating value points in your mind, chances are good that you will be accumulating value with your customer as well.

How do you empirically measure the credibility of a salesperson in the eyes of their customers? The answer is, you can't. Still, teaching salespeople how to establish more credibility sooner can have a tremendous positive impact on the effectiveness and productivity of an entire sales organization. Similarly, you can't empirically measure competitive differentiation with a slide rule, or some fancy computer program. Just because something can't be measured empirically, however, doesn't mean it's not important to the sale. Hence, these subtle but very important intangibles often end up being the difference between earning the customer's confidence and commoditizing your value proportion because you sound the same as everyone else.

By the way, what's the cost of not differentiating yourself in a job interview, or on a sales call? It turns out that some of your most valuable attributes will never show up as line items on your résumé, nor are they listed in your company's product brochure. Qualities like integrity, leadership, desire, passion, vision, creativity, confidence, poise, honesty, compassion, resourcefulness, and work ethic tend to be very important to decision makers who are forming impressions about you and the value you can offer. Even though you can't actually touch these things, your ability to convey these valuable character traits will determine not only whether you succeed in selling yourself, but also how much others are willing to pay for your services.

8

Making Prospects More Receptive
to Your Message

Sellers should have a compelling story to tell about their products and services. But you must also have a receptive audience that wants to hear about your potential solutions. Particularly since today's buyer is increasingly cautious and skeptical, decision makers are quick to fend off even the most tenacious salespeople.

Rather than being more aggressive, however, why not take the opposite approach? What if we combined sound logic with proven communication techniques to pique the customer's interest, as a means of securing more time and attention with key decision makers? You can accomplish this by leveraging curiosity as a key ingredient in your new sales strategy.

The days of manipulating prospective customers into buying your products and services are over. Most customers don't want to be smooth-talked, and they are no longer willing to be pushed, pressured, or persuaded by a commission-hungry salesperson who is personally motivated to close deals by the end of the month. I'm not trying to indict our beloved profession, but some of the traditional tactics for dealing with customers could probably use a makeover to align with the current business environment.

The typical standoffishness buyers have toward salespeople is definitely on the rise, but this trend isn't new by any means. Decision makers have been skeptics of the proverbial product pitch for a long time. But the sheer increase in the volume of sales calls customers now receive, and the aggressiveness of vendors who are struggling to hit their numbers in a tough economy, has done a lot to lessen their receptiveness toward the steady stream of vendors.

In the old days, when salespeople literally had to show up in person to call on a customer, decision makers dealt with far fewer vendors under arguably less sophisticated business conditions. The explosion in technology and the recent shift to telesales programs means customers are now being deluged by sales callers, all vying for a precious slice of the customer's time and attention, and ultimately, a share of their budget.

Until now, the strategy most sellers employed when deal with standoffish customers has been to be more aggressive in their attempts to penetrate accounts in an effort to overcome the customer's natural defenses. Many salespeople still believe that forceful tactics are the only way to be taken seriously. Maybe you're familiar with the movie *Glengarry Glen Ross*, where Alec Baldwin plays an obnoxious sales manager who declares that "Coffee is for closers," and that "selling is a simple matter of ABC: Always Be Closing!"

This kind of thinking has created a predictable backlash over time. Persistent hounding on the part of salespeople has caused customers to be even more cautious and reserved. Meanwhile, this increased resistance on the part of prospective customers has ironically caused sellers to be even more aggressive. It's a crazy cycle to be sure.

Let's review what we know. We know that decision makers tend to buy from people they feel comfortable with and trust, right? That's why it's so important to be seen as a trusted adviser within your accounts. We also know that establishing credibility and building relationships with potential customers is the key to understanding the customer's needs and earning the right to recommend potential solutions. As a salesperson, it's easy to set your sights on the goal of making a sale. The problem is, how do you forge new relationships with someone who is holding you off at arm's length? Furthermore, how are you supposed to get past the customer's initial defenses, especially in today's competitive marketplace, to engage them in a productive discussion of their needs and your corresponding value?

Piquing the interest of skeptical prospects is the first hump you must get over in the sales process, and arguably one of the biggest challenges salespeople today face. How (exactly) to pique the prospect's interest is also one of the least talked about subjects in sales training over the last thirty years. That's because the skills required to transform a customer from being cautious and standoffish into wanting to engage are less about positioning your product, and more about selling yourself first.

> **Piquing the interest of skeptical prospects is the first hump you must get over in the sales process, and arguably one of the biggest challenges salespeople today face.**

Building relationships with key decision makers in target accounts is particularly difficult since lots of other sellers are vying for the same customer's time and attention. If you happen to be one of those people who is a natural conversationalist, then perhaps it's easy for you to strike up a dialogue with prospective customers. Most of us, however, fear the awkwardness and traditional risks of rejection that come with reaching out to potential buyers. We understand that decision makers aren't just sitting next to the telephone waiting for the next salesperson to call. And when their phone does ring, we know from experience that buyers default to holding salespeople at arm's length. Heck, that's why they call it cold-calling.

Until now, salespeople have been taught that selling is a numbers game, and that the inherent risk of rejection is just part of the job. Contact as many leads as possible in the hopes of identifying some subset of potential customers. From there, you will presumably identify a smaller subset of bona fide prospects. Some portion of these prospects will turn into qualified opportunities, and then some fraction of those will hopefully turn into closable deals. The prevailing thought with people who have a numbers-game mentality is—to increase sales, you simply have to make more sales calls.

This notion of funneling leads down into a smaller subset of suspects, prospects, qualified opportunities, and then closed sales is still valid. But rather than missing out on tons of opportunities on the way to netting out a few desirable deals, the focus of the strategic salesperson must shift from just making lots of sales calls to increasing the effectiveness and productivity of your calls

The study of sales effectiveness, and the thought that there *must* be a better way, was the catalyst that caused me to create the QBS methodology in the first place. My quest now, as a sales trainer, is simply to teach other people how to increase their return on invested sales effort. Simply put, if it was possible to adjust your approach in a way that would make more customers more receptive to your messages, and boost your results in the process, would you be open to the possibility of doing something different? If so, then let me call your attention to an important ingredient in the success formula for selling yourself. Allow me to set the stage.

My grandmother (Nana, we called her) always made the best brownies in town. These delectable delights would literally melt in your mouth. Anybody can whip up a batch of brownies, but there was definitely something special about Nana's brownies that raised them head and shoulders above all others. Of course, I can't tell you the exact ingredients because that's a closely guarded family secret. However, I can share a different secret with you—the secret to making customers more receptive to your voice-mail messages, e-mails, live presentations, and overall messaging, that will raise you head and shoulders above other sales reps who are also banging the phones and making calls every day.

The magical ingredient in the strategic sales process is *curiosity*. It's a simple formula really. If a decision maker is not the least bit curious about who you are or what you can do for him, then you probably won't succeed in getting his or her time or attention. Fortunately, the opposite is also true. If you are able to do something to pique the prospect's curiosity, you will not only get more mind share within target accounts, you will also enjoy a competitive advantage throughout the sales process.

Curiosity: The Genesis of Every Sale

Because I was a salesperson in the field before becoming a trainer, my focus when delivering QBS methodology courses (and when writing books) has always been on the implementation of the material, not just the transfer of information. What you learn at a QBS training course or by reading one of my books is only valuable if you can apply it in the real world. Of course, when you try something and it works, the goal then is to understand why it worked so you can repeat your success in future customer situations.

The QBS methodology was designed to be a recipe for repeatable success. Rather than expecting everyone on the sales team to reinvent the wheel through trial and tribulation, what if we provided them with a blueprint that could be duplicated across the organization? My goal here isn't to transform your sales team into a bunch of script readers. But to the extent that the larger sale is a cumulation of smaller successes throughout the sales process, we should be able to identify the ingredients that are necessary to implement and repeat an effective step-by-step formula. In Question Based Selling, I assimilated the logic of a successful sales call into a simple formula, which I call the Conversational Layering Model™.

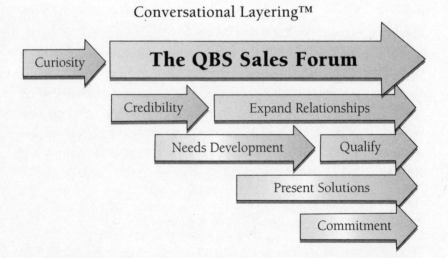

Conversational Layering™

Curiosity

The QBS Sales Forum

Credibility

Expand Relationships

Needs Development

Qualify

Present Solutions

Commitment

This diagram tracks the logical flow of a sales conversation. Starting in the upper left-hand corner and cascading down toward the lower right, each of the arrows in the graphic represents an important element (or ingredient) on the way to achieving the larger goal of making a sale. The direction of the arrows gives us a road map for identifying each of the prerequisites necessary to transition to the next appropriate step in the sales process. If you are able to identify and execute each of the steps in this logical progression, your likelihood of making a sale is significantly enhanced. The best way to understand how Conversational Layering works is for me to explain it in reverse, working backward from the desired result.

Ultimately, the goal of every salesperson is to secure a commitment of some kind from qualified customers (lower right of diagram). Because people on the sales team have different roles, securing a commitment could include anything from front-end lead generation to having the customer fax you a signed purchase order. Either way, we want potential decision makers to choose to engage with us as opposed to a competitor, and we want them to recognize enough value to move forward with a decision that favors our solutions.

Working backward in the Conversational Layering diagram, in order to secure this level of commitment from potential buyers, you must present valuable solutions. Very few prospects will commit without some sense of how they might benefit from your product or service. Working backward once again, before you can present a viable solution, you must first identify a need—some problem, issue, goal, or objective. It's impossible to provide value without the existence of a need. Qualification is another part of the discovery process, which is why it's on the same level as needs development. Mutually beneficial business transactions should be good for the customer and vendor both. Are you following the logical progression of the prerequisite steps needed in the sales process so far?

Unfortunately, this is where the logic ends in most traditional sales models, as "probing" for needs often marks the beginning of the older school sales mind-set. You can ask whatever questions you want once a customer sees you as a valuable resource and "wants to" share information. But if you are forging relationships with new prospects, you should expect a certain level of standoffishness, as potential buyers in the real world are generally reluctant to share information with just any salesperson who calls.

So here's the multimillion-dollar question. How is a salesperson supposed to engage potential customers in a productive conversation about their needs when customers default to being standoffish toward salespeople they don't yet know or trust? The answer can be found in the upper left of the Conversational Layering diagram. The two most important ingredients for engaging prospects in productive conversation are *Curiosity* and *Credibility*, both of which are enablers for the entire rest of the sales process.

We already talked about establishing credibility (chapter 6) by kicking your needs development conversations off with a series of short-answer, diagnostic questions. When forging new relationships, sellers can earn a lot more credibility by asking intelligent questions than by making claims about their products. But before you start barraging customers with questions, however, you must first secure their time and attention. In QBS, we say you have to have a "forum for selling."

How do you secure a prospect's time and attention in today's competitive marketplace when they are accustomed to fending salespeople off on an daily basis? That's where one of the least talked-about ingredients in sales comes into play—leveraging curiosity.

I would argue that curiosity is the genesis of each and every sale. I'll say it again. If a prospect or customer is not the least bit curious about who you are or what you can do for them, then you probably won't succeed in getting their time or their attention. The opposite is also true. As prospects and customers become more curious about what you or your products can do for them, you get more mind share with key decision makers in important target accounts.

One of the questions I end up asking salespeople, managers, and executives at companies all over the world is: "So, what are you currently doing to leverage curiosity as part of your strategic sales process?" The most common answer I hear back is "Huh?"

Don't be alarmed if you haven't spent much time thinking about how to leverage curiosity before now. You can go to your local bookstore and pore through every business book on the shelf; the topic of curiosity is essentially unmentioned. Isn't that strange—sales drives every company, and curiosity drives every sale, but we're not even talking about it?!

Creating Sparks of Interest

Just making people curious is not the goal in Question Based Selling. What we really want is to engage potential buyers in a productive conversation about their needs in a way that enables us to establish credibility, build relationships, convey the value of our solutions, and ultimately secure commitments to move forward with appropriate next steps in the sales process. Piquing the customer's interest simply becomes the springboard to accomplishing these goals.

Curiosity is actually a powerful emotion. It's the spark that causes people to want to know more about whatever it is they're curious about. Whenever someone becomes curious, they tend to focus all of their attention on whatever has piqued their interest, and everything else fades to the background. This is particularly good for salespeople, since one of our primary functions is to grab the attention of key decision makers in targeted prospect accounts.

> **Curiosity is a powerful emotion. It's the spark that causes people to want to know more about whatever they have become curious about.**

If you are on board with the notion that curiosity provides the spark that ignites the rest of the sales process, let's talk more specifically about how to induce curiosity, and how to incorporate this into your daily interactions with prospective and existing customers. Ironically, some of the techniques we've already talked about are also some of the most valuable for piquing the prospect's interest.

Mini-Invitations Are HUGE!

Mini-invitations are terrific conversational tools, as we discussed in chapter 4. They are also great curiosity inducers. In an account where you already have an existing relationship and the customer is open and willing to share with you, you may not need a curiosity strategy. But if your job function includes business development, and you are responsible for creating revenue opportunities that otherwise wouldn't exist, then using mini-invitations to make people more receptive can pay huge dividends.

Basically, a mini-invitation is the customer's way of saying "Tell me more." It's the equivalent of a decision maker saying, "Mr. Salesperson, I'm interested enough to continue the dialogue, so can you please take a few minutes and explain your solutions?" Of course, their interest (in the form of an invitation) paves the way for you to educate them. Similarly, if a customer said, "Ms. Salesperson, could you please ask me a couple specifics to better understand my needs?" that would instantly change the complexion of your sales interactions. Customers would go from being standoffish to being intrigued, to the point where they are actually inviting you to take the lead in the conversation. Look again at the words from one of the examples I referenced earlier.

Salesperson: Hi, Ms. Jones, my name is Bart Burton with Integrity Office Solutions here in Little Rock. I realize that you may have a source for office equipment already, which is perfectly fine. We specialize in print supplies. But the value we offer to customers is unique because we basically solve the problems that traditional toner vendors have created, and we can save customers money in the process.

Office Manager: What problems do you solve?

Bingo! When a customer asks for more information, they instantly become more receptive to what you have to say. This technique doesn't guarantee that you will make a sale, but I can pretty much guarantee you won't sell anything if you aren't able to pique the customer's interest.

Let's dig deeper for a moment and look at the meaning of the words. The customer in this example is basically saying, "Can you please take a few minutes and explain how you can be a valuable resource to us?" That's a nice invitation from a curious prospect, don't you think?

Inducing curiosity, as a positioning strategy, is applicable in every industry. While one could argue that some of this is just common courtesy, using curiosity to create mini-invitations is highly strategic because it generates a predictable outcome. A salesperson in the financial services industry, for example, could easily say, "We solve many of the problems that traditional investment vehicles have created for investors." Unless the customer was dead set against talking to this person, he or she would be compelled to ask, "What problems do you solve?" Just like that, this customer has suddenly become more receptive.

A medical supplies rep selling therapeutic devices could easily say to a doctor or clinician, "This device was designed to solve some of the issues that traditional treatment protocols have created." And so on, and so forth. Using curiosity to engage potential buyers goes hand-in-hand with the notion of pointing to the elephant in the room. If you truly are a valuable resource selling beneficial solutions, then it's perfectly reasonable for you to articulate the challenges that customers currently face, many of which were created by other solutions that you are able to improve upon.

Curiosity Facilitates Needs Development

I mentioned earlier that my first needs development question is almost always the same. At the point when it's appropriate to inquire about the customer's needs, I say, "Can I ask you a couple specifics about your current _____ environment, so I can give you accurate information?" Virtually everyone responds by saying yes or sure. Besides being invited to ask relevant questions, this is also a great way to induce curiosity. The underlying logic is simple. When someone invites you to ask questions, which you then ask, you will get in return more information that's in more depth and is also more accurate. As a bonus, you also get the customer's time and attention because they will instantly become curious to know what you are about to ask.

Try this experiment. Strike up a conversation with someone at a dinner party or in the bleachers at your child's basketball game, and say to that person, "Can I ask you about something that I've been wondering about?" Then, notice the expression on their face. The other person will instantly lock in on you as if nothing else was happening in the world. You will have their complete attention, to the point where if they have just taken a bite of food, they will literally stop chewing. It's human nature—when someone becomes curious about something, they focus all of their attention on whatever they're curious about, and everything else fades into the background.

A word of caution: Just because someone gives you permission to ask questions doesn't mean they will remain curious forever. This initial spark of interest must be followed with good technique, in the case of Question Based Selling, by asking diagnostic questions that allow you to establish some initial credibility that will blossom into a longer-term business relationship.

Another way to create sparks of interest is to use the PAS positioning model we talked about in chapter 3, as opposed to the traditional SPA approach. As we discussed, the typical elevator pitch is full of statements. Ironically, unleashing a litany of claims about a product or service usually does more to satisfy a prospect's curiosity than to create it. On the other hand, facilitating a conversation about what's most important to a decision maker (focusing on their problems, issues, and concerns) does the exact opposite. Rather than satisfying the customer's curiosity with a self-serving rant about your value, every time you ask a relevant and intelligent question about the customer's needs, you pique their interest even further about how you might be able to address those needs.

Let me show you what I mean as we play out the earlier dialogue.

Salesperson: Hi, Ms. Jones, my name is Bart Burton with Integrity Office Solutions here in Little Rock. I realize that you may have a source for office equipment already, which is perfectly fine. We specialize in print supplies. But the value we offer to customers is unique because we basically solve the problems that traditional toner vendors have created, and we can save customers a significant amount of money in the process.

Customer: What problems do you solve?

Salesperson: Well, there are a number of tricks that sometimes get pulled on customers in the toner business. Things like overstocking supply shelves, substituting lesser-quality products, or not keeping enough inventory on hand such that customers run out of product at the least opportune times. We make these issues disappear because of how our customer service center is set up. Would it make sense for me to give you a quick overview of how we do it?

At the end of the day, you bond with people on their problems, and your value proposition is only as good as the customer's perception of what they need. Customers who are curious and have lots of reasons to buy from you will to have a much greater sense of urgency to move forward. They will also have more interest in listening to your advice and recommendations.

Leveraging Curiosity with Voice Mail and E-mail

Voice mail has become an enemy for many sellers, and e-mail is similarly losing ground as an effective prospecting tool. Isn't it strange how technological advances in communication have, in many cases, distanced salespeople from prospective buyers? That's because in our new electronic age, you're not the only one who's trying to leverage technology to penetrate new accounts.

For example, when leaving a voice mail, the average call back rate has been reduced to between 2 and 5 percent, depending which survey you happen to believe. That means there are lots of salespeople making calls and leaving voice-mail messages with prospects, but the vast majority of those calls are not being returned. Treating sales as a numbers game does little to motivate a salesperson when their percentage chance of success is so astronomically low. Add in the disheartening reality that if a prospective customer listens to your voice mail and decides not to call you back, your chances of getting through next time are reduced even further.

> **Treating sales as a numbers game does very little to motivate a salesperson when their percentage chance of success is so astronomically low.**

What if it was possible to reverse this trend? Seriously, if you were able to leave voice-mail messages that caused 70 to 80 percent of the recipients to promptly return your calls, wouldn't voice mail suddenly become a valuable sales asset, rather than a liability? How about a similar turnaround in results with e-mail? This reversal can absolutely happen if you are open to changing your messaging strategy, or more specifically, changing how your voice-mail and e-mail messages are being perceived.

Let's boil this down to make it easy. There are only two reasons people to respond to voice-mail messages. One is obligation. If the president of your company calls and leaves you a voice-mail message, you will return that call, probably sooner rather than later. Likewise, if an important customer calls and leaves a message, you will surely call them back. If your mom calls, call her back—she's your mom! But what percentage of prospects feel obligated to return cold calls from salespeople? In that context, is anyone surprised the average callback rate is low?

The only other reason people to respond to voice-mail messages is curiosity. Let me say it one more time. If someone is not the least bit interested in who you are or what you can do for them, then they are not going to engage with you—in this case, they won't return your call. On the other hand, if you are able to induce curiosity with the voice-mail messages you leave, your probability of getting a return call increases dramatically.

I am not a fan of sales tricks, so I can tell you there's no place for clever one-liners when leaving voice-mail messages. Getting a high callback rate on voice-mail (or when sending e-mails) is more about technique than gimmickry. In fact, if I left five voice-mail messages for five different prospects, I might leave five completely different messages. But my strategy for inducing curiosity and getting a high response rate would be consistent, though the script could change significantly based on the context of the call.

The big mistake sellers make with voice mail is sounding just like everyone else. That's the quickest way to commoditize your value, or in the case of voice mail, it's the quickest way to get deleted. The second biggest mistake sellers make is leaving a voice-mail message that satisfies the recipient's curiosity, which is the opposite of our objective.

Here's a standard-sounding voice-mail message from a typical vendor:

Voice mail: Good afternoon, my name is Joe Smith and I'm with XYZ Company, the leading provider of widgets in North America. We offer valuable solutions for companies like yours and I wanted to see if I could get a few minutes of your time to see if there might be an opportunity to benefit you as well. If you get a chance, I would love to have the opportunity to talk with you today. I can be reached at (770) 123-4567. Have a great day!

Blah, blah, blah . . . get in line! Most prospects won't return this call because the message sounds just like dozens of other voice mails they've already deleted from other vendors so far today. They're not likely to feel obligated to respond, and since it's just another cold call from an eager salesperson, they're certainly not going to be curious. Of course they won't call back!

The alternative to sounding like everyone else is leaving a curiosity-inducing voice-mail message that actually piques the prospect's interest. How exactly can you do this? The key to success when using voice mail or e-mail is being purposeful, relevant, and specific in the context of your message, as opposed to sounding generic. Let me give you a few samples. Try saying the words aloud as you read them.

Curiosity-Inducing Voice-Mail Samples:

- "Hi, George, this is Pat Wilkins calling from the Dynamic Systems Group—I'm on the team that works with large industrial accounts in the Southeast. I was on a conference call with one of your counterparts last Wednesday afternoon just before lunch, and two issues came up that I thought might impact your platform decisions moving forward, one of which is time sensitive. I wanted to be proactive and try to catch you in the office this afternoon. If you get a chance today, could you please call me back at (770) 123-4567? I know you're busy but I'd appreciate a callback."

- "Hi, Dale, this is Lane Patterson with HJK Corporation. I'm on the team that supports health care accounts in central Ohio. I was hoping to catch you for a minute because we've had thirteen new announcements in the last three and a half months, two of which will likely impact your patient statistics for the rest of this year. If you get a chance this afternoon, could you please call me at (770) 123-4567?"

- "Hi, Susan, this is Jocelyn Thompsin calling from Premier Partners. I manage a team that works with financial brokers in the tri-state area. A file came across my desk yesterday morning that raised a flag regarding [insert something relevant] and I wanted to try and catch you in the office. If you get a chance today, could you please call me back at (770) 123-4567?"

Please note that these are just sample voice-mail messages, and they are not intended to be used as generic cold-calling scripts. You don't want to leave scripted messages anyway, because anything that sounds generic will cause your calls to be perceived as purposeless and not credible. I merely pulled a few hypothetical scenarios out of the air as examples of possible curiosity-inducing voice mails. The point that should be made is that the context of all the voice-mail messages I leave is intended to be relevant and valuable, and the information I referenced would have been 100 percent accurate, or else I wouldn't have said it.

My own callback rate, along with the success rates of the students we teach, tends to be very high simply because specific voice-mail messages that are purposeful and relevant also tend to be curiosity-inducing. If the person who listens to your message wonders, "What two issues?" or "A file came across your desk that raised a flag?" they will surely call you back. While there is an opportunity to recycle good ideas, it's critical that the context of your voice mails is tailored to be congruent with whatever might be important to your target audience.

If you dig a little deeper, you may have noticed a few strategic nuances in the voice-mail samples above. For example, if you are initiating contact with new prospects, the first thing people want to know is who are you, and why are you calling? Just saying your name and company does not satisfy the need to know who you are. Are you the owner of the company, a customer service rep, or might you be in some other role? Don't worry about having an impressive-sounding title. You just need to be relevant. Thus it's easy to say, "Hi, Dale, this is Lane Patterson with HJK Corporation. I'm on the team that supports health care accounts in central Ohio." Lane may be an inside rep or a senior executive, but the fact that she's on the team that handles health care accounts in central Ohio instantly makes her relevant to those accounts.

When you wrap up your voice-mail message at the end, it's important to have a respectful request for action, but one that is also clear and forthright. Usually I'll say, "If you get a chance today, could you please call me back at (770) 123-4567?" It's direct and to the point, but not overly forceful.

Sandwiched between the announcement of who you are and your request for action at the end of your voice mail is the gist of the message. The difference between the hundreds of generic voice-mail messages left by the masses and using question-based approach is one word—*curiosity*. I try to leave voice-mail messages that not only grab the prospect's attention, but also spark a desire for them to call me back. Ultimately, I want people to feel compelled to return my calls.

When I deliver live QBS training programs, people ask, "How exactly do you 'spark a desire' to get people to return your calls?" It's a fair question, and one that needs to be addressed in order to implement this technique and repeat your successes.

The first step is to understand the strategy behind the idea of leveraging curiosity. If you want to get a return call when leaving a voice-mail message, you must depend on either obligation or curiosity. Since very few customers feel obligated to return sales calls, leveraging curiosity is clearly the best option.

What is it exactly that makes people curious while listening to voice-mail messages? If you were sitting in my classroom, I would go to the board and draw a simple cause-and-effect diagram.

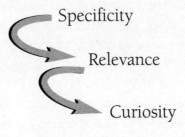

Specificity

Relevance

Curiosity

If the goal when leaving a voice mail is to induce curiosity, the intangible ingredient that creates curiosity is relevance. You cannot pique someone's curiosity by leaving generic or irrelevant voice-mail messages. How can you make your calls more relevant to potential customers? Working backward again, the magic when leaving effective voice-mail messages is specificity.

The main difference between my voice-mails and less effective ones is the fact that the messages I leave are intentionally specific. Did you notice how I mentioned there were "two issues, one of which is time sensitive"? In the second voice mail, I referenced "thirteen new announcements in the last three and a half months." Note that I didn't just say that we had "a bunch of new announcements," because that sounds generic. Specificity is about conveying details to increase relevance and communicate greater value. I even went so far as to indicate that the conference call last Wednesday occurred "just before lunch." To a customer who gets tons of cold calls, this level of specificity conveys that something of importance is really happening, as opposed to just another cold caller reading a script.

Using specificity to create relevance (which breeds curiosity) is like adding seasoning to a steak before you throw it on the grill. Adding specificity causes customers to form the impression that you're calling for a reason, and it also gives them the impression that you know what you're talking about. I want prospective customers to have that impression. Frankly, if you are not calling for a reason, then I would tell you not to even bother calling. On the other hand, if you convey messages that are indeed relevant to customers, of course they will want to call you back and expand the dialogue

This strategy of leveraging curiosity to increase your return call rate can be just as easily applied when reaching out to potential customers via e-mail. I realize that people use e-mail to accomplish a variety of different objectives. We all send, forward, and reply to lots of e-mail messages during the course of a normal business day. E-mail has become a wonderful communication tool. But if you want to use e-mail as an effective prospecting device, you need to do something that will compel and motivate potential customers to prioritize and then respond to your e-mail messages, which can be an excellent stepping-stone to generating a live telephone conversation or a face-to-face meeting.

Once again, it's critical to recognize that you aren't the only salesperson using e-mail to troll for new prospects. I can assure you that dozens of other vendors are targeting your same customers on a daily basis. As with voice mail, most vendor e-mail messages do more to satisfy a customer's curiosity than to induce it, and you don't want to seem like a cold caller on e-mail any more than you would on the telephone. If your e-mails seem valueless, customers will do the same thing you do when you open Outlook and discover a lengthy list of e-mails featuring special discounts, limited one-time offers, and free shipping through the holidays. Delete, delete, delete.

If you want your e-mail messages to be seriously considered, and more important, responded to, then you'd better do something to pique the recipient's curiosity. How do you induce curiosity when sending e-mails?

Good news—the same logic we used for voice mail applies to e-mail. Specificity creates relevance, and relevance breeds curiosity. In other words, stop sending generic e-mail messages! Even if your e-mail makes it past the customer's corporate filter, generic e-mails are quickly discarded. Specificity tends to give e-mail messages purpose and credibility. Let me give you a quick example to illustrate.

Subject: Per Joe Davis . . .

Kim,

My name is Jason Darden with XYZ Company and I'm on the team that works with manufacturing accounts in Northern California. I left you a quick voice mail late last week and wanted to follow up this morning.

Last Wednesday, I talked with one of your managers in the Birmingham office and two performance issues came up that I think might impact your broader technology platform. One of those issues is time sensitive, so I wanted to be proactive and see if it would make sense to brief you on the details.

Any chance we can set up a time to discuss later in the week? Please advise.

Jason
p.s. Joe said to tell you hello . . .

Again, please don't just copy this message and send it to your entire prospect database. You can only expect a high response rate if the context of your e-mails is indeed relevant to the intended recipient. That simply won't happen if you send out a bunch of generic e-mail messages.

Instead, I would encourage you to pay attention to the tone and theme of this sample e-mail message. Notice that Jason is clearly contacting this customer for a reason—because two performance issues came up that he thought might impact her technology platform, one of which is time sensitive. Furthermore, he is also being proactive by following up on the voice mail he left late last week, and he is specifically asking for a response to see if it makes sense to update her on the details—"Please advise."

There's no magic here. If the recipient of the e-mail wonders, "What two issues?" or "How will that affect my business?" Jason will get a prompt response.

To glean some specific ideas of what types of things might be relevant to your customers, I will refer you to the exercise in chapter 5, where I recommended that you build a repository of potential business issues and implications that could be important to potential customers. If you have completed this assignment already, just take any industry issue and sprinkle in a couple "specifics," and you will be well on your way to a significantly improved response rate, whether you leave curiosity-inducing voice-mail messages or send more purposeful e-mails.

Leveraging Curiosity Throughout the Sales Process

Using specific techniques to leverage curiosity is one of the two most important ingredients in the recipe for engaging new prospects—credibility being the other. If customers are not at all curious about what you bring to the table, and they don't believe that you are a credible resource, the sales profession can be a really tough way to make a living.

These strategies for leveraging curiosity and establishing credibility are not limited to the introductory part of the sale, however. As you will see in chapters 9 and 11, where we talk about "Competitively Positioning Your Solutions" and "Wrapping Up the Sale," your ability to apply these foundational themes to the rest of the sales process will enable you to convey significantly more value than your competitors, and facilitate a very comfortable buying atmosphere.

9

Positioning Your Solutions Against the Competition

Whether you are making a sales call, working in the booth at a trade show, or delivering a product presentation, your ability to competitively position your solutions is critical to your success in sales.

Positioning an effective value proposition is more than just rattling off a bunch of features and benefits, however. For decision makers to register real value, they must conclude that your product's capabilities are the most cost-effective as compared to other options. Note that I'm not saying you have to be the cheapest. You just have to be the most valuable solution that satisfies their particular needs.

What's the goal of a sales presentation? Is it to educate potential buyers on the value of your solutions? Is it an opportunity to differentiate yourself from the competition? What about justifying the decision to prospective customers? Seasoned sales professionals would have all of these goals in mind when delivering a sales presentation.

Presentation skills have long been thought to be the key to being successful in sales. Everyone knows that an excellent presentation can help you win you the business, and a subpar presentation can just as easily kill your opportunity to close a sale. If you've ever attended a presentation skills course, however, then you know that most of the instruction tends to focus on style, and the manner in which the material is being presented. While I agree that having an effective presentation style is undoubtedly a valuable asset, sellers also need to realize that how they position themselves and their company's offerings is a strategic opportunity in and of itself.

It's difficult to alter someone's personal style, so I am more than happy to leave your style alone. Instead, let's assume that one of the reasons customers choose to deal with you is because they like your style. But that doesn't mean we should turn a blind eye to positioning logic or what it takes to have a winning presentation strategy.

Once more, we come to a philosophical crossroads in your professional development as a salesperson. For years, sellers have been taught to position themselves and their solutions using an SPA approach, which doesn't necessarily coincide with how buyers process information (PAS). Sorry to rock the boat yet again, but the traditional mindset of conveying value by focusing on the features and benefits of your product or service, and ignoring the elephant in the room, no longer cuts it in a competitive business environment.

I don't have a problem with sellers talking about the capabilities of their products. At the appropriate time in the decision cycle, you're supposed to educate prospective buyers on the value of your proposed solutions and set expectations with regard to the benefits they can expect to receive. My worry is that simply running through a list of features and benefits doesn't maximize your product's value.

One of the themes throughout this book is that the actual value of a product or service is only as good as how it is being perceived by potential buyers. Even if you represent the most wonderful solution in the world, customers will only purchase your product or service if the value perceived is great enough to justify the cost. But in addition to being cost effective, you must also prevail over other comparable options in order to be selected as the vendor of choice.

If your product or company offers some feature or benefit that gives you a whopping technical or functional advantage, one that customers definitely need, then by all means, you should exploit your advantage as long as possible. It's easy (and fun) to sell if your product offering is the only game in town. Enjoy it while you can.

If you sell in a competitive market, however, where other providers offer comparable solutions, the true differences between your proposal and a competitor's may be very slight, if not indiscernible. In those cases, the customer's perception of your value is going to be largely influenced by how your solution is being positioned, which brings the intangible nature of your positioning strategy into play. This is terrific news, because if the outcome of a sale comes down to whoever has "the ability" to convey the most value, then having superior positioning skills can absolutely give you an unfair advantage.

> **If the outcome of a sale comes down to whoever has the ability to convey the most value, then having superior positioning skills can absolutely give you an unfair advantage.**

The only question now is: what can you do to put yourself and your products in the strongest possible position to win business? Rather than trying to come up with a magic bullet, however, the rest of this chapter focuses on a number of presentation nuances that can give you a significant differentiable advantage over the competition.

Winning the Battle for Conversational Control

One of the topics we must talk about with regard to positioning your products and services is conversational control. If it were totally up to you, who would you rather be in control of your sales conversations, you or the customer? Given the choice, most sellers would absolutely want to be in control of their sales presentations, presumably to maximize time spent with potential buyers. However, if we did a survey and asked the typical customer who they want to control the conversation when dealing with vendors, you would quickly discover that decision makers usually aren't eager to yield the floor to a salesperson.

Suddenly, a battle for control is brewing. Salespeople want to be in control of their conversations with customers, but so do the customers. Who is going to win this battle for control? That depends on the answer to this question: why is it in the customer's best interest for you to be in control? I ask because I know that if it doesn't benefit the customer for you to be in control of the conversation, you probably won't be.

To me, the most important reason to have at least some control over your dialogue is to make the best use of the customer's time, by keeping the conversation on track. As a salesperson, you should have a pretty good idea of how you can provide value prior to making the call. Thus, it stands to reason that if you are able to steer the conversation toward those areas that are most beneficial to the customer, you will accomplish much more than if you just let the conversation wander. Whether you get five minutes or two hours in front of a customer, providing maximum value during this window of time not only is good for customers, it also places you in a strong competitive position.

So, how exactly is a salesperson supposed to control their sales conversations, especially when decision makers are cautious or standoffish? Strangely, the answer to this question comes down to simple punctuation—use questions, not statements.

With most sales presentations, flow is very important. Presumably, you are going to present a logical argument or sequence of ideas to support the assertion that customers will be better off purchasing your product or service, rather than selecting a competitor's proposal, or doing nothing at all. The operative word here is *logical*.

Some of your success when delivering an effective sales presentation is content dependent. For our purposes here, let's assume you represent a viable company that offers a robust product or service, and you have a compelling story to tell. Even so, part of what makes any story compelling is the logical flow of the presentation, in terms of how your proposed solution is being justified to your target audience.

For example, if you took a compelling presentation and you totally shuffled the delivery sequence by putting your slides in random order, the effectiveness of your message would be greatly reduced. The opposite is true. Enhancing the logic flow of your company's message can significantly increase a customer's perception of your value.

For now, let's agree that we want our sales presentations to start off well and we also want them to stay on track—not only to maximize our opportunity to sell, but also to make the best use of the customer's time. In addition to just controlling the flow of the presentation, we would also like to establish credibility as a valuable resource, lower the decision maker's natural defenses, and make our target audience more receptive to our advice. The way to do all of this is by controlling the flow of your conversations using strategic questions.

Kicking Off Your Sales Presentations

Unless I am dealing with a spectacularly large audience, I generally shy away from using formal agendas to kick off my sales presentations. I know, I know . . . sellers have been taught for years to kick off their sales calls and presentations by reviewing a formal agenda. In some cases, sellers are even encouraged to secure verbal contracts that supposedly commit the audience to giving the vendor an agreed-upon amount of time during the presentation. No thanks!

The problem with starting off a meeting by reviewing your agenda is that it's too easily perceived as just that—*your* agenda. Granted, you should come to meetings fully prepared and you should absolutely have a clear picture of what you hope to accomplish. But it's important to make sure your opening comments sound mutually beneficial as opposed to one-sided or self-serving.

My rule of thumb on sales calls and during product presentations is to save the chitchat and small talk for the end of the meeting. It's perfectly okay to be professional and courteous. But especially early in your interactions, when customers are sizing you up and forming their initial impressions, you want to be perceived as valuable as opposed to just friendly and nice. First and foremost, customers understand all too well that some vendors are more valuable than others. Hence, they will be quietly assessing you to figure out to what extent you are smart, knowledgeable, capable, competent, experienced, confident, and trustworthy, and whether you are planning to make valuable use of their time. Therefore, I try to err on the side of being purposeful and relevant as a means of gaining early traction in my sales calls or presentations.

Just being chatty and convivial doesn't do a lot to prove you're competent or capable.

At the beginning of a call, for example, I might say, "Mr. Customer, I know that you're busy, so if it's okay with you, I'll get to the part of our offering that might impact you the most. We have announced two new programs in the last five weeks, one of which will enable your customers to reduce their production costs and the other can boost your revenue by as much as twenty percent. Would it make sense for me to take a few minutes and bring you up to speed?" Being purposeful up front makes the customer's decision on whether or not to spend time with you relatively simple. If you say something that piques their curiosity, they will absolutely invite you to educate them further. With your own words, you create a more receptive audience. By being forthright and relevant, you have also boosted your credibility. Of course, once the customer grants you permission to fill them in on the details, you are in a good position to transition into a more in-depth needs development conversation by saying, "I'd be happy to give you all the details. Can I ask a couple specifics about your . . . ?" Bingo! You're off and running.

Basically, you are manufacturing a mini-invitation. Once you are invited to proceed, the customer subtly transfers control of the conversation, by either giving you permission to ask them questions or, in this case, they are inviting you to get into the details, which provides a seamless transition into your sales presentation. If you instead started off with a statement like "I'd like to tell you about our products and services," you might still get into your presentation, but you do so at the risk of customers bracing for what sounds like a typical vendor's self-serving agenda.

If you are presenting in a more formal setting, such as to a decision committee or board of directors, let me offer a few pointers on how best to kick off that type of presentation.

First, I always ask my champion in the account, or whoever scheduled the meeting, to kick off the presentation and introduce each of the participants. Important people like to be introduced. This takes away much of the awkwardness that would otherwise ensue if you just dove into your spiel. I'm not looking for some fabulous introduction, just someone to welcome everyone, communicate the objectives of the meeting, and then turn it over to me.

Once the floor of the meeting is mine, I usually start by thanking people for their time—not profusely—just enough to be respectful and acknowledge that I'm aware their time is valuable and I plan to make good use of it.

Next I state the purpose of the meeting. In doing so, my strategy (and my style) is to pull back the proverbial curtain and verbally point at the elephant in the room, just as we talked about in chapter 1. Verbalizing that there are a host of challenges facing decision makers is without question the quickest way to get a group's attention. There's no point in beating around the bush. If a customer wants to know about your solutions, you might as well frame your value proposition by first demonstrating a knowledge of the challenges they face. I might even throw the sales establishment under the bus by suggesting that the customer doesn't need a sales pitch, they need viable solutions.

Let me give you an example of what my introductory comments in a formal presentation setting might actually sound like.

Seller: Thank you, everyone, for your time. I know we're coming up on your busy season, so I'll jump right in. Over the past several weeks, I have met with a number of people regarding your IT implementation and I think I have a decent understanding of your objectives. Although I don't know everything about your business, I have done some homework in advance of this meeting and I put together several options for your consideration.

Frankly, there are a couple of ways we can do this. If you like, I can pull out my slides and give you a standard marketing pitch. We have plenty of glossies and I can ramble on with the best of them. Or, we could put the canned pitch aside, roll up our sleeves, and have a more in-depth conversation about our solution options and how they would impact your project.

Let me ask the group, which would you rather I do?

As you can see, my style is respectful but very direct. Of course, I also want to sound professional. Frankly, customers are visibly relieved when you let them know that yours is not a sales pitch, rather you actually have something valuable to say.

The next thing that happens is—I pause and wait for someone to answer my question. What I'm looking for is a mini-invitation from the audience. Invariably, someone in the meeting will say, "Great, let's put away the marketing hype and talk specifically about the project." Others in the room will nod and think to themselves, "Whew, I'm so glad this isn't just another sales pitch." You can literally see people lean forward in their chairs with a sense of anticipation, once you have clearly signaled you are headed down a different path from most.

Notice that I didn't just open my presentation up to the audience by asking what they'd like me to cover, or how they wanted it to proceed. I offered them a choice, for me to either deliver a standard marketing pitch or facilitate a more productive conversation about how our solutions would impact their business. Of course, I already know which option they will choose, because of the way my question was phrased. Essentially I subtly poisoned one of the options, knowing that nobody wants "standard marketing hype."

Once your audience invites you to get specific, it's easy and natural for me to then say, "Well, can I ask the group a couple specifics about your _____?" Invariably, they'll say yes. Notice how this formal presentation has suddenly turned into an interactive session. Perfect! I don't really want to get up in front of a group and deliver a boring monologue.

The same strategy we used to kick off the needs development conversation (diagnostic questions) provides a perfect jumping-off point in your sales presentations as well. But since you've already done your homework and prepared for the presentation in advance, you can now do more than just gather information. You can leverage the technique of narrowing the scope of your questions to demonstrate competence, earn credibility with new participants coming into the process, and verify that the information you have based your recommendations on is indeed correct.

Here's how that might sound.

Seller: My understanding from talking with Dave and Terry is that your current operation supports approximately 125 employees across four locations. Correct? *(They nod yes.)* And while most of these employees have similar desktop computers, their application mix differs from user to user . . . right? *(More nodding.)* And the short-term objective is to implement a consistent architecture across the organization within the next sixty days, certainly prior to the start of the new fiscal year, yes?

As part of my Question Based Selling philosophy, I would argue that "He who asks the questions controls the conversation." It's one of those immutable laws of nature. Once you secure the customer's permission to proceed, it's easy to ask a series of diagnostic questions, thus enabling you to initiate an interactive dialogue with the audience. From there, it's a simple transition into needs development, where you can either explore or confirm a customer's issues and implications, particularly to get the issues on the table that you plan to address in your presentation.

Think about it this way. The only reason a customer would want to sit through a vendor's presentation is to understand how your solutions match up to their needs. That said, the best way to begin this matching exercise is to roll up your sleeves and facilitate a more in-depth conversation that begins with some confirmation that you do actually understand the customer's needs.

Confirming a Mutual Agenda

Kicking your sales presentations off in an interactive fashion is good, but you also want to get key issues on the table for discussion and set a direction that will allow your company's story to provide the best fit. Ultimately, the purpose of a sales presentation is to match your solutions up to the customer's needs. Getting the customer's problems, issues, and concerns into the discussion requires a little finesse, however. For example, just telling people what their problems are is a good way to sound presumptuous or offend people in the room who may have been involved with the previous decision. Asking too many questions, and thinking that you will engage them in a lengthy needs development conversation, eats into your time to educate the customer, particularly if you are there to "present" solutions.

Most corporate presentations have a logical flow. Through trial and error and real-life experiences, presentations have been meticulously crafted to follow a path that is designed to convey the company's message in a way that maximizes the presenter's probability of success. The trick is getting people to buy into your agenda early in the presentation, thus giving you the opportunity to position your product in its best light. To secure the necessary buy-in from your audience, try making your agenda *their* agenda.

You do this by securing the customer's permission to have a "roll up our sleeves" discussion about details, rather than a generic overview. You then kick off the audience interaction by asking a series of diagnostic questions to verify details that you have based your recommendations on. Just like at the beginning of a regular sales call, asking diagnostic questions at the beginning of a presentation allows you to establish credibility with those who are forming their initial impressions of you.

Next, you want to get the customer's issues on the table for discussion. This is a simple exercise in question-based facilitation. Pointing at the elephant in the room, you could easily say, "There is a problem in the world of (your industry) where it has become very unclear (to customers) which options are going to provide the best solution because of _____, _____, and _____." From there, it's easy to bring up challenges or topics that you know are most important to customers, having done your homework in advance.

Seller: Richard, several issues came up during our last conversation, including: growth, security, uptime, training, cost effectiveness, support, upgrades, and performance. The options I put together for you would provide benefits in each of these areas. Is there anything else that we need to include on the list of business issues?

As the facilitator of the meeting, I usually take the opportunity to write the customers decision issues on a flip chart or whiteboard, or even on a piece of paper if we are sitting at a table. This gives your audience a chance to see where you are headed, and it also gives them an opportunity to elaborate on any specific concerns they want you to be sure and address in your presentation.

As a way to uncover any hidden concerns someone may be harboring, I will usually ask, "Is there anything else you would like me to cover?" If so, simply add it to the bottom of your list. If not, the customer will say, "No, that's pretty much it for now."

Suddenly, you have the perfect agenda for your presentation. But whose agenda is it? By leading the audience down a question-based path from the onset, and involving them in the development or verification of issues that are important to them, you have successfully created a *mutual* agenda. But since *you* were the one who facilitated the discussion, you essentially control the sequence of the presentation because you raised (and wrote down) issues in the order that best suits the delivery of your message.

The notion of proactively raising a customer's issues should look familiar. Remember back in chapter 2 when we talked about differentiating yourself in a job interview? Again, an employment interview is the ultimate product presentation, where you are totally responsible for selling yourself. That being the case, if you are able to facilitate a more in-depth conversation about the customer's goals and your solutions, you are in a stronger position to separate yourself from the competition.

Here's what the product presentation on your next job interview might sound like. "In addition to being a good person and having a track record of success, my guess (Mr./Ms Hiring Manager) is that you might be looking for more than just a good person—perhaps some of the intangibles that don't necessarily show up as line items on a résumé. For example, you might want someone who can ramp up quickly, blend in with the existing culture but also bring some fresh ideas to the team, defuse tough account situations, and perpetuate solid relationships, etc. . . ."

This is classic PAS positioning, and it's just as appropriate in a presentation as it is in a sales call or job interview. After all, you are attempting to do the same thing in all three scenarios—match your solutions up to the customer's needs. In order for someone to be ready and willing to make a purchase decision, they must conclude the following. They must say to themselves, "Because I have certain problems, issues, goals, needs, or requirements (P), that other alternatives don't address as effectively (A), that's why I choose to purchase your particular solution (S)." When you establish a mutual agenda that accurately reflects the customer's PAS goals, you put yourself in a strong position to facilitate a compelling argument about how your offerings compare more favorably than other alternatives the customer might be considering.

Let me alert you to one common mistake. It's generally not a good idea to kick off your sales presentations by asking, "What do you want me to cover today?" This is a strategic miss because it does not communicate that you have a reasonable understanding of the customer's goals, or that you have even prepared for the meeting. Inviting the audience to take you off on random tangents is a surefire way to end up with mayhem in the conference room.

The Traditional Feature/Benefit Model Is Dead

If the traditional feature/benefit sales presentation isn't already dead, it's definitely on life support. Your next prospect is probably thinking, "I would rather slit my writs than sit through another boring, generic sales presentation."

For as long as I have been in sales, the feature/benefit presentation model has been regarded as the recommended way for sales professionals to deliver their value propositions. The idea is that you highlight a feature of your product or service, and then tell your drooling audience about all the wonderful benefits they will receive.

I suppose it's natural for sellers to want to describe the features of their products and then explain how those features will benefit the customer. As with many long-standing practices, people sometimes argue that positioning features and benefits is the way to go because that's how everyone else does it. The problem is sounding like everyone else is not a viable differentiation strategy unless your strategy is to claim to be the same, and then simply undercut their price. If you are selling products that require differentiation, then it might be time to adjust your thinking relative to how you want to position your solutions.

In fact, how you choose to position yourself in future opportunities might depend on the answer to this question: would you rather be perceived by potential buyers as a "solutions provider" or as a "problem solver"?

> **"We sell solutions" has become the standard battle cry of the perenially average businessperson.**

For the last fifteen years or so, the idea of "providing solutions" has been batted back and forth between competing marketing departments like a corporate shuttlecock. For some reason, "We sell solutions" has become the standard battle cry of the perennially average business-person.

Is that what customers really want—your solutions? Earlier, I asked: what is more important to the typical customer, their problems or your solutions? If you agree that customers are more interested in their own problems, issues, and concerns than they are in the salesperson's sales pitch, then it seems to me we should align our value proposition with the customer's primary focus (solving problems) and not the vendor's primary focus (selling solutions).

Customers in all industries are much more worried about achieving their own goals than trying to help a corporate sales organization achieve their quarterly sales quotas. Consequently, I would much rather be seen as a problem solver than a solution provider.

While it's true that achieving trusted adviser status within key accounts gives you an opportunity to provide advice on important issues, perhaps we should pause long enough to realize that the thing customers want advice about is the actual problems, issues, goals, and concerns they are dealing with. In fact, selling solutions is really just another way to say you want to help customers solve important problems.

Are we splitting hairs with semantics here? Isn't the act of solving a problem and the act of providing a solution one and the same? Yes, good point. A salesperson cannot actually solve a problem without providing a solution. Likewise, providing a solution is only beneficial if it actually solves a problem.

But if you think about it in sales terms, the only real reason a customer would want to spend time with a certain vendor is if the salesperson could help them solve a problem of some kind. Surprisingly, most vendors position themselves in a way that is exactly the opposite of this. In the feature/benefit model, for example, sellers run around telling customers about all the cool features of their products, and then relate how those features might provide a benefit to them. Taking an SPA approach (talking about solutions/features first) creates a logic problem because it's backward from how most customers make decisions.

PAS is much more effective as a positioning strategy, not only because it aligns with the decision process, but it's also the most effective way to educate customers on the value of your intangible benefits. Remember, in order for someone to purchase your product or service, they must conclude the following: Because we have a problem (P), which the alternatives don't address as effectively (A), that's why we choose to purchase your solution (S). So rather than randomly pointing out features of your product and explaining why they're good for customers, you will be more successful using a PAS opposite approach.

Most Buyers Are Comparative Thinkers

When we talk about PAS positioning, it's easy to focus much of our energy on understanding the customer's problem (P), and then positioning the corresponding value of our solutions (S). But don't forget to spend time with potential customers talking about (A)—the alternatives to purchasing your product or service.

I assume most of the people who are reading this book sell in a competitive environment. If this is true in your world, then it's safe to assume that prospects and customers are going to consider other options besides your own.

Most decision makers are comparative thinkers. I am, and you probably are as well. Granted, I won't visit every store in the area to compare prices or products, but I usually explore my options before pulling the trigger on an important purchase. This includes exploring the option to do nothing and maintain the status quo.

If you are the only vendor that can offer a certain solution and your customer has to make an immediate decision, then you may not even need a sales strategy. However, this level of exclusivity is rarely the case. Most buyers will consider options other than yours in an effort to make the best decision. That's where your role as a salesperson comes into play. You have to figure that decision makers are going to turn to someone for advice. And if you aren't proactive in helping customers compare and contrast the different alternatives being considered, then your competitors will be. Since you are the most equipped to position your products against competitive offerings, then it is definitely in your best interest to be the one who compares and contrasts the various options, as opposed to leaving that to one of your rivals. I can guarantee they're not going to position you in your best light.

I actually look for opportunities to bring up alternatives (A) when talking with potential buyers. My logic is simple. Given that most customers are going to consider options other than mine anyway, I want to at least be involved in the discussion. Moreover, because I look for opportunities to speed up the sales process, if I can lead a conversation that compares and contrasts the various options up front, we might be able to knock some key vendors out of contention before the decision process even begins.

Never bring up or bad-mouth a competitive vendor by name, however. I figure my competitors have their own marketing departments, so it's not my job to introduce them into prospect accounts. Let them find their own leads. But if a customer asks me to compare my offering to a competitor's, then it's "game on" and I'm definitely ready to position my strengths against their weaknesses. Still, I don't talk badly about them. Mud-slinging usually backfires, because it makes the person who's doing the bad-mouthing sound defensive.

Ultimately, you want to facilitate a comparative thought process that differentiates you in the customer's mind. You do this in part by demonstrating your knowledge of the customer's problem (P). Ultimately, I try to win the close ones on two things: volume and depth. If I can bring up more ideas and have more in-depth conversations with the customer, then they are more likely to take advice from me than from a salesperson whose message is based on superficial buzzwords.

I also want to increase the customer's comfort level that they are indeed making the right choice, thus widening the separation that exists between my offering and other alternatives (A). I like to call it "subtly poisoning." Let me show you what this sounds like in the context of what I sell—strategic sales training. Listen for the (P) as I characterize the problem, and then the alternatives (A):

Sales VP: Tom, tell me about QBS and the programs you deliver.
Freese: I'd be happy to. We obviously are a sales training company, except

for the fact that we spend most of our time un-teaching many of the concepts that sellers have been conditioned to believe over the last thirty years.

If you are looking to increase revenue, shorten the sales process, and strengthen your position in the marketplace, then you basically have three options. One option is to simply continue with your current approach, which would likely produce the same results.

A second alternative would be to hire one of the name-brand training companies to come in and redefine your sales process. The challenge with that is, just "defining" the sales process doesn't address the real problem. I bet your people don't need a refresher course explaining that Step 1 in the sales process is "Identify New Opportunities," Step 2 is to "Qualify," Step 3 is to "Uncover Needs," and so on. They've already attended countless classes on "what" to do. So has your competition.

Thus, rather than just redefining the process, QBS solves a different problem. Because in most cases the steps of the sales process have already been defined, Question Based Selling is very specifically focused on teaching salespeople "how" to execute more effectively within each of those areas. If you look around any sales organization, you will see that some salespeople are more effective than others, selling the same solutions to the same types of customers. But instead of making each person figure out how to tweak their approach through trial and error, QBS shortens the ramp-up time by showing sellers how a series of small adjustments can significantly improve their sales results.

Did I bad-mouth anyone else's training program? No. In fact, I didn't mention any other program by name. I did, however, plant a few seeds of doubt that might dampen the customer's enthusiasm for pursuing a "refresher course." In essence, I make the point that continuing with the current approach probably won't accomplish the client's goals of improving revenue or gaining market share. I also point out that redefining the sales process won't make your salespeople more effective than your competition. That's not some covert sales strategy on my part; its the truth.

Your Sales Presentations Tell the Story

The best piece of sales advice I ever received was from my sales manager and mentor, Barry Gillman, back in 1992. I had just accepted a position selling NetFrame Superservers into an emerging market, and very few people had even heard about our technology. Barry, my boss and a seasoned technology veteran, once told me, "Tom, when you present your solutions to a customer, if you take the time to say it, be sure and also take the time to explain it."

In sales, you need to have a good story to tell. Presumably, you represent a viable company that offers valuable solutions, so the easiest part of telling your product's story is rattling off the various bullet points that make up your value proposition. I'm sure you have access to brochures, handouts, PowerPoint slides, or other marketing aids that enhance your presentation. But it's no longer enough just to "have" a good story. In a highly competitive marketplace you must also position your products and services in a way that conveys the full extent of your own personal value proposition.

The key to maximizing your value proposition boils down to one word—*translation*. In addition to covering key points in your presentation, you also have to explain how your product or service will impact the customer, and translate that into real value for them. This can happen in two ways. Either customers must figure out for themselves how you provide value, or you (as the advice giver) must present enough evidence to help them recognize the value of your offering— essentially, by weaving your message into a cohesive story and connecting the dots along the way. My preference is to be a "dot connector," mostly because I want to make sure key points that get made during my presentation positively influence the customer's perception of my value.

If you have already built a repository of business issues and implications to facilitate your needs development conversations, this will serve as a nice guide for translating value during your sales presentations. The repository itself is basically a physical list of *what* issues are important to potential buyers, and *why* those issues might be important. Your job (as translator) is to map the capabilities of your solution back to how it will affect the customer—i.e. implications. Just as we said that depth of conversation was important during needs development, depth is equally valuable when it comes to positioning and cost-justifying your proposed solutions.

To illustrate, suppose you took your newfound insight from this book and embarked on a new career selling umbrellas. We talked about the real value of owning an umbrella earlier. I'm sure your umbrellas would protect people from the rain. The brochure that comes with the umbrella might even point out that it helps the person standing underneath to avoid getting wet. But I might also take the opportunity to educate potential customers further, by pointing out that our umbrellas would protect their clothes (a silk tie or leather jacket), not to mention protecting them from catching a cold, possibly getting sick, or unnecessarily having to miss work. I might also make the point that it's important for people look their best if they are meeting a client or someone special after work.

Students in our live training courses sometimes ask, "Tom, couldn't the umbrella salesperson in the next kiosk say the same things about their products?" The answer is, sure they could, but only if they are thinking as strategically as you. Our logic here is simple and repeatable. Once again, ask yourself: how many reasons do you want customers to have to buy from you? More implications translates into more reasons to buy from you, and giving customers more reasons to buy (from me) is clearly my strategy to win more sales in an otherwise highly competitive environment.

Note that the goal when delivering a sales presentation isn't necessarily to make the prospect an expert on every facet of your product or service. You don't have to teach a customer how to be an attorney to sell legal services. Similarly, the fact that I don't understand all the engineering behind how an automobile engine actually works does not negate my desire or ability to purchase a well-built automobile. My goal during a sales presentation is simply to convey enough value for customers to make a sound business decision, and to build enough credibility for decision makers to feel confident they are dealing with someone who understands their needs, can offer sound advice, and will support them after the sale.

Positioning Yourself During a Job Interview

We know from earlier discussions that the question that kicks off the "official" portion of a face-to-face job interview is almost always the same. At some point after the initial pleasantries, the hiring manager will say, "Tell me about yourself." A similar thing happens during sales calls, when a customer says, "Tell me about your product." They could just as easily ask, "What are you selling?"

> **Decision makers are not so concerned about your résumé during a job interview, just as customers don't really care what's printed on the product brochure during a sales call.**

As we saw in the interview scenario from chapter 2, most candidates simply answer the question. But rather than listening to you rattle off a bunch of selling points about yourself, maybe the hiring manager is really looking to discover whether the person on the other side of the conversation is customer-focused or self-centered. By the same token, if a customer is truly focused on their own agenda rather than on your pitch about yourself, then your best strategy when selling yourself will be to focus on them.

Again, I'm not trying to dodge the question. I just want to position myself (and my services) in a manner that gives my target audience a clear picture of how I provide the greatest value.

Always remember that decision makers are not so concerned about your résumé during a job interview, just as customers don't really care what's printed on the product brochure during a sales call. What potential buyers are interested in is how those details will affect your performance in the job, or how a salesperson's advice will help them accomplish their goals. Recognizing this will make you exponentially more effective when it comes to competitively positioning yourself and the value of your solutions.

10

Paint Pictures with Your Words

Most people think in pictures, not words. Thus, if you want to be an excellent communicator, your words must enable customers to visualize the potential value of your proposed products and services.

Painting pictures with words is an extremely valuable sales skill, but one that is generally left up to the individual to figure out on their own. As a complement to the other positioning techniques we've discussed in this book, let me now give you some very specific ways to convey significantly more value with more ease.

Words, words, words . . . in sales, there are so many words! Particularly in today's competitive marketplace, hungry vendors are always trying to out-describe each other, and the abundance of words (even fancy marketing words) has become so deafening that many of the claims salespeople make about their products and services are instantly disregarded, if not totally ignored.

I'm sure you've heard the saying that a picture is worth a thousand words. It's true. Try reading a short written paragraph describing something, and then look at a picture of the same item. When you see the visual image, your brain begins to process specific shapes, color, shading, and depth. You will automatically recognize visual contrasts between the various objects that exist in the picture. An emotional response may also be triggered if you associate something in the picture with an experience you've had in the past. The neurons in someone's brain fire instantaneously when they see an actual picture rather than just hearing a bunch of words.

Have you ever noticed that you don't dream in words? You dream in pictures. When you sleep, there's no message ticker running across the bottom of the screen as if you were watching the cable news network. When you dream, it's more like you're watching a movie, as your subconscious mind enables you to visualize your thoughts.

During live QBS training courses, I sometimes invite audiences to try an experiment. I say, "Close your eyes for a few moments and pretend you are walking across an expansive rolling meadow of green grass in the early springtime. In the background you see tall trees blowing in the wind, against a bright blue sky dotted with a few large billowy white clouds. In the foreground, you see a single flower standing tall against the surrounding bright green grass. As you approach, you can see that the flower is a long-stemmed daisy, with a circular fan of brilliant white petals surrounding a yellowish-orange center."

Then I'll say, "Now open your eyes. Did you see the word D-A-I-S-Y, or did you actually visualize a picture of a daisy?" I already know the answer—people tend to think in visual pictures, not just words.

> **The neurons in your brain fire instantaneously when you see an actual picture rather than just hearing a bunch of words.**

The ability to verbalize ideas and concepts is rapidly becoming a lost art in our modern society. Given the accelerated pace of life, coupled with our narrowing attention spans, much of the information that is now communicated is netted out into a list of succinct bullet points. As a result, the art of storytelling is being replaced by the practice of condensing one's thoughts down into a few terse marketing bullets that can be texted or e-mailed.

If you want prospective buyers to recognize the full value of your product or service, then your company's story and the messages you convey must be articulated in a way that creates visual images in the mind of your target audience. You do this by painting pictures with your words. Essentially, this is the skill of storytelling.

How to Better Relate to Your Audience

The underlying themes that drive any sales process are pretty basic. Sellers ultimately want to communicate the value of their offerings to potential buyers, and decision makers want to understand their alternatives in order to choose the best solution.

Perhaps the most important lesson for how to better relate to your audience has been driven home several times already in this book. Let me ask the key question again: What is more important to the typical customer when you first engage—their problems (P), issues, and concerns, or your solutions (S)? The core philosophy in Question Based Selling is also the foundational thought that enables you to bond with potential buyers on what's most important to them (P), rather than what's important to you (S).

We have also talked about specific conversational techniques like leveraging mini-invitations, diagnostic questions to earn credibility, and escalating the strategic focus of your questions to increase the value of your needs development conversations.

One of the best ways to communicate with people as you execute the various steps in the sales process is to leverage stories, anecdotes, metaphors, analogies, and parables to enhance key points you want to make. Just open to any chapter in one of the books I've published (including this one), and you will notice that I almost always use some form of explanation device to paint (for the reader) a more in-depth picture of the concepts I am trying to convey.

Using stories to better relate to your audience enables you to translate the capabilities and potential benefits of your recommended solution into real value for the customer. Given that most people who evaluate your product or service are comparative thinkers, they will naturally try to put your value proposition into some type of context, mostly likely by relating it to something they are already familiar with or understand.

For example, when I explained earlier that using diagnostic questions to kick off your needs development conversations will open the floodgates of communication, there are no gates that really open. "Opening the floodgates" is just a figure of speech. However, the expression is valuable because of the image it conveys to the reader. It communicates that the technique of using diagnostic questions will act as a catalyst to initiate an impressive flow of information from an otherwise reluctant customer to the salesperson.

Speaking of floods, I have yet to train a sales organization that actually sells water pumps. Nonetheless, I take virtually every student through a hypothetical planning exercise to discuss the dos and don'ts of how best to position yourself if you were selling a water pump. I use this analogy to intentionally separate sellers from whatever distractions or special circumstances that may have affected their last deal. This allows students to focus exclusively on strategy and sales technique. Of course, once you understand how to extrapolate the customer's issues into more specific implications, and you have a handle on the logic of PAS positioning versus the traditional SPA approach, the lessons learned using the water pump metaphor can be adapted to virtually any sales situation.

From my perspective, a better understanding of the underlying logic leads to quicker implementation, whether we're talking about a student of mine putting QBS techniques into practice, or a potential customer of yours deciding to move forward with a purchase.

As an example, in the first chapter of my very first book, *Secrets of Question Based Selling*, I draw a parallel between dating and selling, where I refer to dating as the ultimate sale because it represents the ultimate risk. Has my advice actually helped unmarried people have more success in their respective dating careers? I bet it has. More important, the risk reduction strategies built into Question Based Selling have helped thousands of salespeople to fill their respective pipelines with more customers. It has also enabled them to navigate more effective sales conversations and significantly improve their chances of success in and throughout the sales process.

Even the metaphor I used to characterize your next job interview has a much broader application, which extends way beyond your next official employment interview. It basically foreshadows your next sales conversation, where you will definitely need to *sell yourself first*.

Take your pick—whether we're talking about Gold Medals and

German Shepherds, my first home buying experience, or *The Wizard of Oz*, you can bring your stories to life by creatively weaving relevant anecdotes, metaphors, analogies, and parables into the context of the messages you're trying to convey. I always say that relating to your audience is a function of distilling concepts down to the customer conversation level. If the person who is on the receiving end of your words thinks, "I've had something like that happen to me before," then the point you are trying to make will forever be cemented in their mind.

Specificity Brings Your Messages to Life

I hope you do have a good story to tell about your products and services and the company that ultimately supports them. Your ability to tell this story in a compelling manner, however, will determine the degree to which you are able to influence potential buyers to choose your offering instead of other comparable solutions.

Some people are natural storytellers. When they speak, everybody listens. These people are said to have a certain charm, personality, or charisma. What they really possess is the secret to being a good storyteller. Nobody talks about it, but there's definitely something that makes their messages more compelling. The secret to effective storytelling is specificity. What makes a story compelling are the interesting details.

One of the quickest and easiest adjustments a salesperson can make is to replace standard clichés, industry buzzwords, and promotional sound bites with more specific details. I'm not suggesting that you should necessarily be more technical when it comes to describing your solutions, just more colorful and detailed in how you convey your descriptions and key points.

I can't give you an exact formula for how much color to add in your conversations, but I can give you an example. Watch what happens when the same thing is said in two different ways below. Can you spot the difference?

Option A: "I went to the store and rented a movie."
Option B: "After I devoured a nine-ounce fillet that my wife, Laura,

cooked for me on the patio grill last night, my two daughters and I hopped into the van and cruised down to the local supermarket (a mile from my house) and we rented a Disney movie to watch on my big-screen TV."

Which version of the truth paints a more vivid picture of what actually happened last night? Obviously the answer is Option B, because it provides a more detailed depiction. It's simply more interesting to the reader. In a single sentence, we now know when the events occurred, what we ate for dinner, who went with me to the grocery store, how far the supermarket is from my house, what kind of car I drove, and our purpose in making the trip. We even know what kind of movie was rented and where it was watched.

> **While it's true that a picture does paint a thousand words, a thousand words can also paint a pretty clear picture.**

While it's true that a picture does paint a thousand words, a thousand words can also paint a pretty clear picture. The goal here is not to be verbose, just more compelling. Let me give you an example of how this notion of increased specificity can be applied to the sales process.

Seller: Speaking of customer references, Emory University Hospital initially deployed an earlier version of our inventory system in March 2004, back when John Thompson had just become director of materials management. They recently upgraded again in November 2008, and they are getting ready to install three other financial modules. In fact, I had lunch with the COO from Emory two weeks ago at the Atlanta Chamber of Commerce meeting, where the speaker ironically talked about government-funded health care programs versus the private sector.

The seller in this example could have just said something cursory like "Emory is one of our best customers." So why am I suggesting you even bother to say all those extra words, when you can say essentially the same thing much more succinctly?

One of our jobs as salespeople is to educate potential buyers on the value of our solutions. Consequently, there is some responsibility on our part to communicate the relevant facts about the products and services we offer. Another important responsibility of the salesperson is to make customers feel comfortable that they are indeed making a good decision. While partial or incomplete information from a salesperson tends to make customers less comfortable, the opposite is also true. The clearer the customer's vision of the value of your offerings, the more comfortable they will feel with regard to moving forward with a purchase.

What's the alternative to being purposeful and specific? Being generic! Particularly when you want to talk with customers about issues they face or the implications of those issues, very few customers have generic problems, and even fewer are looking for high-level generic solutions.

The Art of Question Based Selling

I definitely believe there is some science behind having a repeatable model that maximizes your sales effectiveness. That's partly what has motivated me to write five books on the subject. But I would point out that there is also an "art" to being a successful communicator.

The science includes understanding the underlying logic that enables sellers to manage the Scope, Focus, and Disposition of their questions, so that they will ask the right question at the right time. The science of Question Based Selling also includes a philosophical toolbox filled with a host of other communication techniques like using Global Questions, Conversational Dynamics, PAS, Conversational Layering, Diagnostic Questions, Building a Mutual Agenda, and closing on appropriate next steps in the sales process.

The artistic portion of sales communication lies in choosing the actual words that either best deliver the questions you want to ask, or best convey your value proposition. Like a painter standing in front of a canvas, holding a palette with the full spectrum of colors from which to choose, you must color and blend your words to translate your message and ultimately create the visual images you want the customer to picture. Your ability to articulate your message will likely determine the customer's perception of your value, their comfort level, and where you stand relative to competitors who are also vying for market share.

The best advice I can give you about articulating a valuable message is to think less about what you are trying to say, and more about what the customer needs to hear in order to move forward with a favorable decision. If the roles were reversed and you were the customer, what is it that you would want to hear from a salesperson in your industry, in order to feel comfortable that you were making the right decision? Would you form the impression that you were dealing with a knowledgeable, thoughtful, credible resource, or just another vendor pushing their wares? There is definitely an art to communicating in a way that best aligns with the customer's perspective.

Let everyone else use sound bites and talk in terms of high-level generalities. You should make a personal commitment to yourself, and to your customers, that if you take the time to say it, you will also take the time to explain it. Helping customers clearly see the value of your solutions by describing them in more creative ways is a tremendously valuable selling skill, and one that will make the difference time and time again.

11

Wrapping Up the Sale

Closing can be relatively simple once you reach the point where your customer is ready to move forward with a purchase. But, if a decision maker isn't yet convinced that your product or service provides the right solution, then more selling needs to occur.

Since a sales transaction usually represents the culmination of several smaller victories on the way to closing the larger sale, a savvy salesperson can revisit many of the same strategies and techniques used earlier in the sales process to close more deals.

What's the best way to increase the number of transactions you close per month, per quarter, or per year? One way is to make more calls and try to increase the number of opportunities coming into the top of the funnel. Another way is to focus on the end result, and to do those things that will secure more mind share from key decision makers within target accounts. You can also help yourself by expanding your needs development conversations to include a broader range of issues and implications, in order to differentiate yourself from the competition. You would additionally want to implement the positioning strategies we talked about in chapter 9, and maximize the customer's perception of your value by painting pictures with your words. Doing these things should put you in good shape to close more sales. So, let's use these last few pages to talk more specifically about the salesperson's role in wrapping up the deal.

Honestly, the act of closing a sale should be an anticlimactic event. If a client clearly recognizes the value of your product or service and agrees that your solutions will help them address important needs, then wrapping up a sales transaction shouldn't be more difficult than just saying, "Press hard, five copies." However, if the customer does not see the value of your solutions, using manipulative closing gimmicks is probably not going to help you win the business against a viable competitor.

As far as I'm concerned, you can take all the books, tapes, and train-ing videos that claim to offer "surefire closing tricks" and throw them in the trash can—every last one of them. If your customer truly wants to move forward with a purchase, then you don't need tricks to wrap up a sales transaction. And, in those cases where a customer (for whatever reason) isn't yet ready to move forward with a decision, then it might be true that the sale is not ready to be closed. Ask yourself, what trick can a salesperson use in today's business climate to make you buy something you don't really want?

The real "trick" to being successful in sales is causing customers to see the value of how your solutions will address their needs, and within the process, make them comfortable enough to justify a decision to move forward with a purchase. So far, much of our focus has been on filling the pipeline, securing mind share, conveying value, and differentiating yourself from the competition. Now, it is time to "pull back the curtains" on the end of the sales process and focus on what you can do to expe-dite customer decisions and wrap up more sales.

First, Find Out Where You Stand

I have never considered myself to be a pushy salesperson. I am forthright and direct with people, for sure, but that's different. Maybe it's because I don't appreciate being pushed when I'm the customer, especially not by some salesperson who seems more intent on achieving their own goals than on helping me achieve mine.

A point will come in every sale, however, when the buyer must choose whether or not to move forward with a purchase. At the same time, sellers must decide whether to continue pursuing the opportunity, and if so, how to proceed in a way that's not pushy but still mutually beneficial.

The end of the sales process is notorious for creating awkward moments between salespeople and their customers. Potential buyers are well aware that you want to close the deal, so there's no point in being timid. It's perfectly acceptable for a salesperson to have goals. But invariably the moment of truth will arrive, where you are either going to find out that your efforts will be rewarded with the completion of a sale, or you will learn that the customer has decided to go in some other direction. Essentially, that's the point when a salesperson feels like they are putting their neck on the proverbial block and hoping that it doesn't get chopped off.

Recently I heard a sales executive quote a statistic saying that 78 percent of all salespeople hesitate when it comes to asking for the order. I believe it, knowing that the inherent risk of rejection is the single largest demotivator in the sales profession. Even so, sellers must find a way to ask for the order, because it's the only way to know where your customer actually stands relative to making a purchase. It's also the only way to know how best to pursue the opportunity from there.

Putting the awkwardness of the situation aside, closing is really about getting an accurate report as to where you really stand in the sales process. Is the customer ready to move forward with a purchase? If not, what things might be holding them back? Are there sticking points, contract terms, or outstanding issues that still need to be addressed? Does anyone else need to be involved in the decision?

Knowing the true status of the sale is the only way a salesperson can know how best to proceed. Ever had an objection come up in the eleventh hour of a deal that you were able to successfully address and still complete the transaction? I have experienced this many times. No one wants customers to raise objections, but it's definitely true that you can't address obstacles you don't know about. With objections, sound logic and good closing techniques become an extremely valuable assets for the proactive salesperson who strives to manage their sales opportunities all the way through closure. The alternative would be just let sales situations play out on their own and hope for the best.

If you happen to discover that one or more of the opportunities you have in the pipeline is not going to happen, my philosophy is that it's better to find out now rather than chase phantom deals on your sales forecast. Frankly, this level of insight enables a realistic salesperson to redeploy their time, effort, and resources to other, more legitimate opportunities. Finding out that the customer is ready to move forward with a purchase is equally important, so you can get on with the details of wrapping up the transaction.

There are several schools of thought on the best way to actually pop the closing question. Much of it is situational and will depend on the context of your conversation, the mix of personalities involved, and your relationship with the customer. I purposely use the phrase "closing question" because as you've probably noticed, I'm not very good at pussy-footing around. With customers, I would rather be direct and to the point, knowing that an effective question-based approach gives me the best chance to achieve the desired result, with the least amount of risk.

When you aren't sure exactly where you stand at the end of the sales process, trying to somehow guess what to do next is a high-risk strategy. Should you chill out and give the client some more time to make a decision so they can get comfortable with your proposal? Or would it be better to show some initiative and recommend more strongly that they should move forward now? Guessing where you stand in the sale also leaves you to wonder whether a price discount would provide enough incentive for the customer to act, or would that just end up eroding your profit margin? Moreover, is it appropriate to take the customer to lunch or dinner, and do those events obligate decision makers in key accounts to buy into your solution anyway? Because it's so easy to guess wrong, sellers who just take shots in the dark end up making mistakes, like unnecessarily discounting their price or wasting valuable sales resources.

To me, the best way to find out where you stand in the sale is to put your closing question in hypothetical terms. After you have identified the customer's needs and educated them on the full extent of your value proposition, go ahead and summarize the progression of events that brought the decision process to this point. Then you can simply ask the customers if it "makes sense" to take the appropriate next step. Here's how that sounds in an actual dialogue.

Seller: Mr. Customer, given that you are looking to improve manufacturing efficiency, cut costs, and preserve quality, which is exactly what this product provides, would it make sense to move forward with the process of finalizing the contract so you can begin to realize the benefits of our solution?

The phrase "Would it make sense to . . ." is particularly effective when suggesting possible next steps in the decision process. I talked about this briefly back in chapter 4, in the context of securing mini-invitations. "Would it make sense . . ." essentially brings logic into play, suggesting that the reason to move forward is to benefit the customer. That takes away any sense that you're focused on raking in a commission check. Whether it does or does not "make sense" for the customer to take your suggested next step, asking in a way that's forthright and direct gives you the opportunity to find out where you stand, so you can either wrap up the terms of the sale or work with customers to resolve any outstanding issues.

> **The only legitimate reason to consummate a transaction is because yours is the product or service that most effectively addresses the customer's need.**

I usually recommend that sellers avoid older-school closing euphemisms like "Can we shake on it?" or "Do we have a deal?", because they tend to sound sales-y and self-serving. Customers know you probably stand to earn some sort of bonus or commission from the transaction, but a salesperson's income doesn't ever justify a purchase. In fact, the only legitimate reason to consummate a transaction is because yours is the product or service that most effectively addresses the customer's need.

Use Trial Closes for a Softer Touch

I personally don't like the idea of twisting a customer's arm to try and close a sale. The last thing I want to do is forge a budding relationship with a prospective client and then create an awkward situation at the end of the sale by attempting to close too aggressively.

It's a balancing act—sellers must be forthright enough to find out where they stand in the sale and know how best to proceed, but there isn't any upside to being harsh, pushy, or manipulative at the end of the decision cycle.

One way to minimize your risk of sounding aggressive is to use *trial closes*. A trial close is a question that gives you a gentler way to be direct, yet sensitive and respectful during that part of the decision where customers often don't want to be pressured. Trial closing is essentially a risk reduction strategy. Rather than putting your neck on the block and hoping it doesn't get chopped off, you simply ask something like:

Seller: Ms. Prospect, now that you have a pretty complete perspective regarding our products, would it make sense for us to think about sitting down and wrapping up the details?

If you notice in the dialogue, the salesperson's trial closing question isn't actually asking the customer to commit to moving forward with a purchase. He is simply asking if it "makes sense" to "think about" sitting down. The prospect's response will generally tell you where they stand. If they agree that "Yes, it does make sense for us to sit down and wrap up the details," then the suggestion to move forward with a transaction is a relatively easy one to make. On the other hand, if the customer responds cautiously, or for whatever reason they say that it doesn't even make sense for them to "think about" sitting down, then you probably are not close to making a sale. At that point, I would be inclined to say to the customer, "Something's not right, is it?" If something is indeed holding them back, getting the obstacle out in the open can be a relief to the customer, and it accomplishes your objective of knowing where you stand in the sale.

The advantage of using a trial close versus going for the jugular is that customers tend to respond more openly when you take a softer approach. More information is always better with regard to closing sales transactions. And it's always easier to navigate this otherwise sensitive area of asking for a commitment when the customer "wants to" share information with you, rather than when they feel pressured. With most customers, if they even get so much as a whiff of aggression from an eager salesperson, their defenses will quickly go up and you're back to guessing how best to proceed.

Trial closes are also valuable tools for assessing the validity of potential deals on your sales forecast. Managing the pipeline is important to salespeople and managers alike. And depending on your industry and the types of products you sell, sales cycles can range from a simple one-call close to a much more complex, multifaceted decision process that can span several weeks or months. Does your deal have a 30 percent chance of closing, or an 80 percent chance? What is the likelihood of closing a transaction this month, or within the current quarter? What is the customer's approval process? Who else in the account needs to sign off on the P.O.? Are there any next steps? Is there anything that you can do to accelerate the purchase?

One of the ways to avoid sounding like a money-grubber is by focusing on the broader decision, and not just the impending purchase. For example, I might ask, "What is the typical administrative process for this type of decision?" Asking about the "typical" decision process tends to lighten the conversation and minimize any pressure that a customer might feel about an impending transaction. Even if a specific deal is up in the air, customers can still talk abstractly about the typical administrative process for these types of decisions.

Sellers must also be sensitive to the fact that large decisions can sometimes seem overwhelming to customers, thus creating emotional hurdles that can stymie the decision process. Thus, trial closing is a good way to make sure customers do not feel overwhelmed by your closing questions.

Essentially, trial closing is a divide and conquer strategy, where sellers test a customer's "readiness" by focusing on smaller aspects of the larger sale. For example, you might ask, "Mr. Customer, have you talked to the bank about financing?" Or, "Where are you planning to warehouse the equipment once it arrives?" You could ask, "Have you thought about when you would like to take delivery?" If the buyer has already talked to the bank, and he already has a plan for where to warehouse the equipment when it arrives, then you are probably in very good shape to move forward.

A medical equipment salesperson could ask a doctor, "Do you have any surgery cases scheduled in the next week to ten days?" An advertising salesperson could ask, "How far along is the art design for your upcoming advertising campaign?" A real estate agent might ask a prospective homeowner, "Have you thought about how you might furnish the kitchen in this particular house?" Look at it this way: If the potential buyer of a house hasn't even "thought about" how it would be furnished, then they probably aren't close to making a decision, and you, in turn, probably aren't close to making that particular sale. On the other hand, if they've already measured the dining room to purchase new furniture, that's a good indication that they might be ready to moving forward with a purchase.

Humbling Disclaimers

Sellers are always being encouraged to ask specific qualifying questions—to identify key players, understand the customer's time frame for making a decision, and find out if they have budget money to spend. Most salespeople understand, however, that a fine line exists between being appropriate in your efforts to qualify an opportunity and sounding overly invasive by probing too aggressively for information. Moreover, if a customer chooses not to share specific details with you about the opportunity, this puts you at a competitive disadvantage, because you must then assume that they are probably sharing information with someone else.

To minimize your risk of being shut down by potential buyers and maximize the amount and quality of information you receive, a savvy salesperson can use a very effective question based technique called a *humbling disclaimer*. A humbling disclaimer is a conversational device that desensitizes a salesperson's more delicate questions. The humbling disclaimer is a precursor of sorts, whereby the asker verbally acknowledges the sensitivity of his or her question in order to proactively defuse any invasive feelings that could otherwise come from asking such a probing question. That's a lot of words, I know, so let me give you some examples.

Inquiring about the customer's budget provides a great illustration.

Sellers always want to know if a certain project is budgeted, or at least, that the customer indeed has money to spend. Inquiring about a customer's budget is a fair question to ask at some point to see if the deal is even worth pursuing. It is just as important to know if there is a certain time frame in which the customer's budget has to be allocated. Understanding a customer's budget requirements is, therefore, one of the most important qualifying criteria in any pending sales transaction. But, just because a salesperson wants to ask about the customer's budget doesn't necessarily mean decision makers will openly share this information with you. Consequently, sellers often end up saying back to their managers, "I asked about the budget, but the customer is playing it close to the vest."

Should we be surprised that customers are reluctant to share budget information with a salesperson? Picture yourself standing in a car dealership admiring a shiny new sports car on the showroom floor, when an eager salesperson scurries over and asks, "How much money have you got?" I bet you wouldn't be eager to share your W-2 or credit score with someone you don't know or trust. Still, sellers are expected to find out about the budget, and when customers don't share, everyone gets frustrated.

The customer's natural reluctance to share budget details tees up a perfect example of how to use humbling disclaimers. Note that budget usually isn't the first thing I would ask about in a sales call, but the time will come when it's appropriate to bring it up in the conversation. When you reach that point in the dialogue, you simply say: "Mr. Customer, I don't want to step out-of-bounds and bring up something I'm not supposed to ask about, but do you mind if I ask the budget question?"

Technically, the answer to this question is either yes, you may ask about the budget, or no, you may not. However, when you precede your question with a humbling disclaimer, it's uncanny how often people will open right up and start sharing their financial landscape relative to the purchase. In essence, the humility that's built into your disclaimer disarms the customer even before you even deliver the question. Can you see why they are called a humbling disclaimers?

Of course, the customer could respond by saying, "You can ask about the budget, but I'm not going to share details with you." At that point, you aren't going to get specific information about their budget no matter what you had asked. But don't give up. It's better to get a little information than no information. In those situations, I would probably follow up my original question by saying, "That's fine, Mr. Customer. I understand that budget information is often confidential. But could I ask you this? If we put together a proposal that ends up being in the forty- to fifty-thousand-dollar range, do you have the ability to pull the trigger on that type of purchase, or do we need to be thinking about some other approval process?" Even if a customer won't share specific budget details with you, you can generally get some indication of whether they are able to approve this type of expenditure in addition to finding out where you stand in the approval process.

> **If you are verbally respectful of someone else's right to not share information with you, it's amazing how much information you can get.**

Humbling disclaimers are similarly effective when it comes to expanding your needs development conversations. Have you ever asked so many questions in the discovery phase that you start to feel yourself running out of runway? The customer's responses get progressively shorter as their indulgence wanes and a sense of impatience creeps into the conversation. When a customer starts to feel that they are being "probed" for information, you basically have two options. One is to cut needs development short and jump immediately into your value proposition. The other option is to say something that builds a longer runway in the conversation. You can easily do this using a humbling disclaimer. An example would be to say, "Mr. Customer, I appreciate that you have explained the current manufacturing process and your upcoming reengineering initiatives. And while I don't want to seem presumptuous by asking too many questions, I would like to understand how these projects could impact your growth plans. Do you mind if I ask a couple of specifics about your longer-term strategy?"

Here are some other examples of humbling disclaimers:

"I'm not sure the best way to ask, but would you mind if . . ."
"Without stepping on anyone's toes, could I ask about . . ."
"I don't want to say the wrong thing, but would it be okay to . . ."

To fully appreciate the strategy of using humbling disclaimers, I'll let you in on a little secret about human nature. If you are verbally respectful of someone else's right to *not* share information with you, it's amazing how much information you can get. Humility is a very attractive human quality, and one that people are naturally drawn toward. Thus, you can significantly enhance the value of the responses to the questions you ask by strategically preceding your more sensitive questions with a humbling disclaimer. Simply put, causing people to "want to" share more information with you gives you a strategic advantage over other sellers who are just out there probing for needs.

Neutralize the Disposition of Your Questions

When the time comes to wrap up the details of a sale, the salesperson naturally hopes everything will go well. Perhaps that's why sellers have a tendency to ask hopeful questions, with what I would characterize as questions with a positive disposition. I introduced this phenomenon in my first book, *Secrets of Question Based Selling*. Sellers tend to ask positive questions in the hopes of receiving a more positive response. It's subconscious, but especially easy to do if your livelihood is contingent on receiving good news from potential buyers.

What do I mean by hopeful questions? And what exactly does a positively dispositioned sales question sound like? Let me give you a few examples. Note that some of these questions may sound very familiar.

"Would next Tuesday work for a conference call?"
"Does your boss like our proposal?"
"Do you think we're still in good shape to wrap this deal up by the end of the month?"

If you try saying any of these questions aloud, you can literally feel your head bobbing up and down as you ask. That positive undertone happens because the deliverer of the question is hoping to receive a positive response.

It turns out that asking hope-filled sales questions is a bad strategy. Soliciting good news (only) tends to reduce the amount of information people share with you, and it also tends to reduce the accuracy of the information you receive. Let me ask: if a problem is brewing somewhere within one of your accounts, would you want to know about it? Granted, no one wants problems to arise within their sales opportunities, but if something is indeed happening in one of my accounts, I would absolutely want to know. An issue can only be successfully addressed if you realize it's happening. That's why I don't ask "hopeful" questions.

Delivering bad news is understandably difficult, particularly when the message being conveyed is not something the other person would necessarily want to hear. Buyers are often put in this situation, particularly when they are dealing with an enthusiastic salesperson whose livelihood depends on making sales. In the real world, it's quite possible that a decision maker is not "ready to move forward by the end of the month." Perhaps their budget has been slashed, or the decision committee is leaning toward a competitor's product. Whatever the reason, if bad news is brewing, prospects are often reluctant to share this information when they know it's something the salesperson would not want to hear.

If you are in sales and you want to know where you truly stand in one of your accounts, then you must be open to hearing good news and bad news. That's why in Question Based Selling, we teach sellers to neutralize the disposition of their sales questions.

> **If you are in sales and you want to know where you truly stand in one of your accounts, then you must be open to hearing good news and bad news.**

If you break this idea down, you will notice that every question you ask has a certain "personality," or disposition, that can be characterized as being either positive, negative, or neutral. The purpose of neutralizing your questions is to solicit more accurate information about the status of your opportunities. This requires a proactive effort from the salesperson to uncover any potential obstacles. Simply put, I don't ask questions to solicit the answer someone thinks I want to hear. Instead, I strive to get the real answer.

Rather than fishing for good news by asking a hope-filled question like "Are we still in good shape to get the deal?", I would be much more inclined to ask, "Mr. Customer, do you think we're still in good shape to wrap this contract up by the end of the month, or is it possible that something might cause this deal to get pushed out?"

Notice that I am actually inviting the customer to share bad news, if there is any. I don't actually want bad news, but I do want to know if the customer can foresee any obstacles that might prevent the opportunity from moving forward. Another way to neutralize this question would be to ask, "Is there anything that might prevent you from moving forward on this decision?" Can you see how these questions don't ask for good news only? Instead, they seek the whole enchilada.

A variation of this technique would be to reverse roles in the conversation. Ask the customer, "If you were the salesperson on this account, would you be doing anything differently?" This question is neither hopeful nor negative. It's completely neutral. In fact, this is one of the most insightful questions you can ask your customers, coworkers, boss, or employees. You may even want to ask your kids or your spouse, "If our roles were reversed and you were me, what would you be doing differently?" I guarantee that this will generate some of the most accurate and valuable feedback you will ever receive. The only question is, do you really want to know what those around you are thinking?

Work Backward from the Implementation Date

A couple months ago I had a conference call with a sales VP who said, "Tom, I think we're going to postpone our plans for sales training for about six months." That struck me as funny. I understand that companies have expense budgets and timing issues that need to fall into place in order to bring people together for a corporate training event. And I'm certainly not the only salesperson who has encountered a scenario where customers want to delay their decision until some point in the future.

But this particular comment was a bit strange. When do you suppose is the best time to schedule a sales training course? Given the hustle and bustle of our fast-paced business culture, it's never a "good time" for training. So why would it ever make sense to schedule a QBS course? The only justifiable reason to bring me in to train a sales team is to boost results. Therefore, if you aren't anticipating a significant upside in terms of increased productivity, you shouldn't bother to schedule one of our courses—ever! On the other hand, if you believe QBS will significantly increase your team's sales effectiveness and results, then why would you wait six more months to boost productivity?

In this example, I simply worked backward from the desired result by asking, "When would you like to start seeing an increase in your team's sales productivity?" I guess the answer was, "Soon," because I literally delivered a QBS training class last week, for the same VP who originally wanted to delay the training six months.

Not surprisingly, very few of our clients are motivated by my desire to fill my calendar with training events. Instead, clients are motivated by *their* desire to accomplish specific business objectives—like filling their sales pipelines, differentiating themselves in a competitive marketplace, boosting profit margins, and closing more business. Hence, the real question that should dictate when a client schedules a training class is: *When would you like to start seeing results?*

I had several similar experiences when I sold technology solutions. Customers don't really care about when the salesperson receives the purchase order. That's why I didn't spend much time hounding decision makers to find out when certain deals were going to close. Instead, I focused more on what needed to happen to ensure a successful implementation.

Working backward from the implementation date made it easy to create a greater sense of urgency for moving forward. For example, if you were working on an equipment sale of some kind, you could easily ask a customer, "Mr. Prospect, if you look past the initial purchase for a moment, when would you like to have this equipment installed and fully operational?"

This is a valuable qualifying question. If the prospect hasn't even thought about their implementation time frame, then they probably aren't close to making a purchase. Focusing on the time frame for implementation rather than the status of the purchase order is also valuable because it allows the salesperson to follow up on the timing of a deal without making customers feel like they are being hounded for money, or making you sound like you are focused on your commission check. Prospects are well aware that you want to consummate a sale, but they can only take so much pestering about when the order will be placed.

Therefore, let's suppose that you inquired about the customer's implementation plans and the decision maker said, "We would like to have the system up and running by January 15th." If it's only September, January might seem like a long way off; in which case, people might drag their feet because there's no sense of urgency. Therein lies the value of working backward from a specific date. With a couple quick calculations, you can increase the customer's sense of urgency by showing them that the window to make a decision is much shorter than they might have thought.

Working backward from the customer's January 15 implementation date, I would ask, "How much time should we allow for testing before the equipment actually goes into production?" Few technology solutions are put into production on the very day they are taken out of the box. A fully integrated solution needs to be staged, assembled, tested, installed, and then inspected, before being deemed ready for service.

"Let's allow six weeks total—two weeks to install hardware and thirty days to test our internal procedures," the prospect might say.

I would continue working backward by asking, "Once you make a technical decision, how long do you think it will take to get the signatures needed to cut a purchase order?"

"Negotiating the contract could take a couple weeks, depending on the availability of the legal department, but once that's done, we can probably cut a PO fairly quickly," the prospect replies.

The next step is critical. Once you've identified the various elements of the decision process, and you understand the lead times involved, you simply calculate a mathematical timeline by calculating how big (or small) the window is for the prospect to make an actual decision. I might summarize by saying: "Mr. Prospect, if your system needs to be live on January 15th, and we must allow six weeks for testing, two weeks for staging, and another two weeks for the holidays in December, that means we would need to have an order by the first week of November in order to meet your implementation schedule. Basically, that leaves thirty days to evaluate the product and make a decision."

The net effect is—suddenly, a project that was slated to happen "sometime next year" now requires a decision within the next thirty days. Can you see how this approach can impact the customer's sense of urgency? As an added bonus, revising the customer's timeline places you in more of a consultative role. At that point, you are working with them to plan ahead and visualize the future, as a way to help ensure that their project goes smoothly. That's much more valuable than just badgering customers to hurry up and make a decision.

Wrapping Up an Employment Interview

Now that we have talked about everything from piquing the prospect's curiosity, to establishing your credibility early in the sales process, to needs development, positioning your value, and securing a commitment toward closure, let's take one more look at the metaphor of selling yourself in a job interview.

As I said at the beginning of this book, every formal employment interview is a sales situation, and every sales situation is a job interview. The comparison becomes especially apparent when you break the critical elements of the sales process down into its various component parts. Whether you are meeting a potential customer (or hiring manager) for the first time, or you are differentiating yourself later in the decision cycle, the value of the products and services you offer is ultimately a reflection of the customer's perception of you. In that vein, your success will almost always come down to your ability to *sell yourself first*.

Following your interview, you will either be offered a position or you won't. You will have made the sale, or you haven't. Granted, it may take a few days for the hiring manager to complete the current round of interviews and narrow a larger pool of candidates down to a short list. Your patience may also be tested by the bureaucracy we affectionately call human resources. But at the end of the day, companies conduct employment interviews for a reason, and they are ultimately going to make a choice to go in one direction or another. Whether they choose you has a lot to do with your approach and how you have chosen to position yourself with the customer.

First impressions are critically important. That's why we invested so much time in earlier chapters to talk about bonding with potential customers on their problems (PAS), versus your solutions (SPA). If you have done your homework in advance, then you should have a pretty good idea of what a hiring manager wants before you darken their doorstep. This will enable you to be very direct, essentially pointing at the elephant in the room, in order to pique the customer's interest and establish your own credibility.

Once you get the interview or meeting off to a strong start, it's easy then to find an opportunity to then say, "Can I ask you a couple specifics about the opportunity?" On the heels of demonstrating that you are ultimately focused on helping the hiring manager address their goals of a quick ramp-up to full productivity, blending with the existing culture, bringing new ideas and a fresh perspective to the team, etc., securing the customer's permission to "ask a couple specifics" will likely be music to an interviewer's ears.

In addition to being thoughtful enough to ask relevant and intelligent questions, hiring managers are looking for candidates to be interested in knowing more about the position. But you can't just declare that you are interested in being hired. You must demonstrate your interest in the position, along with eliciting the hiring manager's impressions of what they think it takes to be successful at this particular company. Communicating in this manner is a piece of cake for the question-based salesperson, because there is no better way to demonstrate true interest than to ask intelligent questions that show that you have appropriately prepared in advance of the meeting. From the interviewer's perspective, there's a big difference between someone whose thoughtful questions seem to just roll off their tongue, and the nervously shallow candidate who is working hard just to think of something relevant to say.

After reading this book, you will handle your next job interview, and all sales situations, much differently than before. You will let the other candidates competing for the position make the mistake of trying to claim their own credibility. You will know that the more they talk about themselves or their résumé, the more they will end up commoditizing their value to the customer. You, on the other hand, will know how to secure the hiring manager's permission in advance to facilitate a free-flowing exchange of ideas and information.

As your meeting winds down and the hiring manager asks if you have any more questions, you will have one. Using the humbling disclaimer technique we talked about earlier, you will say something like, "I don't want to seem overly forthright or inappropriate in any way, but is it a fair question to ask your impression?" Technically, the answer to this question is either yes (it is fair to ask) or no (that's not an appropriate question). Before you even deliver the actual question, your understanding of conversational dynamics enables you to know that the hiring manager won't just answer with a simple yes or no. Instead, they will openly share their impressions about you right then and there, and they will appreciate that you were forthright enough to ask. Of course, knowing where you stand with respect to an opportunity is the first step to closing the sale.

> **You will be the only candidate who asked the hiring manager for permission at the beginning of the interview, and also, the only one who asked for their impression at the end.**

Especially if you are interviewing for a sales position, the hiring manager will see that you are comfortable and willing to ask for the order. You will have also positioned yourself perfectly to be the one who is focused on helping the customer address their goals, objectives, issues, and concerns. I can tell you that you will likely be the only candidate who asked the hiring manager for permission at the beginning of the interview, and also the only one who asked for their impressions at the end. Note that it doesn't take courage or bravery to be successful if you put yourself in the position of having superior technique.

Who knows, you may get hired on the spot. Or, you may find out from the interviewer that there are a couple of gaps in your credentials relative to what the employer is looking for from the ideal candidate. Becoming aware of these gaps is actually a good thing. Remember, you can't address an issue you don't know about. Since there is no such thing as the perfect candidate anyway, the hiring manager's concern actually affords you a unique opportunity to reiterate your strengths and shore up any potential shortcomings while wrapping up the meeting. You can also echo key points in your subsequent correspondence.

As an extra bonus, asking the interviewer for their "impression" usually leads to some valuable expectation setting with regard to what happens next. Will the hiring decision be made in a matter of hours, days, or weeks? Will subsequent interviews be necessary to gain the support of other managers or key executives? Is there anything the interviewer would suggest you do in the meantime?

One of the biggest secrets to being successful in any kind of selling is having the knowledge and perspective to understand that potential customers are willing to share their thoughts, feelings, and concerns with only some fraction of the sellers/candidates who are out there offering goods and services. Fortunately, for those sellers who are willing to demonstrate the level of commitment that you have shown by reading this book, the extent to which people will choose to deal with you has everything to do with your philosophy on selling yourself in today's competitive marketplace.

Now it's up to you to put these proven strategies into practice, have some fun helping customers accomplish their objectives, and get paid handsomely in the process. Game on!

Epilogue

For Sales Managers Only

What's the definition of insanity? Maybe it's insane to write five how-to books for a target audience of highly intelligent people who aren't always open to hearing constructive feedback. Do you know any salespeople with big egos? Ah, but how quickly things can change, especially now that so many sellers have been humbled by recent market conditions, coupled with the realization that their success moving forward will likely require some modifications to their current approach.

Never before have salespeople or sales organizations been so hungry for change or for a fresh set of ideas that will help their customers, colleagues, and company, in addition to helping themselves. In fact, the status quo might be a salesperson's worst enemy at this point, as current clients are reevaluating their existing vendor agreements, and new opportunities will be predictably more difficult to penetrate. It's simply not logical to believe that while the whole business climate is changing, yet your approach to sales can remain the same and still get acceptable results.

But even with a tumultuous economy sales are still going to happen. You have to assume that someone is going to earn the customer's trust, and that person is also most likely to earn their business. Well, that person might as well be you. That's essentially the case I've made throughout this book—that your success moving forward is contingent on your own personal effectiveness, more so than ever before. And, the notion of developing your own sales effectiveness can no longer be thought of in terms of mere motivational buzzwords.

It's easy to talk about adapting to a new economy. The challenge for sales organizations is, there's never a "good time" for change, not to men-

240

tion training. I hear it from salespeople and managers who have monthly, quarterly, and annual sales objectives they are desperately trying to meet. I am neither surprised nor offended that sitting in a sales training class isn't near the top of anyone's fun list. If I had a nickel for every time I felt this way when I was as a salesperson, I wouldn't have to write any more books. People are busy, and there probably won't ever be a convenient time to put that your to-do list down long enough to sharpen your tools and techniques.

Even though I'm a sales trainer by trade, I would quickly tell you that this is not the time to revert back to traditional approaches. Instead, this *New Era of Salesmanship* may provide the perfect opportunity for you to leverage logic and innovation in order to update your sales skills, rather than simply gravitating back to old habits that will commoditize your value and make you sound just like everyone else.

> **Sellers must do everything in their power to make themselves invaluable to their customers, their colleagues, and their company.**

My beef with the corporate establishment comes when salespeople are given lofty quotas, but then left to their own devices to figure out how to achieve such monumental goals. With the exception of the previous experiences sellers bring to the table, not much detail is being provided with regard to *how* to be effective in this new environment.

Most salespeople don't need motivation and encouragement. Everyone knows it's time to perform. Now, it's all about giving your sales team the coaching and direction they need to perform at their best. One of the key points in my first book simply states: In order to achieve above-average sales results, one must first be open to thinking about above-average concepts.

More than ever before, sellers must do everything in their power to make themselves invaluable to their customers, their colleagues, and their company. This will require a conscious effort on the individual's part to hunker down and honestly evaluate their current sales process, strategic mindset, and interpersonal skills. Can you change or adapt without having to wait for the rest of your sales team to get on board? Of course you can. The question is, are you ready to take your game to the next level by making a few small adjustments in your sales strategy?

We have reached a defining moment where companies will be handsomely rewarded for partnering with their sales teams in an effort to leverage the current appetite for change. Identifying what to do and how to do it more effectively should dominate your strategic focus at this point. Building a cohesive sales strategy that the entire team can rally around, and then seeing perceptible results, is going to be the key to your success moving forward. The good news is, most salespeople are hungry for success, and they will respond very favorably if you can just light a fire under their competitive spirit.

At the end of the day, give me a salesperson who is eager to succeed and has a proven methodology for differentiating his or her strategic sales efforts, and I will show you someone who has an unfair advantage in today's competitive marketplace.

ACKNOWLEDGMENTS

The recent economic turmoil has given me a renewed sense of purpose to help clients reexamine how they conduct business, and in many cases, to help them reinvent their approach to the entire sales profession. It is true that tumultuous times tend to bring people together. Thus, I have been fortunate to be surrounded by a world-class team of professionals and all-around good folks, as this (my fifth) book was definitely a collaborative effort.

Let me start by thanking my good friend and marketing guru, Scott Whitney. In addition to building the best Web sites on the planet, Scott's expertise as a podcaster and master of live streaming video has enabled us to create QBS "Live" Custom Training Modules, essentially leveraging the Internet to provide interactive QBS coaching broadcasts for clients who either want to enhance the effectiveness of Question Based Selling, or culturalize the QBS methodology across the entire sales organization.

The unsung hero of this project is my executive assistant, Robin Decker. In addition to being a rock of sanity when things get crazy around the office, her quiet confidence inspires me on a daily basis, and her dedication to helping clients in every way possible is incomparable. I also wish to thank Alan Rohrer and Jim Russell for their commitment to delivering QBS Methodology Training at the highest level.

I would also like to thank my editor in chief, Laura Freese, along with Emily Gilreath (my proofreader in chief), whose combined editing contributions have convinced me that three heads are better than one. Craig Moonshower and Warren Caldwell were also instrumental in helping me develop graphics that would bring the text to life. Last, I wish to give a shout-out to my literary agent in chief, Al Zuckerman, who believed in me from the beginning, and made me feel just as accomplished as his many other client authors including Ken Follett, Stephen Hawking, Christopher Paolini (*Eragon*), and Stephenie Meyer (the *Twilight* series).

I also wish to thank the entire Portfolio team at Penguin Group. From my very first meeting with Adrian Zackheim to my frequent interactions with my competent editor, Brooke Carey, and others on the publishing team, it has certainly been nice to connect with people who understand that the dedication and quality of the effort put in on the front end will ultimately determine the value of the finished product.

A special note of gratitude to goes to a handful of special people (in no particular order), including Mark Reed, Gregg Quisito, Jerry Saunders, Jarrett McConnico, Monte Mickle, Evan Steiner, Kenny Matula, Mathew Gore, Steve Johnson, Mark Selleck, Barry Gillman, Dan Hess, Jim Hardee, Mitch Little, Mike Henderson, Danny Jones, Tom Mathews, Kevin Madden, Terry Edge, Larry Freese, Richard Sites, Bart Burton, Bill Burton, and Charlie King. I cannot put into words the positive impact these people have had on my work and on the resulting success I have experienced over the years.

Last but not least, I would like to thank my wife, Laura, for her unconditional support throughout my entire QBS journey, and my two daughters, Sarah and Mary Claire. Truth be known, I may be the fourth-best salesperson in the Freese household.

INDEX

FIND OUT MORE INFORMATION

To inquire about or schedule a QBS Methodology Training course for your sales team, or if you would simply like more information about QBS books, QBS audio CDs, QBS OnLine, Ongoing Coaching, or QBS Licensing, please contact us at:

QBS Research, Inc.
5600 Spalding Drive, 922933
Atlanta, GA 30092
Ofc: (770) 840-7640
Fax: (770) 840-7642
E-mail: admin@QBSresearch.com
Web Site: www.QBSresearch.com